D0926654

Race and Schooling in the South, 1880 1950

Long-term Factors in Economic Development
A National Bureau of Economic Research Series
Edited by Robert W. Fogel and Clayne L. Pope

Photo: *Children leaving school at the close of the day's sessions* (Alabama, 1937), The Library of Congress (photo by Arthur Rothstein).

Also in the series

Claudia Goldin
Understanding the Gender Gap: An Economic History of American Women (Oxford University Press, 1990)

Roderick Floud, Kenneth Wachter, and Annabel Gregory
Height, Health and History: Nutritional Status in the United Kingdom, 1750–1980 (Cambridge University Press, 1990)

Samuel Preston and Michael Haines
Fatal Years: Child Mortality in Late-Nineteenth-Century America (Princeton University Press, 1990)

In preparation (tentative titles)

Robert W. Fogel
The Escape from Hunger and Early Death: Europe and America, 1750–2050
Kenneth L. Sokoloff
In Pursuit of Private Comfort: Early American Industrialization, 1790 to 1860

Race and Schooling in the South, 1880–1950: An Economic History

Robert A. Margo

The University of Chicago Press

Chicago and London

ROBERT A. MARGO is associate professor of economics at Vanderbilt University and a research associate of the National Bureau of Economic Research.

The University of Chicago Press, Chicago 60637
The University of Chicago Press, Ltd., London

Library of Congress Cataloging-in-Publication Data

Margo, Robert A. (Robert Andrew), 1954–
    Race and schooling in the South, 1880–1950 : an economic history /
Robert A. Margo.
        p.   cm. —(Long-term factors in economic development)
    Includes bibliographical references and index.
    ISBN 0-226-50510-3 (alk. paper)
    1. Education—Economic aspects—Southern States—His-
tory.   2. Discrimination in education—Southern States—
History.   3. Segregation in education—Southern States—History.   4. Economic development—Effect of education
on.   I. Title.   II. Series.
LC66.5.S68M37   1990
338.4′7370′975—dc20   90-11249
                                                            CIP

⊗The paper used in this publication meets the minimum requirements of
the American National Standard for Information Sciences—Permanence
of Paper for Printed Library Materials, ANSI Z39.48–1984.

Relation of the Directors to the
Work and Publications of the
National Bureau of Economic Research

1. The object of the National Bureau of Economic Research is to ascertain and to present to the public important economic facts and their interpretation in a scientific and impartial manner. The Board of Directors is charged with the responsibility of ensuring that the work of the National Bureau is carried on in strict conformity with this object.

2. The President of the National Bureau shall submit to the Board of Directors, or to its Executive Committee, for their formal adoption all specific proposals for research to be instituted.

3. No research report shall be published by the National Bureau until the President has sent each member of the Board a notice that a manuscript is recommended for publication and that in the President's opinion it is suitable for publication in accordance with the principles of the National Bureau. Such notification will include an abstract or summary of the manuscript's content and a response form for use by those Directors who desire a copy of the manuscript for review. Each manuscript shall contain a summary drawing attention to the nature and treatment of the problem studied, the character of the data and their utilization in the report, and the main conclusions reached.

4. For each manuscript so submitted, a special committee of the Directors (including Directors Emeriti) shall be appointed by majority agreement of the President and Vice Presidents (or by the Executive Committee in case of inability to decide on the part of the President and Vice Presidents), consisting of three Directors selected as nearly as may be one from each general division of the Board. The names of the special manuscript committee shall be stated to each Director when notice of the proposed publication is submitted to him. It shall be the duty of each member of the special manuscript committee to read the manuscript. If each member of the manuscript committee signifies his approval within thirty days of the transmittal of the manuscript, the report may be published. If at the end of the period any member of the manuscript committee withholds his approval, the President shall then notify each member of the Board, requesting approval or disapproval of publication, and thirty days additional shall be granted for this purpose. The manuscript shall then not be published unless at least a majority of the entire Board who shall have voted on the proposal within the time fixed for the receipt of votes shall have approved.

5. No manuscript may be published, though approved by each member of the special manuscript committee, until forty-five days have elapsed from the transmittal of the report in manuscript form. The interval is allowed for the receipt of any memorandum of dissent or reservation, together with a brief statement of his reasons, that any member may wish to express; and such memorandum of dissent or reservation shall be published with the manuscript if he so desires. Publication does not, however, imply that each member of the Board has read the manuscript, or that either members of the Board in general or the special committee have passed on its validity in every detail.

6. Publications of the National Bureau issued for informational purposes concerning the work of the Bureau and its staff, or issued to inform the public of activities of Bureau staff, and volumes issued as a result of various conferences involving the National Bureau shall contain a specific disclaimer noting that such publication has not passed through the normal review procedures required in this resolution. The Executive Committee of the Board is charged with review of all such publications from time to time to ensure that they do not take on the character of formal research reports of the National Bureau, requiring formal Board approval.

7. Unless otherwise determined by the Board or exempted by the terms of paragraph 6, a copy of this resolution shall be printed in each National Bureau publication.

(Resolution adopted October 25, 1926, as revised through September 30, 1974)

Contents

Preface

This book is about the interrelations among race, schooling, and labor market outcomes for men, principally in the American South, from the late nineteenth century to the mid-twentieth. Two decades of quantitative research by social scientists and historians have greatly expanded our knowledge of slavery and its economic consequences for blacks, but the post-slave experience of blacks in the American economy has received less detailed attention. The goal of my book is to deepen our understanding of that experience and the context it provided for changes in racial economic differences after World War Two.

I have been fortunate to have had my work critiqued by colleagues at various stages. For their advice, I would like to especially thank Richard Freeman, David Gray, James J. Heckman, J. Morgan Kousser, Joel Perlmann, Jonathan Pritchett, and Paul Taubman. Many helpful comments were also provided by seminar participants at the American University, Colgate University, Harvard University, Indiana University, the National Bureau of Economic Research, Northwestern University, the University of California at Los Angeles, the University of Chicago, the University of Illinois, the University of Pennsylvania, the University of Massachusetts at Amherst, Vanderbilt University, Washington University at St. Louis, and Yale University.

The empirical research undertaken in this project required immense amounts of computer time and expertise. Most of the computer work was conducted while I was a member of the economics faculty of Colgate University. I am grateful to Colgate University for providing the computer time and to Richard Grant of the Colgate Computer Center for providing the expertise. Some of the data analyzed in Chapter 4 were collected as part of a project with Joel Perlmann on the social and economic history of American teachers, which has been financed by the Spencer Foundation and the National Science Foundation. I am grateful to both foundations for their support.

I owe special thanks to Stanley Engerman and Claudia Goldin, both of whom commented extensively on the penultimate version of the manuscript. My mentor, Robert Fogel, always encouraged me to turn my research articles into a book. I hope the end product aspires to the ideals and high standards set by these economic historians. I am also grateful to my editor, Julie McCarthy, for her comments on an early draft.

This book is dedicated to my wife, Wendy, and my son, Daniel.

R.A.M.   Nashville, Tennessee, 1990

1   Two Explanations of Economic Progress

The difference in economic status between blacks and whites is one of the most pressing social issues in the contemporary United States. The interrelations among race, schooling, and labor market outcomes are important factors behind these differences. By placing these interrelations in a particular historical and geographic context, a richer understanding of the dynamics of social change and economic development can emerge. This study will focus on the American South, from the late nineteenth century until the middle of the twentieth. Significant gains in relative black status since World War Two, as measured by the black-to-white earnings ratio, contrast with a period of little change between the turn of the century and the eve of World War Two (Figure 1.1).[1] In fact, between 1900 and 1940 the black-to-white earnings ratio for adult men showed an improvement of just 3 percentage points, while in the subsequent forty years the ratio increased a dramatic 13 percentage points.[2] Thus, in 1940, the average annual earnings of black men were about 48 percent of those of white men, but by 1980 the earnings ratio had risen to 61 percent (Smith 1984, 695). Associated with the increase in the earnings ratio, and perhaps a better indicator of social change, is the postwar emergence of a "new" black middle class composed of persons employed in a wide variety of skilled blue-collar and white-collar occupations (Landry 1987).[3]

Two frameworks have been advanced to explain the initial stability and subsequent rise in the earnings ratio: a supply-side, or "human capital" model, and a demand-side, or "institutionalist" model. Proponents of the human capital model argue that the initial stability of the earnings ratio can be explained by large and persistent racial differences in the "quantity" and "quality" of schooling in the first half of the twentieth century (Smith and Welch 1979; Smith 1984; U.S. Commission on Civil Rights 1986). Black men born in the late nineteenth and early twentieth centuries completed far fewer years of schooling, on average, than did white men. In addition, the vast majority had

1

Black-to-white earnings ratio

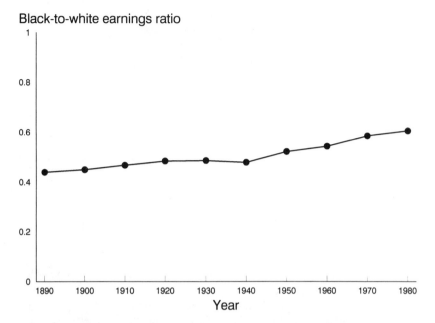

Figure 1.1   Black-to-White Earnings Ratios: Males, Ages 20 to 64
Source: Smith (1984).

attended *de jure* racially segregated public schools in the American South where the education they received was generally inferior in quality to that provided to southern whites. The combination of low educational attainment and poor educational quality made it extremely difficult for black men to compete successfully for better jobs and higher pay. Because these cohorts of black men "remained a large part of the labor force" during the first half of the twentieth century, "there was no reason to expect, on the basis of human capital factors," an increase in the earnings ratio (Smith 1984, 696). Eventually, however, the racial schooling gap declined, as successive generations of black children achieved higher levels of educational attainment than their parents had. Once the older generations had left the labor market, replaced by younger, better-educated black men, an improvement in the earnings ratio could, and did, commence.

Institutionalists do not dispute the long-term narrowing of racial differences in schooling. But they reject the claim, implicit in the human capital model, that a narrower schooling gap in the first half of the twentieth century would have done much good in fostering black economic progress at that time. Rather, institutionalists believe that, early in the century, the majority of black men were trapped in very low income jobs, primarily in southern agriculture. The absorption of black labor into better-paying jobs in the nonfarm economy was initially slow not because blacks were poorly educated, but because of historically determined patterns of employment segregation in the South, and because of racism and the availability of competing supplies of labor (European immigrants) in the North (Mandle 1978; Wright 1986). To speed up the process of absorption, positive "shocks" to the labor market were required, which permanently increased the nonfarm demand for black labor. During World War One the supply of immigrants was reduced and northern employers turned to southern blacks to fill their labor needs (Whatley 1990). Large increases in labor demand during World War Two again hastened the flow of black labor from the rural South.[4] But, for a variety of reasons, wartime shocks alone were not sufficient to set in motion a large and sustained rise in the earnings ratio. Additional shocks—the civil rights movement and associated antidiscrimination legislation—were necessary. It was only after such shocks had occurred that the earnings ratio could increase and a "new" black middle class, made up of better-educated, younger cohorts, could emerge.

Research on the relative merits of the human capital and institutionalist models has been inconclusive. Smith (1984) presented national average, cohort-specific series of earnings ratios and of racial differences in average educational attainment.[5] A regression of Smith's earnings ratios on the racial gap in educational attainment produces a statistically significant, negative coefficient: the smaller the schooling gap, the higher the earnings ratio.[6] Yet the relationship between the schooling gap and the earnings ratio is not very robust to minor modifications to the regression specification, which suggests that Smith's data are not sufficiently informative to distinguish between the human capital and institutionalist models (Kiefer and Phillips 1988). Indices of relative (black-to-white) occupational status compiled by Becker (1957, 113) show an increase in the North and a decrease in the South from 1910 to 1950, which suggests that national data mask important regional differences.

In this book I will critically examine the empirical relevance of the human capital and institutionalist models during the first half of the twentieth century. My basic conclusion is that the human capital model has merit, but that an eclectic synthesis of it and the institutionalist model, along with an additional factor that I call "intergenerational drag," does a better job of explaining the initial stability of the earnings ratio than either framework does alone. The synthesis has three parts.

1. *Human Capital*. Racial differences in educational attainment were an economically significant factor behind the initial stability in the earnings ratio. Had the racial schooling gap been smaller, more blacks would have been employed in nonfarm occupations and industries in the South and more would have migrated North. Racial differences in educational attainment were, to a significant extent, a consequence of public sector discrimination. According to constitutional doctrine, the black public schools of the American South were supposed to be "equal" in quality to the white schools, but were not. The

violations of the "separate-but-equal" doctrine hindered the educational attainment of black children and consequently their ability to enter the nonfarm economy as adults.

2. *Intergenerational Drag.* Even if the equal part of the separate-but-equal doctrine had been enforced in the southern public schools, the educational achievement of black children would have lagged behind white children, because of "family background" effects. Poverty and high rates of adult illiteracy, as much as the poor quality of the schools, kept black children out of the classroom. These family background effects, in turn, can be partly traced to educational backwardness in the nineteenth century and ultimately to slavery.

3. *Institutionalist.* Equalizing educational outcomes between the races would not have been enough to equalize earnings. Shocks to the labor market that increased the nonfarm demand for black labor were essential if earnings ratios were to start on a sustained upward path. Most of the black migration from the South cannot be accounted for by secular improvements in schooling; significant flows of black labor out of southern agriculture were associated with the world wars. Further, black men were underrepresented in the growth of nonfarm employment in the South from 1900 to 1950 because of their race, not because of inadequate schooling.

Part of the support for the synthesis rests on this book's econometric analyses of a rich and newly available body of evidence: the public use samples of the censuses of 1900, 1910, 1940, and 1950 (Center for Studies in Demography and Ecology 1980; Population Studies Center 1989; U.S. Bureau of the Census 1983a, 1983b). The principal advantage of the public use samples is that they allow the study of racial differences at a highly disaggregated level. In addition to the public use samples, I make extensive use of the published reports of state superintendents of education of various southern states, which provide detailed race-specific data on the characteristics of southern public schools.

Methodologically the book's analysis of labor market outcomes differs somewhat from most studies of racial differences. Such studies are frequently conducted within the framework of an *earnings function,* a regression of an individual's earnings on various personal characteristics, such as schooling, age, and geographic location (U.S. Commission on Civil Rights 1986; Smith and Welch 1989). My approach is to focus primarily on employment categories: industry, occupation, and region.[7] The selection of employment categories as the dependent variable is appropriate for my study, because the evidence of initial stability in the black-to-white earnings ratio is based on census data on employment categories.[8] In any case, it is an approach partly dictated by the nature of the 1900 and 1910 public use samples which contain no information on earnings. But, even if such data were available throughout the period, I contend that analysis of employment categories yields valuable information about racial differences in labor market outcomes beyond that contained in earnings data.[9] My approach is similar to that employed by James Heckman, Richard Butler, and Brooks Payner, who recently studied racial differences in employment in South Carolina after World War Two.[10] "Highly aggregated" data on black-white earnings ratios "do not isolate well-defined labor markets . . . [m]uch valuable institutional detail may be lost in the process of data aggregation . . . across diverse [economic] sectors" (Heckman and Payner 1989, 139).

Chapter 2 sets the stage by reviewing the historical evidence on racial differences in the quantity and quality of schooling in the South. Although racial differences in school attendance rates and child literacy declined over time, racial differences in the educational attainment of the adult population remained persistently large during the first half of the twentieth century. Chapters 3 and 4 are concerned with the political economy of resource allocation in *de jure* segregated schools. In Chapter 3 I demonstrate that racial differences in various indicators of the quality of schooling, such as per pupil expenditures, increased around the turn of the century and did not begin to narrow significantly until the 1940s. Chapter 4 is a study of racial differences in teacher salaries, which were a major proximate cause of racial differences in per pupil expenditures in the South. I find that, prior to World War Two, much of the difference between the wages of black and white teachers was a pure discriminatory "wedge."

The results of Chapters 3 and 4 demonstrate that the South violated the equal part of the Supreme Court's separate-but-equal doctrine established in *Plessy v. Ferguson* in 1896. Chapter 5 examines the impact of the violations on educational outcomes. Results from three case studies show that the violations hindered the educational achievement of black children, and thus their ability to enter the nonfarm economy. But, even had the equal part of separate-but-equal been enforced, a large part of the racial gap in educational outcomes would have remained because of family background effects. I conclude that only a radical redistribution of school resources might have compensated for these effects.

Chapters 6 and 7 are concerned with the impact of schooling on employment in the South and on migration from the South. Utilizing the public use samples, I show that schooling enhanced the probability that a black man would enter the nonfarm economy, in the South or elsewhere. But I also find that shifts of black labor out of southern agriculture cannot be explained by trends in schooling, and that black men were underrepresented in the expansion of nonfarm occupations and industries in the South because of their race. Thus, while the census samples provide support for the human capital model, demand-side factors, as described by institutionalists, were fundamentally important. A summary of my findings and their implications is contained in Chapter 8.

2   Race and Schooling in the South: A Review of the Evidence

In the South before 1950, racial differences existed in the "quantity" of schooling, as indicated by literacy, school attendance, and educational attainment. Differences also existed in the "quality" of schooling, as measured by the nominal characteristics of public schools, such as per pupil expenditures, class sizes, and the length of the school year. Although racial differences in illiteracy and school attendance declined steadily over time, racial differences in educational attainment remained persistently large, declining only towards the end of the period. Racial differences in the quality of schooling followed an inverted U-shaped pattern, increasing around the turn of the century, and then diminishing in the 1940s.

2.1   Illiteracy in the South Before 1950

Prior to 1940 the U.S. Bureau of the Census collected information on illiteracy—in essence, whether a person could read or write, at all, in any language. Panel A of Table 2.1 shows race-specific illiteracy rates in the South from 1880 to 1950 derived from the published census volumes, for all persons aged 10 and over, and for adult males ages 20 to 64. The figures for 1940 and 1950, and all of the adult figures, were computed from the census public use samples. In 1940 the census inquired about years of schooling (highest grade completed) instead of illiteracy. To make long-term comparisons it is necessary to convert the 1940 and 1950 data on years of schooling into illiteracy rates. Because the conversion procedure is an inexact one, a plausible range of figures is given.

In 1880, 76 percent of southern blacks (age 10 and over) were illiterate, a rate 55 percentage points greater than that for southern whites. The huge racial difference could hardly have been otherwise. On the eve of the Civil War the overwhelming majority of slaves were illiterate. During the late antebellum

Table 2.1 **Illiteracy in the South**[a]

A. By Race

	Ages 10 and Over			Males, Ages 20 to 64		
	Black	White	Dif	Black	White	Dif
1880	76.2%	21.5%	54.7			
1890	60.7	14.9	45.8			
1900	48.0	11.7	36.3	50.0%	11.9%	38.1
1910	33.3	8.0	25.3	40.4	9.4	31.0
1920	26.0	5.7	20.3			
1930	19.7	3.8	15.9			
1940	10.7–15.1	3.8–5.0	6.9–10.1	12.0–16.7	4.0–5.0	8.0–11.7
1950	8.9–12.0	2.4–3.3	6.5–8.7	9.6–13.3	2.5–3.3	7.1–10.0

B. For Blacks, by Age and Sex

	Age					
	10–14	15–24	25–34	35–44	45–54	55–64
Males						
1880	71.3					
1890	44.3	49.6	54.3	65.7	79.2	86.7
1900	35.6	39.5	40.2	47.9	63.7	77.6
1910	23.2	27.9	28.1	31.7	43.0	59.8
1920	14.5	21.7	23.9	26.9	34.5	47.5
1930	7.4	16.6	20.5	22.9	28.4	36.1
Females						
1880	69.1					
1890	40.0	48.8	69.3	84.9	91.1	93.4
1900	28.7	33.6	47.8	66.6	82.8	88.8
1910	17.3	20.6	28.2	41.9	62.0	77.2
1920	10.4	13.9	20.2	29.1	45.4	64.6
1930	4.9	8.8	14.2	20.7	30.9	45.6

[a]South: Delaware, District of Columbia, Maryland, West Virginia, Virginia, North Carolina, South Carolina, Georgia, Florida, Kentucky, Tennessee, Alabama, Mississippi, Arkansas, Louisiana, Oklahoma (1910–), Texas.

Notes: **Panel A:** figures in Black and White columns are percent illiterate; figures in Dif columns are differences between black and white illiteracy rates, in percentage points.

Sources: **Panel A:** AGES 10 AND OVER—*1880,* U.S. Census Office (1883, 919–25); *1890,* U.S. Census Office (1897, 218–19); *1900,* U.S. Census Office (1902, 436–37); *1910,* U.S. Bureau of the Census (1914, 1203); *1920,* U.S. Bureau of the Census (1922, 1159); *1930,* U.S. Bureau of the Census (1935, 235); *1940,* calculated from 5% random sample, 1940 public use sample. (A range is given. The lower bound assumes that 87.9% of persons reporting zero years of schooling and 82.5% of persons reporting one year of school were illiterate; the upper bound adds to the lower bound 52.8% of persons reporting two years of schooling. All other persons are assumed to be literate. The conversion factors between years of schooling and illiteracy were taken from U.S. Bureau of the Census 1948); *1950,* calculated from public use samples. Assumes same conversion factors between years of schooling and illiteracy as in 1940. MALES, AGES 20–64— *1900, 1910,* calculated from public use samples; *1940,* calculated from 5% random sample, 1940 public use sample; *1950,* calculated from 10% random sample, 1950 public use sample. **Panel B:** *1880,* U.S. Census Office (1883, 1651); *1890,* U.S. Census Office (1897, 112–13, 218–19); *1900,* U.S. Census Office (1904); *1910–1930,* U.S. Bureau of the Census (1918, 412; 1935).

period it was generally illegal to teach slaves to read and write. Even if it had been legal, it is doubtful that slave literacy rates would have been very high. Only a small percentage of slaves were involved in making economic decisions in which literacy would have been an asset to the slave owner.[1] A literate slave was presumed to be discontent chattel—or worse, a potential trouble-maker or runaway.

In the immediate aftermath of the Civil War the Freedmen's Bureau was established to ease the adjustment of ex-slaves to freedom. Historians have written extensively about the Bureau's educational programs (Morris 1981; Jones 1980). Northern teachers—the "Soldiers of Light and Love"—went South as part of these efforts. At the peak of operations in 1869, some 150,000 students were enrolled in Bureau schools. The educational impact of the Freedmen's Bureau, however, was less than often supposed. Its schools were primarily located in towns and cities, not in the countryside where the majority of southern blacks lived. Few adults benefited from Bureau schools (Ransom and Sutch 1977).

Some progress in combating adult black illiteracy came in the 1880s. Black illiteracy stood at 61 percent in 1890, down 15 percentage points from the 1880 figure. By 1900, slightly more than half of southern blacks claimed to be literate, a remarkable achievement in light of conditions a generation earlier. The postbellum decline in illiteracy was larger among blacks than whites. Nevertheless, the racial literacy gap in 1900 was still considerable (36 percentage points).

The black illiteracy rate continued to fall during the first half of the twentieth century, dropping to slightly more than 25 percent in 1920. By 1950, I estimate that between 88 and 91 percent of southern blacks were literate, as measured by the census.

Southern white illiteracy, too, declined between 1900 and 1950 but at a slower pace than black illiteracy. Consequently the racial literacy gap fell steadily. In 1910 the racial literacy gap stood at 25 percentage points. By 1950, the gap had decreased to 7–9 percentage points.

Literacy rates of adult males followed a path similar to that of the population aged 10 and over. Using the 1900 census sample, half of the adult black males in the South were illiterate, compared with 12 percent of the adult white males. In the 1940 sample between 12 and 17 percent of adult black men are classified as illiterate. By 1950 the racial literacy gap among adult men was 7–10 percentage points, slightly higher than among the population aged 10 and over.

Panel B of Table 2.1 displays literacy rates of southern blacks arrayed by age group and sex. Moving down a column gives the literacy rate of a particular age group in each census year. For ages 15 and over, moving along a diagonal shows how the literacy rate evolved for a birth cohort.[2] For example, 48 percent of black males aged 35–44 were illiterate in 1900; moving ahead ten years, 43 percent of black men aged 45–54 were illiterate in 1910.

The long-term decline in black illiteracy was achieved by a succession of literate younger cohorts replacing illiterate older ones. Fully 71 percent of black male children ages 10 to 14 were illiterate in 1880. Illiteracy among this age group was cut in half by the turn of the century (to 36 percent) and by another 29 percentage points by 1930.

Among older blacks illiteracy rates were extremely high during the immediate postbellum period and remained high as these cohorts aged. In 1890, for example, 66 percent of black men aged 35 to 44 (virtually all of whom had been enslaved at birth) were illiterate. In 1900 the illiteracy rate of this cohort, now aged 45 to 54, was 64 percent, virtually unchanged over the intervening decade. A black man (or woman) who reached adulthood illiterate was very unlikely to learn to read or write later in life: "The idea that after slavery was abolished large numbers of adult blacks successfully acquired, on their own, elementary reading or writing skills is a myth" (Smith 1984, 691).

Among black children, females had higher literacy rates than males. For example, 83 percent of females in 1910 could read and write, compared with 77 percent of males. In the late nineteenth and early twentieth centuries the gender difference in literacy rates was opposite in sign among older age groups. Among 35- to 44-year-olds in 1900, the female illiteracy rate exceeded that for males by 19 percentage points. Eventually, the gender difference in literacy among older blacks declined as younger black females, who had higher literacy rates than younger males, replaced the older age groups in the population.

The high rates of adult illiteracy inherited from slavery had serious consequences for black economic progress. Later I shall demonstrate that schooling expanded a black man's economic options by increasing his probability of holding a nonfarm job in the South or moving from the South. Illiterates had fewer options, and most were condemned to a life of very low incomes. Illiterates were less likely to accumulate wealth than were literates (Higgs 1982; Margo 1984a). The negative effects of adult illiteracy were felt across generations; as I shall demonstrate, children of illiterate parents were less likely to attend school than were children whose parents could read and write.

2.2   School Attendance in the South, 1880–1950

The spread of literacy among southern blacks was a consequence of the acquisition of literacy by the young. Because high rates of adult black illiteracy persisted into the twentieth century, it is implausible that the majority of black children learned to read and write at home. Rather, as will be shown, school attendance rates of black children rose over time. Further, the racial gap in school attendance that existed after the Civil War narrowed over time as well.

Table 2.2 shows race-specific school attendance rates, by sex and age group. The rates were calculated from data collected by the U.S. Bureau of

Table 2.2	School Attendance Rates in the South			

	Ages			
	5–9	10–14	15–20	5–20
Black Males				
1880				21.1%[a]
1890	22.4%	48.6%	17.1%	29.5
1900	21.6	49.7	14.9	28.5
1910	38.5	63.7	23.7	41.8
1920	50.8	75.8	26.8	51.6
1930	58.2	86.4	31.4	57.6
1940	64.7	88.6	34.2	61.3
1950	69.2	93.5	45.4	69.3
Black Females				
1880				21.1[a]
1890	23.2	53.1	18.4	31.1
1900	22.6	56.2	19.7	31.9
1910	40.6	70.0	29.2	45.6
1920	52.3	79.4	31.5	53.7
1930	60.3	89.1	35.3	59.6
1940	66.4	91.5	39.1	63.7
1950	70.3	94.6	45.0	69.0
White Males				
1890	38.4	79.4	33.9	49.6
1900	35.0	74.3	32.0	46.4
1910	52.5	84.8	40.6	58.5
1920	61.3	89.8	37.2	62.8
1930	64.4	93.6	42.5	66.6
1940	64.5	93.4	45.3	66.5
1950	69.9	93.2	53.5	71.6
White Females				
1890	38.4	76.6	30.1	47.6
1900	35.0	77.3	31.5	47.0
1910	51.9	85.8	39.2	57.8
1920	61.4	89.9	42.0	63.2
1930	65.3	94.4	42.7	66.2
1940	65.6	94.0	43.8	66.1
1950	71.0	96.5	49.1	71.2

Notes: Figures are total number of children attending school divided by the population aged 5 to 20. **Black Children:** *1890, 1900,* adjusted for nonreporting bias, see Appendix to this chapter; *1950,* attendance rates for Delaware were estimated by (1) estimating ratio of attendance rates, Delaware/Maryland in 1940, (2) multiplying ratio by attendance rates for Maryland in 1950, and (3) estimating numbers of black children in Delaware in 1950, using 1940 ratio of Delaware to other states. **White Children:** *1890, 1900,* adjusted for underreporting (see Appendix to this chapter); **1940,** adjusted for underreporting in Kentucky; *1950,* attendance rates for Delaware were estimated using procedure described above for black children.

[a]To estimate the black attendance rate in 1880, a state-level logit regression of the child literacy rate for ages 10–14 (LIT) on the attendance rate for ages 10–14 (ATT) was estimated using data for 1910. The results (with *t*-statistics in parentheses) were:

$$\text{logit (LIT)} = -3.56 + 7.63 \text{ ATT} \qquad N = 17, R^2 = 0.75$$
$$(5.14) \quad (8.01)$$

Next, I used the regression to estimate ATT (ages 10–14) in 1880 (LIT is known in 1880). I then multiplied ATT by the ratio of attendance for ages 5–20 to attendance for ages 10–14 in 1890.

Sources: *1890–1940,* U.S. Bureau of the Census (1943). *1950,* U.S. Bureau of the Census (1952) for black children, and for white children the figures were estimated from a 25% random sample of the 1950 public use tape.

the Census.[3] Like the literacy question, the census question on school attendance was a minimal indicator; in general, a person was counted as having attended school provided she attended at least one day during a specific period prior to the date the census was taken.[4] In 1890 and 1900, however, the question pertained to the number of months children attended school. It has been suggested that the question on months attended led to an undercount of black children enrolled in school (Smith 1986). The Appendix to the chapter considers this question at length, concluding that small upward adjustments to the original data are warranted. These adjustments are included in Table 2.2.

In 1880 about 20 percent of black children (ages 5 to 20) attended school, and attendance climbed to about 30 percent in 1900. From 1900 to 1950 the attendance rate rose continuously, increasing by 22 percentage points between 1900 and 1920. By 1950 69 percent of southern black children attended school in the previous year, more than double the proportion fifty years earlier.

In the late nineteenth and early twentieth century school attendance rates of southern white children exceeded those of black children by a considerable margin. In 1890, for example, the white attendance rate (ages 5 to 20) was 48 percent, 18 percentage points higher than the rate for blacks. By 1920 63 percent of white children were attending school at some point during the census year, about 10 percentage points higher than the black attendance rate. Growth in white attendance continued during the 1920s, slowed during the Great Depression, and then rebounded again in the 1940s. In 1950 about 71 percent of southern white children were attending school. This was, however, only 2 percentage points greater than the black attendance rate in 1950. Thus, like racial differences in literacy rates, racial differences in school attendance declined over time, with the bulk of the decline occurring after 1910.

Consistent with the gender differences in literacy rates, black female children attended school more frequently than black male children. The gender difference was larger among children over the age of 10 than among younger children. The gender difference declined over time as school attendance became a universal phenomenon among black children. Attendance followed an inverted U-shaped pattern with respect to age. Rates of attendance were lowest among the age groups 5–9 and 15–20, peaking in the age group 10–14. In 1900, for example, about half of black male children aged 10–14 attended school, compared with 22 percent of 5- to 9-year-olds and 15 percent of 15- to 20-year-olds. But the growth in attendance over time was greater in the younger and older age groups than in the middle. The inverted U flattened as the century progressed.

Except in 1920, the overall attendance rate of white female children was slightly less than that of white male children, reflecting slightly lower female attendance in the older age group. Attendance rates of white children peaked in the age group 10–14, and over time, the inverted U-shaped pattern flattened. Growth in white attendance was greater among the younger and older age groups than among children between the ages of 10 and 14.

Despite the long-term narrowing, it is clear from Table 2.2 that a significant racial gap in school attendance existed prior to 1940. Earlier I suggested that high rates of adult black illiteracy may have contributed to keeping the gap wide. The reasons for a negative relationship between adult illiteracy and school attendance are complex: Illiterate parents had lower incomes and wealth—they needed their children to work, on the family farm or in the market; illiterate parents were more likely to live in rural, predominantly black counties (the "black belt") where educational opportunities were most limited; and illiterate parents could not help their children learn to read and write. The quantitative significance of the relationship between adult literacy and school attendance of children is explored in more detail in Chapter 5. My goal here is to establish that a relationship existed.

Panel A of Table 2.3 shows the relationship between the school attendance of southern black children and the literacy status of their parents, using a sample drawn from the 1910 census tape. The date refer to two-parent families, but the substantive findings would not change if single-parent households were included. A majority of children (64 percent) lived in families in which one or both of the parents was illiterate. Both parents of about 34 percent of the children were illiterate. Consistent with the gender differences in adult literacy discussed earlier, in 16 percent of the cases the father was literate and the mother illiterate, while a smaller fraction (14 percent) had literate mothers and illiterate fathers.

It is clear that school attendance was correlated with the literacy of the parents. In households with both parents illiterate, 36.8 percent of the children attended school, compared with 56.8 percent in households in which both parents were literate, or a difference of 20 percentage points. Attendance was higher, as well, in households in which at least one parent was literate. The effect was slightly greater if the mother, rather than the father, was the literate parent.

Panel B of Table 2.3 reports a regression of census data on black school attendance rates from 1910 to 1930. The data are state aggregates: the independent variables are dummy variables for gender, age group, decade, whether the state had a compulsory schooling law, and the illiteracy rate of adults, ages 35 to 44. The dummy variable for compulsory school legislation was included to see if such laws had their intended positive effect on school attendance.

The results confirm the existence of an economically and statistically significant relationship between adult literacy and school attendance. Holding constant other factors, a reduction of 10 percentage points in adult illiteracy increased the school attendance rate by 4.2 percentage points. The coefficient of the compulsory schooling dummy is positive and significant at the 10 percent level but it is small in magnitude, consistent with other studies showing that such legislation had only minor impacts on school attendance (Landes and Solmon 1972).

Table 2.3   **School Attendance and Parental Illiteracy: Southern Black Children, Ages 5 to 20**

A. 1910 Census Sample

	Number of Observations	Attending School (%)
Both parents illiterate	2,147	36.8
Father literate, mother illiterate	1,046	45.1
Father illiterate, mother literate	909	45.5
Both parents literate	2,308	56.8

B. Regressions of School Attendance

	Without State Dummies		With State Dummies	
	β	t-statistic	β	t-statistic
Constant	0.552	23.65	0.665	10.22
Female	0.036	5.11	0.038	6.11
Age group:				
10–14	0.273	31.04	0.272	37.29
15–20	−0.207	−24.56	−0.207	−28.91
Adult illiteracy rate, ages 35–44	−0.420	−8.21	−0.692	−4.87
Compulsory schooling law	0.027	1.91	0.011	0.82
Decade:				
1920	0.029	2.39	0.015	1.02
1930	0.076	5.98	0.046	2.17
Number of observations	306		306	
R^2	0.918		0.948	

Notes: **Panel A:** Sample is from the public use tape of the 1910 census and consists of all black children residing in the South in 1910, both parents present. **Panel B:** Dependent variable is age- and sex-specific school attendance rate of black children, in state j in year t (= 1910, 1920, 1930), from Table 2.2 and Landes and Solmon (1972).

2.3 Years of Schooling

National data on educational attainment, or "years of schooling," were first collected by the Bureau of the Census in 1940. For persons born since 1915, census data provide a reliable time series of the average educational attainment of the adult population. For persons born before 1915, the data must be arranged by age group (or birth cohort) to get at the long-term trend. When the data are so arranged, they measure the average educational attainment of persons who *survived* to at least 1940 (i.e., survived to answer the census question; see below).

Figures 2.1 and 2.2 chart race-specific estimates of average years of schooling by birth cohort, for persons born in the South, and for the entire male population, regardless of place of birth. The average educational attainment of southern blacks born before the Civil War was only 2.4 years of schooling.

Years of schooling

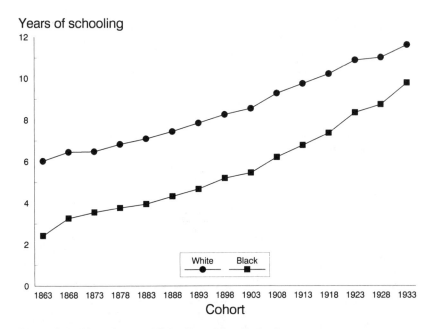

Figure 2.1   Mean Years of Schooling: Born in the South
Notes: Cohort is midpoint of five-year birth cohort, for example, 1913 refers to the birth cohort
1913–18; 1863: born before 1865.
Source: Smith (1986, 1227).

Years of schooling rose to more than double the pre–Civil War level for cohorts born at the end of the nineteenth century. Still, it is clear that the average
educational attainment of the southern black population was extremely low in
the late nineteenth and early twentieth centuries, absolutely and compared
with southern whites.

Black educational attainment rose with each successive birth cohort. The
average educational attainment of southern blacks born between 1916 and
1920 was 7.4 years, a full three years longer than the average among those
born between 1886 and 1890. Mean years of schooling increased to 8.75
years—an elementary school education—among southern blacks born between 1926 and 1930, and to 10.4 years—some high school—among those
born in the late 1930s.

Average years of schooling among southern whites born before the end of
the Civil War was 6.0 years, 3.6 years longer than for southern blacks. Among
white cohorts born after the war but before 1880—that is, during Reconstruction—average years of schooling rose but at a slower pace than among southern blacks, and the mean racial schooling gap declined, to about 3 years. The
gap then remained stable among cohorts born between 1876 and 1915.

The cohort of southern whites born just after World War One was the first

Years of schooling

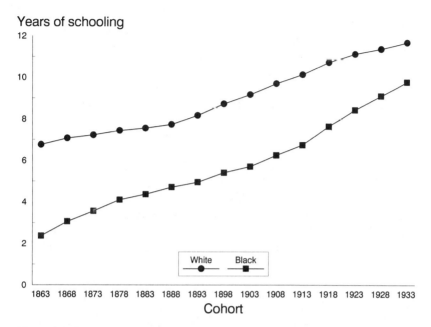

Figure 2.2   Mean Years of Schooling: Males, U.S. Average
Notes: Cohort is midpoint of five-year birth cohort; 1863: born before 1865.
Source: Smith (1984, 687)

to complete, on average, a substantial amount of high school. Mean years of schooling among whites born between 1916 and 1920 was 10.2 years. Average years of schooling for southern whites continued to increase among cohorts born in the next twenty years, to nearly 12 years for those born in the late 1930s. The growth in white educational attainment was slower than for blacks, however, and the racial schooling gap once again began to decline. The racial gap stood at 2.5 years among those born in the early 1920s, falling to 1.6 years among those born between 1936 and 1940.

The national data (Figure 2.2) show that, for both black and white males, average educational attainment was far lower in the South than elsewhere in the country. The national data also indicate that the racial gap in educational attainment widened for male cohorts born between 1886 and 1915. After 1915 the gap declined continuously, as it did in the South.

Cohorts born between 1880 and 1915 formed the bulk of the labor force during the first half of the twentieth century (Smith 1984). Thus census data imply that racial differences in educational attainment were persistently large among persons in the labor force in the South prior to 1950. In the nation as a whole, this conclusion holds a fortiori because the racial schooling gap appears to have increased for cohorts born between 1880 and World War One.

The persistently large racial gap in educational attainment may seem paradoxical in light of the pronounced declines over time in the racial gaps in literacy and school attendance. Literacy and school attendance, however, are very crude indicators of schooling. Two persons can be "literate" according to the census definition and have vastly different educational backgrounds—a fourth grade education, for example, versus a high school diploma. A school attendance rate measures the fraction of the population attending school in a particular year, not their educational level.

More fundamentally, a school attendance rate does not reveal whether attendance behavior was "homogeneous" or "heterogeneous." In 1890 the average school attendance rate of southern black children ages 5 to 20 was 29.5 percent (Table 2.2). This could mean that *every* black male attended school for 29.5 percent of his childhood years, a total of 4.7 years (0.295 × 16 years).[5] Or it could mean that 29.5 percent of black male children achieved a fairly high level of educational attainment while the rest never attended school at all, or attended only rarely. The former is what is meant by "homogeneous" behavior, the latter by "heterogeneous" behavior.

Black school attendance in the late nineteenth century South was far from homogeneous because, if it had been, the literacy rate of black children (ages 10 to 14) would have been much higher than it actually was (56.7 percent in 1890; see Table 2.1).[6] Between 1880 and 1920 it became much more likely that a southern black child would attend a sufficient amount of school to be considered "literate" according to the census definition. Black attendance behavior was more homogeneous in this sense, but it was not until the cohorts born after World War One that black children began to stay in school long enough, on average, to narrow the racial gap in years of schooling. Even then, black attendance in the 1920s and 1930s was still very heterogeneous, as indicated by a skewed distribution of enrollments by grade. In the early 1930s 34 percent of all southern black children enrolled in elementary or secondary schools attended kindergarten or the first grade; fully 72 percent were enrolled in grade four or below (Blose and Caliver 1935, 23). By 1950, 20 percent of southern black enrollments were in kindergarten or the first grade; 14.1 percent of those enrolled attended high school compared with 5.8 percent in 1931–32 (U.S. Department of Health, Education, and Welfare 1954, 102; Blose and Caliver 1935, 23).

Thus a portion of the persistent racial gap in years of schooling can be attributed to the initial heterogeneity of black school attendance. Over time *some* school attendance became universal, but average black educational attainment as a result increased more slowly *across* cohorts than either literacy or school attendance rates.[7]

Not all of the persistence, however, can be explained in this manner. The underlying census data are not above suspicion. As pointed out earlier, the data on educational attainment are retrospective—persons had to survive at least until 1940 in order to report their educational attainment to the census. Educational attainment and life expectancy, however, are positively correlated: those who survive longer tend to be better educated than the average member of their birth cohort. Another problem is the potential for educational "creep" or "self-promotion." As educational norms rise, individuals may exaggerate their schooling accomplishments as they age. Making generous allowances for mortality and creep bias, however, does not change the conclusion that the racial gap in years of schooling remained persistently large early in the century (see Margo 1986c, 195–97).

There is another reason, however, to suspect that the meaning of "years of schooling" differed between blacks and whites. The length of the school year in southern black schools was less than in the region's white schools (see Section 2.4). The average length of the school year in the South, black or white, was shorter than in the nation as a whole. Such differences would not necessarily result in biases. A black pupil attending school for four months of the year for eight years would finish, at most, half the grades completed by a white attending eight months for eight years. However, the wording of the census question apparently caused years of schooling to be overstated for many blacks. Although the question was phrased in terms of grades completed, the Bureau of the Census knew that many respondents had been educated in "ungraded" schools. If a person attended an ungraded school—a school without formal age-grade distinctions, although the students would be differentiated by their level of progress—census enumerators were supposed to "enter the approximate equivalent grade . . . or, if this cannot readily be determined, the number of years the person attended school" (U.S. Bureau of the Census 1943, 178). How many enumerators actually followed these instructions is not known, nor is the meaning of "number" certain. But an obvious interpretation of "number" is the literal one. A child attending school from age 8 to age 14 would report her educational attainment as 6 "years," which would then be tabulated (by the census) as the sixth "grade." Ungraded-school bias is a serious problem because most black schools in the late nineteenth century South were ungraded. In Texas, for example, fully 89 percent of the black schools were ungraded in 1900 (Margo 1986c, 196). Graded schools were more common in cities and towns, because the division of students into grades was a function of economies of scale. Urban schools were larger schools, and thus could accommodate a greater division of labor among teachers specializing in certain grades or subjects.

Circumstantial evidence of ungraded school bias among blacks is shown in Table 2.4. The column labelled Years of Schooling is an alternative estimate of educational attainment, giving the average number of *years* spent in school. The column labelled Highest Grade Completed gives the census attainment data. Using the Years of Schooling column, the racial gap in educational attainment shows a decline over time, in contrast to the trend in Figure 2.2.

Dividing years of schooling by highest grade completed provides an estimate of the average number of years necessary to complete a grade. If ungraded school bias were important for blacks, one would expect to find years

Table 2.4   The Bias in Educational Attainment: Black Cohorts

Cohort	Years of Schooling	Highest Grade Completed
1886–90	4.9	4.7
1891–95	5.5	5.0
1896–1900	6.4	5.4
1901–5	7.2	5.7
1906–10	8.0	6.3

Note: Figures are national, cohort-specific averages.
Source: Years of schooling, Margo (1986b, 1222); *Highest Grade Completed,* Smith (1984).

per grade to be close to one. Among black males born between 1886 and 1890 it is 1.05. A similarly constructed estimate for white males in the same cohort group is 1.1 years per grade (Margo 1986b, 1222).[8] In the absence of bias, it is implausible for the white estimate to exceed the black estimate: the black schools were inferior in quality to the white schools, which hampered black educational achievement (Chapter 5).

Over time the black school year increased in length and graded schools replaced ungraded ones. The timing of the replacement cannot be determined with certainty because no state kept adequate records. It is clear, however, that the shift was substantially underway by World War One. Reasonably good national data on the distribution of southern black enrollments by grade level first appeared in 1918. The shift from ungraded to graded schools makes the average educational attainment of blacks appear to increase more slowly over time than it actually did.

Some studies have used the apparent widening of the racial gap in educational attainment to explain the stability of the aggregate black-to-white income ratio before World War Two (Smith 1984). My findings suggest, however, that the widening of the attainment gap was partly an artifact of the way census data were collected. It does *not* follow, however, that racial differences in schooling were unimportant determinants of racial differences in labor market outcomes prior to World War Two; Chapters 6 and 7 will demonstrate that they were. The existence of ungraded school bias is itself a manifestation of large racial differences in the quality of schooling, which are discussed in the next section. No matter how carefully it is measured, the average educational attainment of black people fell well below that of whites during the first half of the twentieth century.

2.4   The Quality of Schooling: The Racial Division of Public School Expenditures in the South, 1890 to 1950

In 1917 the U.S. Bureau of Education published "Negro Education: A Study of the Private and Higher Schools for Colored People in the United States" (Bulletin nos. 38 and 39). Written by Thomas Jesse Jones, the two volumes chronicled conditions in the nation's black schools to a degree far beyond what the title implied. In Jones's view, conditions in private black schools, the majority of which were located in the South, were inextricably tied to conditions in the *de jure* segregated public schools of the South. For example, that there were few public high schools for blacks meant that "[high] schools for Negroes [were] dependent on private aid" (Jones 1917, 7). Jones collected pertinent statistics on the public schools from published state reports, surveys of school superintendents, and personal correspondence, interpreted these carefully, and made numerous policy recommendations. His report was (and is) the most comprehensive survey of segregated schools for its time.

The picture Jones painted was a grim one. Great progress had been made in improving the South's schools for white children since the turn of the century. Teacher salaries had been increased, school terms lengthened, inefficient one-teacher schools consolidated and replaced by multiroom, modern buildings, and public high schools had multiplied enormously. But little of the educational awakening had trickled down to the black schools. "Inadequacy and poverty," Jones lamented, "are the outstanding characteristics of every type . . . of education for Negroes in the United States. No form of education is satisfactorily equipped or supported" (1917, 9).

Statistics on expenditures revealed a shocking indifference to the educational needs of black children. Jones concentrated his attention on expenditures on instruction (teacher salaries), which were the most reliable and widely available figures. For every dollar spent on teacher salaries per white child ages 6 to 14, 29 cents was spent per black child.[9] The lower level of expenditures in black schools was the direct consequence of a shorter school year, classroom overcrowding (a higher teacher-pupil ratio), and lower pay for black teachers.

Geographic variations in conditions in the black public schools received Jones's attention. The situation was worse in the Deep South than in the upper South. In Alabama the black-to-white ratio of state averages of per pupil expenditures was 0.19. In Maryland the ratio was 0.46 (1917, 23). Interstate differences, however, were smaller than differences between counties. In counties in which the black population constituted between 10 and 25 percent of the population (29 percent of white children and 12 percent of black children lived in such counties), 58 cents was spent per black pupil for every dollar spent per white pupil. In counties in which the black population share ranged from 50 to 75 percent (where 10 percent of white children and 37 percent of black children resided), the black-to-white ratio was a meager 0.14—14 cents per black pupil for every dollar spent per white pupil (28).

Expenditures on teacher salaries were not the only important difference between the black and white public schools. Many of the black schools were in privately owned buildings (churches, lodges, or rural cabins) donated to local school boards and pressed into service. The exterior surroundings "varied from untidy to positively filthy. Ash heaps often adorned the front yards, . . . at barely respectable distances leaned ugly outhouses in unscreened and shameful impudence" (1917, 32). School equipment (books, blackboards, chalk, maps, globes) was undersupplied or nonexistent. Many teachers labored valiantly against the odds, but others were "utterly incapable of any responsibility" (34). An adequate supply of well-trained educators was impossible because "public provision for training colored teachers [was] negligible" (34).

It was at the high school level that the differences were most pronounced. In the entire South there were only sixty-four public high schools for black children.[10] A southern black child wishing a post-elementary education had to seek it in one of the region's private schools or else leave the region. Because most of the private schools were located in towns or cities while the black population was heavily rural, a black child's opportunities for a secondary education were severely circumscribed. Inadequate facilities at the secondary level compounded the difficulties of the elementary schools, because the high schools were a chief supplier of the students who might eventually become teachers.

With conditions like these, it was hardly surprising that black children, on average, attended school less frequently than white children. "The low attendance in colored schools," Jones declared, "is the first great problem to be solved" (1917, 32). He laid the blame squarely on the "poor and unattractive" schools and the "low economic status" of the black community (38).

Jones was well aware that the huge divergence between the black and white schools was a phenomenon of comparatively recent origin at that time. Table 2.5 pieces together race-specific estimates of per pupil expenditures on teachers salaries (in 1950 dollars) for various southern states from 1890 to 1950. Racial differences in instructional expenditures were smaller than in the value of school capital or in expenditures on ancillary services, such as transportation. Nevertheless, available data on these other aspects of school quality suggest that the trends in teacher salaries faithfully summarize the general trend in the relative (black-to-white) quality of the black schools.

Around 1890 the public schools of the southern states could be charitably described as backward. It had been so since antebellum days (Kaestle 1983). The North experienced its "common school revival" long before the South did, and was on the verge of mass high school education at the turn of the century, which the South was not. Despite considerable improvement during the postbellum period, southern public schools lagged far behind. In 1890, per pupil expenditures in southern public schools equalled only 43 percent of the average outside the region. The average length of the school year was ninety-two days, two months shorter than the average elsewhere.[11]

When pressed, southerners justified their region's indifference to education by appealing to economic and social constraints. The South was a poor, agricultural region—wealth per adult male was lower than the national average

Table 2.5   **Per Pupil Expenditures on Instruction: Selected Southern States (in 1950 dollars)**

	c. 1890	c. 1910	c. 1935	c. 1950
Alabama				
Black	8.80	10.39	17.50	67.66
White	8.89	33.51	53.18	89.50
Ratio	0.99	0.31	0.33	0.76
Arkansas				
Black	NA	15.48	17.71	46.46
White	NA	37.13	39.80	74.45
Ratio	NA	0.42	0.45	0.62
Delaware				
Black	NA	31.48	129.51	116.12
White	NA	41.80	129.50	133.65
Ratio	NA	0.75	1.00	0.87
Florida				
Black	13.12	9.95	34.66	107.11
White	26.66	36.05	84.74	134.57
Ratio	0.49	0.28	0.41	0.80
Georgia				
Black	NA	8.74	15.12	59.80
White	NA	29.84	55.59	89.59
Ratio	NA	0.29	0.27	0.68
Louisiana				
Black	8.29	9.03	19.91	86.48
White	16.57	53.76	74.60	139.04
Ratio	0.50	0.17	0.27	0.62
Maryland				
Black	27.88	27.88	80.63	134.86
White	42.82	47.34	102.84	142.71
Ratio	0.65	0.59	0.78	0.95
Mississippi				
Black	9.27	7.67	13.36	22.29
White	18.62	27.88	58.61	71.00
Ratio	0.50	0.28	0.23	0.31
North Carolina				
Black	7.75	9.28	32.92	92.84
White	7.67	17.25	51.43	100.37
Ratio	1.01	0.54	0.64	0.93
South Carolina				
Black	NA	6.13	18.62	58.82
White	NA	32.43	67.74	91.77
Ratio	NA	0.19	0.28	0.64
Tennessee				
Black	NA	13.24	32.68	50.67
White	NA	19.76	57.24	73.41
Ratio	NA	0.67	0.57	0.69
Texas				
Black	NA	22.19	42.84	114.32
White	NA	35.06	85.68	137.22
Ratio	NA	0.63	0.50	0.83

(continued)

Table 2.5   (continued)

	c. 1890	c. 1910	c. 1935	c. 1950
Virginia				
Black	13.82	13.64	33.05	82.06
White	19.90	32.79	63.81	93.61
Ratio	0.69	0.42	0.52	0.88

Notes: Figures are expenditures on teacher salaries per pupil in average daily attendance and pertain to public schools only. Price index is Warren-Pearson wholesale price index (U.S. Bureau of the Census 1975). NA: not available. *Sources: 1890,* Margo (1985); *1910,* Jones (1917); *1935,* Blose and Caliver (1938); *1950,* U.S. Department of Health, Education, and Welfare (1954).

and children were needed on the farm, particularly in cotton cultivation. Fertility was high: there were far more children to be educated, per adult, than elsewhere in the country. Population density was low, which drove up school costs on a per pupil basis. Last but not least, the South had the added expense of maintaining a dual system of *de jure* racially segregated public schools.

At the time Jones's study was published, the "added expense" excuse was a poor one. It was somewhat more plausible in 1890. In five of the eight states represented in Table 2.5, per pupil expenditures in 1890 were higher in the white schools than in black schools. Of these, three states—Florida, Louisiana, and Mississippi—recorded the lowest levels of the black-to-white spending ratio, all well less than one. Yet in the other states in the table (Alabama, Kentucky, and North Carolina), per pupil expenditures did not differ much between the races. The dual school systems were certainly not equal, but they were more equal (as measured by per pupil expenditures) than at any time prior to the Supreme Court's 1954 school desegregation case, *Brown v. Board of Education.*

Comments by state school superintendents reprinted by the U.S. Bureau of Education in its annual report for 1890 provide insights into how school funds were distributed in the late nineteenth century. Arkansas is not one of the states represented in the table but, judging by the testimony of Josiah Shinn, the state's superintendent of public instruction, it seems that equal provision was reasonably well adhered to:

> The law apportions to all children irrespective of color. Each child in Arkansas, black and white, . . . receives the same amount of money by State apportionment. Each county in the State, irrespective of color, gets an amount of money equal to the sum of the amounts given to its children of school age . . . [each] district gets . . . a sum of money . . . equal to the multiple formed by the pro rata into the number of children in the district. (U.S. Bureau of Education 1893, 1077)

The total amount of school funds available to be distributed at the district level consisted of the state school fund, county poll taxes, and any property tax voted by the taxpayers of the school district. "Up to this point in our financial management," Shinn continued, "no [racial] distinction whatever has been made." The school fund was to be distributed between the races by local school "directors" (the school board) and "if any discrimination is made . . . the fault will lie with the directors." But there was "no restriction upon the black man's right to hold the office of school director. In eastern Arkansas in a large majority of the districts the [directors are] black" (1893, 1077).

Two types of distribution schemes were generally followed. In the first, money was allocated "to hold a three months' school for each race." If any funds were left over, they were distributed "by taking the ratio of the black and white children of school age, respectively, to the whole number of children." In Shinn's opinion the way in which additional funds were distributed was "always more favorable to the colored race than to the white" because the fraction of black children of school age who were attending school was lower than the white fraction. The second scheme, which held "schools of equal length" regardless of the relative proportions of white and black children, was "on the broadest basis of fairness, and reaches the widest stretch of justice. . . . It would be unjust . . . not to say further that the greater majority of our school directors follow the second plan." Shinn concluded by listing twenty-one cities and towns in which the "terms and all the other arrangements" were equal between the races (1893, 1077).

Alabama's state superintendent of education noted that state law required the state school fund be "apportioned among the townships and districts according to the number of children of school age, the fund of each race being kept separate." Poll taxes, also part of the school fund, were kept separate as well. This method of distributing school funds, the superintendent added, "has caused much dissatisfaction" (1893, 1075), presumably for the same reasons as in Arkansas.

By 1910 school officials no longer divided school budgets relatively equally between the races. Table 2.5 shows that the black-to-white ratio of per pupil expenditures declined in every state between 1890 and 1910. In some states (Florida, Mississippi, Virginia, Louisiana), expenditures per black pupil actually fell in constant dollars. In the others, expenditures per black pupil stayed the same or else grew at a much slower rate than spending per white pupil.

The fall over time in the black-to-white ratio of per pupil expenditures at the state level was not the only change of importance between 1890 and 1910. The negative relationship between the percentage of blacks and the black-to-white ratio of per pupil expenditures became more pronounced over the twenty-year period (Margo 1985).

Fundamentally an optimist, Jones believed the black public schools would eventually improve, even though he had little cause to do so at the time. Subsequent events proved he was right. In 1938 the U.S. Office of Education published "Statistics of the Education of Negroes, 1933–34 and 1935–36" (Bulletin no. 13), written by David Blose and Ambrose Caliver. The fifth such report since Jones's landmark study, it contained an abundance of data on enrollments, attendance, class sizes, expenditures, the value of school property, and other aspects of the schools.

Blose and Caliver (1938, 1) pointed with pride to the "remarkable progress" that had been made "in the education of Negroes . . . during the preceding two decades. . . . Many of the Southern States have more [black] public high schools now . . . than all the Southern States combined had 20 years ago. . . . Public support of education for Negroes had grown at a rapid rate." The overall proportion of black children enrolled in school had increased by 26 percentage points. The school term was lengthened, and children tended to stay in school for more years than they had previously. In 1915 teachers' salaries in the black schools equalled almost $6 million. By 1935 the sum had grown to $35 million. To Blose and Caliver, the trends indicated that "more schools of all types [were] being provided Negroes," as well as "a growing appreciation of Negroes as to the value of education in the solution of many problems which confront them" (2).

But in other respects Blose and Caliver's assessment was as gloomy as was Jones's. Despite the gains for blacks, "the divergence between the two races [had] not lessened" (1938, 2). In the quarter-century from 1910 to 1935, the white schools had not stood still. Spending per white pupil had grown tremendously. In relative terms (black-to-white), the black schools had generally held their ground, but the absolute differentials were larger than in 1910. "Great progress in the education of Negroes" had been made, but there still was "considerable inadequacy of educational facilities and opportunities" (ibid.).

Moreover, the progress had been highly uneven geographically. In terms of instructional expenditures, black schools in Mississippi or South Carolina lagged behind those in Virginia or Maryland. Great disparity was still evident at the county level. A study by the sociologist Charles Johnson (1941) using 1930 data revealed a negative correlation between the black-to-white spending ratio and the percentage of the population that was black, similar to the one Jones had observed earlier. Johnson's investigation also uncovered variations associated with the local economy, or what he called "county types." In counties in which cotton was the dominant crop and "plantation" agriculture was practiced, and in which few blacks held nonfarm jobs, far fewer resources were devoted to the black schools than in counties in more urban settings.[12]

Relative (black-to-white) improvement in the black schools finally occurred during the 1940s and early 1950s. In the South as a whole, real per pupil expenditures on instruction in the black schools were 288 percent higher in 1954 than in 1940. Spending per white pupil also increased, but at a slower pace (38 percent between 1940 and 1954). Consequently the black-to-white

Black-to-white ratio of per pupil expenditures

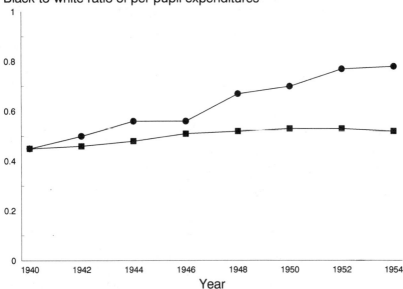

Figure 2.3   **Black-to-White Ratio of Per Pupil Expenditures: The South, 1940 to 1954**

Notes: A circle indicates the actual black-to-white ratio; a square indicates the hypothetical black-to-white ratio assuming no change in the black-to-white ratio of teacher salaries (see text).
Source: Calculated from data in Federal Security Agency, U.S. Office of Education (1942, 1947, 1949–51) and U.S. Department of Health, Education and Welfare (1954, 1957, 1959).

ratio of per pupil expenditures rose from 0.45 in 1940 to 0.78 in 1954 (Figure 2.3)[13]

The data on expenditures suggest two important findings. First, in real terms per pupil expenditures in the *de jure* segregated black public schools of the South increased over time: each successive generation of black children received more school resources. Second, racial differences in the quality of southern public schools followed an inverted U-shaped pattern, first decreasing around the turn of the century, and then narrowing in the 1940s.

It might be argued, however, that per pupil expenditures provide misleading evidence on the relative quality of black schools.[14] Per pupil expenditures on teacher salaries are (approximately) the product of the average monthly wage of teachers, the length of the school year, and the number of teachers per pupil (class size). The U-shaped pattern might be primarily a consequence of changes over time in the relative (black-to-white) wages of black teachers. Racial differences in teachers' pay, however, may mainly reflect wage discrimination against black teachers, not differences in the quality of instruction.

Table 2.6   **Length of the School Year in Days: Selected Southern States**

	c. 1890	c. 1910	c. 1935	c. 1950
Alabama				
Black	75	97	127	177
White	70	131	144	176
Ratio	1.07	0.74	0.88	1.01
Florida				
Black	100	91	168	180
White	100	112	174	180
Ratio	1.00	0.81	0.97	1.00
Louisiana				
Black	90	75	128	178
White	87	153	175	180
Ratio	1.03	0.49	0.73	0.99
Mississippi				
Black	76	104	119	141
White	70	114	145	163
Ratio	1.09	0.91	0.82	0.87
North Carolina				
Black	63	96	161	180
White	61	107	161	180
Ratio	1.03	0.90	1.00	1.00
South Carolina				
Black	NA	75	127	174
White	NA	117	173	180
Ratio	NA	0.64	0.73	0.97
Virginia				
Black	124	124	165	180
White	115	139	170	180
Ratio	1.08	0.89	0.97	1.00

Notes: Figures give average length of school year in elementary and secondary public schools.
NA: not available.
Source: 1890, 1910, Margo (1985); *1935,* Blose and Caliver (1938); *1950,* U.S. Department of
Health, Education, and Welfare (1954).

Adjusted for wage discrimination, the patterns in school quality might look very different (Welch 1973; Donohue and Heckman 1989).

Tables 2.6 and 2.7 report evidence on the length of the school year and average class sizes. Between 1890 and 1910 the average school term in black schools fell relative to the length of the term in white schools. After 1910 the school term in black schools increased significantly. Racial differences in length of the term began to diminish earlier than did racial differences in per pupil expenditures, but it was not until the 1940s that the gap narrowed substantially. Class sizes, too, generally followed a U-shaped pattern. In the late nineteenth century, class sizes were larger in the black schools than in the white schools, and the gap widened between 1890 and 1910.[15] The gap remained roughly stable until the mid-1930s, at which point it began to narrow.

Table 2.7   **Class Sizes: Selected Southern States**

	c. 1890	c. 1910	c. 1935	c. 1950
Alabama				
Black	33.3	39.7	36.7	28.1
White	26.3	27.3	26.1	24.7
Ratio	1.27	1.45	1.41	1.14
Arkansas				
Black	29.8	33.1	35.2	30.5
White	27.5	25.2	27.2	25.5
Ratio	1.08	1.31	1.29	1.20
Florida				
Black	29.4	41.7	27.6	24.7
White	18.9	20.8	23.9	22.7
Ratio	1.55	2.00	1.15	1.09
Louisiana				
Black	43.5	42.5	39.8	28.8
White	25.0	25.6	24.5	23.2
Ratio	1.74	1.66	1.62	1.24
Mississippi				
Black	32.3	38.7	36.5	34.1
White	21.7	18.3	26.3	26.5
Ratio	1.49	2.11	1.39	1.29
North Carolina				
Black	27.0	34.0	28.9	29.3
White	29.4	28.0	30.9	26.7
Ratio	0.92	1.22	0.94	1.10
South Carolina				
Black	48.1	49.4	31.9	25.8
White	25.0	26.4	23.8	23.4
Ratio	1.92	1.87	1.34	1.10
Tennessee				
Black	37.3	38.5	31.2	28.5
White	39.9	34.7	25.9	25.9
Ratio	0.93	1.11	1.20	1.10
Virginia				
Black	34.5	30.2	28.5	27.1
White	23.8	23.2	27.8	24.5
Ratio	1.45	1.30	1.03	1.11

Note: Figures are ratio of pupils in average daily attendance to teachers.
Source: 1890, 1910, Margo (1985), U.S. Bureau of Education (1893); *1935,* Blose and Caliver (1938); *1950,* U.S. Department of Health, Education, and Welfare (1954).

The U-shaped pattern in per pupil expenditures was not solely a reflection of changes over time in the relative wages of black teachers. However, it is also clear that the U-shaped patterns in the length of the school year and in average class sizes were less pronounced than that in per pupil expenditures, which implies that changes in relative teachers' pay occurred. Such changes were especially important in the 1940s, as Figure 2.3 shows. Had the black-to-white ratio of teachers' wage rates stayed constant at its 1940 level, the black-to-white ratio of per pupil expenditures would have increased by 7 percentage points between 1940 and 1950, compared with an actual increase of 22 percentage points. In Chapter 4 I study the determinants of racial differences in teacher salaries, concluding that changes in wage discrimination played an important role in generating the U-shaped pattern in school expenditures.

2.5   Summary

In this chapter I have reviewed evidence on racial differences in the quantity and quality of schooling in the South during the first half of the twentieth century. Although racial differences in literacy and school attendance decreased in successive cohorts, the racial gap in average educational attainment remained persistently large. And, although successive cohorts of black children were educated in better and better schools, racial differences in the quality of schooling followed a U-shaped pattern over time. The next two chapters are studies of the political, social, and economic elements that gave rise to the U-shaped pattern in the quality of schooling.

Appendix
Census Data on School Attendance in 1900

In 1890 and 1900 the U.S. Bureau of the Census collected information on the number of months of school attended by all persons of school age. The school attendance rate in both years is calculated to be the percentage of children reporting a positive number of months attended. In 1910 and subsequently, the census asked whether a person attended school at all during some specified period prior to the census date. It has been suggested that the census question on months attended led to an underenumeration of black school attendance in 1890 and 1900 and, consequently, to too large an increase in the black school attendance rate between 1900 and 1910 (Smith 1986).

The Bureau was well aware of the underenumeration problem in 1890 and 1900. In U.S. Bureau of the Census (1918, 377) it was noted that "some of the apparent improvement [between 1900 and 1910] may be attributed to a change in the form of the schedule inquiry which, it is believed, was more favorable to securing correct answers in 1910 than in 1900." In U.S. Bureau of the Census (1935, 208) the blame was laid on the possibility that "in some instances the person from whom the enumerator obtained his information would not know though he knew the child had attended school. In a few of these cases the enumerator probably made no report at all with respect to school attendance. The returns for 1890 and 1900 are therefore doubtless less complete than those for subsequent censuses and perhaps less complete than those for earlier censuses." The 1935 census report, thus, suggests that if black school attendance was underenumerated, the reason was ignorance on the part of the individual answering the enumerator.

The extent of underenumeration of black school attendance can be investigated using the public use sample of the 1900 census. It is impossible to investigate underenumeration in 1890, because the census manuscripts were destroyed in a fire. However, it is unlikely that results would be different for 1890, because the school attendance question was the same in both years and because the black school attendance rate, as measured by the census, was nearly identical in 1890 and 1900. The public use sample contains a separate code ("99") if the school attendance question went unanswered, but those who answered zero months were coded as "0"—no attendance during the previous year. By examining the correlation between various other answers and the answer to the school attendance question, the extent of underenumeration can be estimated.

I begin by examining the instructions to enumerators of the 1900 census. The instructions regarding school attendance were as follows:[16]

> 224. Column 21. Attended school (in months). For all persons attending school during the year ending June 1, 1900, enter the number of months (or parts of months) of school attendance, as 9, 8, ½, etc. If a person of school age did not attend school at all during the year, write "0." For all other persons to whom the inquiry is not applicable, leave the column blank.

The instructions seem clear, but two problems are suggested on reflection. What should the enumerator have done if the person answering the question did not know how many months a child attended school? Further ambiguity arose with the interpretation of "school age," and "not applicable." If a child was not of "school age," the question was "not applicable" and the column should have been left blank. But the meaning of "school age" was not necessarily the same for the enumerator and the respondent. In its published volumes the census considered "school age" to be "ages 5 to 20," which was a larger range than the legal range (for public school) in most states, and certainly much larger than was the norm in the South.

Table 2A.1 shows the distribution of nonresponse ("99") and zero months ("0") by age groups (ages 5–9, 10–14, 15–20) for southern blacks, southern whites, and children outside the South. Blank columns were common throughout the country, not just the South, so common that it is not credible to claim that large numbers of those coded as "99" should be recoded as having attended school (Smith 1986).

The extent of nonresponse varied by age. The nonresponse rate was much higher for young children (ages 5–9) and teenagers (ages 15–20) than in the prime school-age population (ages 10–14). The age pattern of nonresponse

Table 2A.1   **The Pattern of Nonresponse and Zero Months, School Attendance, 1900: By Age Group, Race, and Region**

	Number of Observations	% "99"	% "0"
Ages 5–9			
Southern black	1,437	69.0	10.5
Southern white	2,695	59.5	6.7
Non-southern	7,197	41.2	2.1
Ages 10–14			
Southern black	1,293	39.5	9.8
Southern white	2,673	19.8	7.1
Non-southern	6,563	13.2	1.1
Ages 15–20			
Southern black	1,435	72.6	10.8
Southern white	2,902	58.1	10.4
Non-southern	7,521	70.3	4.0

Notes: Author's calculations from 1900 census public use sample. % "99": percentage leaving school attendance question blank (coded as "99"); % "0": percentage answering zero months of school attendance.

suggests that the column was left blank because either the enumerator or the person answering the enumerator's questions thought the question was "not applicable"—that is, the child was not of "school age" as defined by the state or by local norms. In regions with low overall attendance, such as the South, law and custom affected the type of response given to the school attendance question. Nevertheless, the high overall rate of nonresponse still leaves open the possibility that, in the case of southern blacks, *some* of the 99's should be recoded to positive months attended, thereby increasing the black attendance rate in 1890 and 1900.

Insight into the recoding problem can be gleaned by examining the instructions to enumerators regarding gainful occupations. Enumerators were to "report a student who supports himself by some occupation, according to the occupation, if more time is given to that, but as a student, if more time is given to study." Under the heading "Nongainful Pursuits," the enumerator was instructed that "if a person is attending school write 'at school'." By examining the cross classification of school attendance and occupation, two pieces of information are derived. Children whose school attendance was coded as "99" or "0" but whose occupations were coded as "at school" are cases of underenumeration, and these children were added to the total attendance figures.[17] It is possible to estimate the percentage of such cases in the population (and the standard error of the fraction), so the probable range of error can be established. The cross classification also yields estimates of the percentage of children with a gainful occupation and the percentage at home without a gainful occupation. If school attendance was underenumerated, one would expect a lower labor force participation rate and a higher percentage living at home

Table 2A.2   **Labor Force Participation by Age Group and Schooling,**
                Southern Black Children in 1900

	School Attendance		
	"99"	0 months	>0 months
Ages 5–9			
In labor force	0.4%	—	—
At home	99.0	94.7%	36.9%
Student	0.6	4.6	63.1
Number of observations	991	151	295
Ages 10–14			
In labor force	59.1%	52.0%	22.4%
At home	37.8	47.2	20.0
Student	3.1	0.8	57.6
Number of observations	511	127	655
Ages 15–20			
In labor force	71.6%	70.3%	37.4%
At home	28.3	27.7	16.8
Student	0.1	1.9	45.8
Number of observations	1,042	155	238

Note: Figures (%) are column percentages.
Source: Author's calculations from 1900 census public use sample.

among children whose school attendance response was "99" than among children whose response was "0."

Table 2A.2 shows the cross classification of labor force participation and school attendance among southern black children. Because the census was not required to collect information on occupations for children under age 10, the vast majority of such children either reported no occupation or else the occupation of student. However, thirteen of the 1,142 children who either failed to respond to the school attendance question or who answered "0" months reported an occupation of "student." Thus the estimate of underenumeration of school attendance in the age group 5–9 is 1.1 percent ($= {}^{13}\!/_{1,142}$).

Among the 511 children ages 10 to 14 coded as "99" on the school attendance question, fully 59 percent reported a gainful occupation while another 38 percent were living at home. A larger fraction (3.1 percent) than in the younger age group reported their occupation as "at school" even though they left the school attendance column blank. Among those who gave an answer of "0" months, fully 52 percent were in the labor force and another 47 percent were living at home. Only 1 child gave an occupation of "student" but reported "0" months of attendance. Thus in the age group 10–14 the underenumeration rate is estimated to be 2.7 percent ($= {}^{17}\!/_{638}$).

In the oldest group (ages 15 to 20) underenumeration was very small. Among those not responding to the school attendance question or giving an answer of "0" months, only 4 children, or 0.4 percent, reported their occupation as "at school." The overwhelming majority of those answering "99" or "0" were in the labor force or at home. By contrast those who attended school were much less likely to report a gainful occupation (37 percent) or live at home (17 percent).

Overall, underenumeration of black school attendance is estimated to have been 1.2 percent in 1900, with a standard error of 0.2 percentage points. The estimate of underenumeration is statistically significant, but not economically so.[18] Were the upward adjustment not included in Table 2.2, the black attendance rate in 1900 would have been 21 percent instead of 22 percent. The similarity between the labor force participation rates of children coded as "0" and children coded as "99" indicates that, with respect to the use of time, both groups of children were statistically indistinguishable. Nonresponse to the school attendance question was common because, in the vast majority of such cases, the children did not attend school. Leaving the column blank seems to have been an easy way for enumerators to avoid writing large numbers of zeros.

3   The Political Economy of Segregated Schools: Explaining the U-Shaped Pattern

Relative (black-to-white) per pupil expenditures in southern public schools followed a U-shaped pattern over time: an initial period of relative similarity in the late nineteenth century, followed by a pronounced shift towards inequality around the turn of the century that persisted for forty years, and then a trend towards equalization in the 1940s. The initial deterioration in the relative quality of the black schools was a consequence of widespread disenfranchisement of blacks and of growth in demand for better white schools. Although there were incentives and institutions that ensured that public funds would continue to flow to the black schools after disenfranchisement, these forces were not sufficient to eliminate the gap in school spending. Rather, the trend towards equalization in the 1940s only took place as the consequence of a concerted legal effort, in the context of changed social, political, and economic circumstances.

3.1   The Disenfranchisement Hypothesis

Between 1890 and 1910 per pupil expenditures in southern black schools fell relative to per pupil expenditures in white schools. Most scholars attribute the decline to two factors.[1] One, southern blacks lost political clout in the late nineteenth century and with it, influence over how school revenues were allocated. Two, the demand for better white schools increased after the turn of the century. This demand was met by a combination of higher school budgets and, in some cases, by shifting resources away from the black schools.

The history of voting rights in the postbellum South is a sorry tale.[2] During Reconstruction (1866–77), southern blacks enjoyed a modicum of political power under Republican governments established after the Civil War and maintained by a federal military presence. Funds for social services were greatly increased or provided for the first time, such as public schools for

33

black children. Blacks were elected to public office, and served in many state and local capacities. Taxes to pay for the expansion in government spending fell largely on the ex-slaveholding planter class.

With the end of Reconstruction the political clout of blacks, and that of poor whites as well, suffered a reversal. Reconstruction governments were replaced by Redeemers, southern Democrats intent on restoring the political supremacy of the white elite. State budgets were reduced and services, particularly education, were cut back. Laws were amended to allow the state government to appoint local officials, who previously had to be elected to office. Whomever controlled the state government—and the Redeemers were in command—controlled the distribution of government spending at the local level. Through a combination of intimidation, violence, and outright fraud, the influence of black voters was reduced. Formal disenfranchisement, in the sense of laws that deliberately restricted the franchise, would come later. The Redeemers feared that such legislation would invite a second Reconstruction, and so settled for informal means of curtailing voting rights.

Key (1949, 533) argued that the informal means were so successful that disenfranchisement was a *fait accompli* by the time suffrage restrictions were formally enacted. An important book by Morgan Kousser (1974) shows, however, that Democratic hegemony was far more precariously based. Pockets of Republican strength survived and occasionally flourished after Reconstruction, and the possibility that the Republican (or another opposition) party might return to office still existed.

The possibility nearly became reality with the Populist revolt of the 1890s. The rise of Populism had many causes, but there is no doubt that a key factor was the devastating economic downturn of the early 1890s. Populist candidates attempted to register poor white and black voters, included members of both groups on party slates, and generally sought to redistribute political and economic power away from Redeemers and their supporters.

To combat the Populist menace, Democrats resorted to the same methods they used in the 1880s—violence, race-baiting, and fraud—only this time they followed up by enacting suffrage restrictions into law. The restrictions did not take the form of explicitly prohibiting the right to vote on the basis of race or party affiliation, although some came very close. Frequently the right to vote was made conditional on literacy, property ownership, residency, or payment of a poll tax.[3] A person might have to demonstrate his ability to read and write by passing a test administered by a local official. Aside from the fact that the official determined who passed the test, near-illiterates never bothered to try, not wishing to reveal their ignorance publicly. A Louisiana law allowed illiterates to register if they owned at least $300 worth of taxable wealth, a sizable amount. Other states made registration conditional on residency in an area for a year or longer, which was difficult or impossible for farm laborers. The poll tax was usually a nominal sum, but it might have to be paid at a time and place different from voter registration. If the registree had neglected to pay the tax in previous years, the tax due would be cumulative. To ensure the laws would not cut too heavily into the white electorate, "grandfather" clauses were enacted which exempted ex-Confederates from meeting certain requirements provided that they registered within a grace period.

The effect of suffrage restrictions was, nevertheless, to curtail voting by poor whites and virtually decimate the black electorate.[4] Overall, white turnout declined by 26 percent and black turnout by 62 percent, comparing gubernatorial and presidential elections before and after suffrage restrictions were enacted (Kousser 1974, 240).[5] The "Solid South" was the product of deliberate actions aimed at restricting the size of the electorate and its racial and economic composition.

Equally deliberate were the consequences of disenfranchisement for the racial distribution of public expenditures. "At the same time" that political rights were being abridged, "southern state and local governments increased their discrimination against blacks in the only important service those governments provided—education. . . . Discrimination in voting, in other words, paralleled discrimination in government services, a condition unlikely to have been coincidental" (228–29).

The effects of disenfranchisement on school spending, however, were more complex than a pure redistribution of school revenues from blacks to whites. The story can be told with the aid of a simple model. Imagine that the preferences (V) of a typical adult white can be summarized by the following equation:

(1) $$V = V(e_w, Y - \mu z)$$

Y is the person's income, e_w is spending per white pupil, z is school budget per pupil, and μ is the fraction of the financing of the school budget borne by whites. Spending per white pupil is related to spending per black pupil (e_b) via the school board's budget constraint:

(2) $$e_w \delta + e_b(1 - \delta) = z = s + t$$

δ is the proportion of pupils who were white; and in per pupil terms, the school board budget, z, consists of state school funds, s, and local school taxes, t. Equation (2) can be rewritten to show the dependence of e_w on e_b:

(3) $$e_w = z/\delta - [1 - \delta)/\delta]e_b$$

Differentiating with respect to z and setting the result equal to zero gives the individual's preferred level of the school budget, z^*, which solves

(4) $$V_1/V_2 = \mu/\alpha$$

Here $\alpha = de_w/dz$, the fraction of a one-dollar increase in the school budget going to the white schools (the subscripts in [4] are partial derivatives). The left-hand side of (4) is the individual's demand curve for expenditures in the white schools, e_w. The right-hand side is the "price" of raising white school spending, that is, the burden on whites of an increase in the budget divided by the fraction of the increase going to white schools. Disenfranchisement caused the "price" of white schooling, μ/α, to decline, and thus the demand for e_w rose.

Only part of the increase in white per pupil expenditures from 1890 to 1910, however, was a pure redistribution from black to white schools from a fixed "pie," that is, with a constant level of z. Consider the case of Mississippi. Between 1890 and 1910 real expenditures per black pupil in Mississippi fell, on average, by $1.60 (see Table 2.6). In 1890 55 percent of the children attending Mississippi's public schools were black. Using equation (3), such a decline in black spending would cause an increase in average white spending of $1.96 (= 1.60 × [0.55/0.45]), holding z constant. The actual increase in white per pupil spending in Mississippi between 1890 and 1910 was $9.26 (see Table 2.6). Thus redistribution of school revenues from blacks to whites accounts for 21 percent (= 1.96/9.26) of the increase in white expenditures in Mississippi. Similar results were obtained for the other states.

The rise in white per pupil expenditures between 1890 and 1910 was facilitated by institutional changes in school finance in the context of rising demand for better white schools. Growing demand and the concomitant institutional changes, which were coincident with disenfranchisement, led to increases in school budgets, frequently through the levying of local school property taxes. Prior to disenfranchisement, some southern states constitutionally limited or even prohibited the levying of local school taxes at the discretion of the electorate. Wealthy white landlords argued against local school taxes because they themselves bore, or so they believed, most of the cost and personally received few benefits. But, as long as the black and white schools received roughly equal per pupil allocations, many middle-class white parents, too, were opposed to higher school taxes because they, as a group, owned much more taxable wealth than blacks (Higgs 1982; Margo 1984a). A superintendent of Oconee County, Georgia thought it was wrong to "tax the whites to educate the blacks. This has made a skeleton of what otherwise would have been a corpulent and muscular man [the school system]" (U.S. Bureau of Education 1893, 1079). The state superintendent of North Carolina noted there was "much opposition to public schools in the State . . . because of the small amount of taxes paid by the negroes" (ibid.). Alabama's superintendent claimed that "in portions of the State the colored race gets well-nigh all the school fund, whilst that race pays a very small per cent of the taxes that make up that fund" (1075). The superintendent of Tipton County, Tennessee, bristled:

There seems nothing at present that promises to discourage the advancement of the public schools in this county further than that there is a growing disposition on the part of the white people of the county, who pay ninety-five one-hundredths of the taxes, to discontinue the public education of the "brother in black" who, notwithstanding the fact that he pays less than five one-hundredths of the taxes of our county, receives more than 50 percent of the public-school moneys. This, the white people argue, is wrong, and should be remedied; and I heartily agree with them . . . the negro should bear the burden of his own education. (1893, 1080–81)

Eliminating blacks from the electorate removed this "obstacle" to white educational progress.[6] It is no accident that state constitutions—Alabama, Louisiana, and North Carolina are examples—were amended after disenfranchisement to permit the levying of school taxes. It is also no accident that the "black balance of payments"—the amount blacks received in school expenditures less the black share of the school tax burden—declined after disenfranchisement (Smith 1973; Kousser 1980a).[7]

Not every county chose to increase expenditures on white schools by levying local school taxes, however. In some cases redistribution from blacks to whites was more profitable. Counties in which the black population share was high—the "black belt"—did not need higher local taxes to finance better white schools. If the black population share was 75 percent, every dollar diverted from the black schools yielded three dollars of additional spending per white pupil; at 90 percent, the rate of return was ten dollars for every dollar diverted (see eq. [2]). State school funds were typically allocated to counties on the basis of the total school age population (or enrollment or attendance) in the county; the funds were distributed to district school boards which had considerable discretion in how to spend the money. Black children had a "cash value" to local school boards because each was worth a certain amount of state educational aid (Bond 1934; Myrdal 1944, 341). In black-belt counties the total amount of state funds might be enough to support a good school for white children (who were relatively few in number) without local taxes, or at least ease the local tax burden on white property owners. "I have a local . . . tax in seven of ten wards," explained the superintendent of Caldwell parish in Louisiana. "In the three wards where there is no tax the principal population is colored and the whites in these wards have all the money they want to run the white schools" (State of Louisiana 1907, 60).

In poor, predominantly white counties, growth in school budgets was heavily dependent on state aid. State school funds typically were derived from taxes, legislative appropriations, interest on public lands, and miscellaneous sources; as a fraction of school budgets, their importance declined after disenfranchisement. Poor whites lacked the taxable wealth to finance better schools on their own (many were disenfranchised themselves); and, in any case, they needed their children to work on the family farm or in the labor market. Disenfranchisement led not only to a gap between white and black per pupil expenditures, but to greater inequality among whites as well (Bond 1934, 1939; Harlan 1958; Kousser 1980a).

3.2   Race, Politics, and Educational Change: A Case Study of Louisiana, 1880 to 1910

In this section many of the points just made are pursued in greater detail in an econometric analysis of the effects of disenfranchisement on school spending in Louisiana between 1880 and 1910.[8] To the best of my knowledge, Louisiana was the only southern state to publish race-specific figures on voter registration. Although the voter registration data are known to be flawed, they still reveal the deleterious effect that disenfranchisement had on expenditures in Louisiana's black schools.

The Democratic party returned to power in Louisiana at the end of Reconstruction. One of the first acts of the "Bourbons" was to reduce the size of the state school fund. According to Hair (1969, 60) the brunt of the decline fell on the state's fledgling schools for black children, which had been established in the immediate aftermath of the Civil War. Statistics for 1879 confirm that the black schools were less well funded than the white schools. On average, expenditures per black pupil enrolled equalled 67 cents for every dollar spent per white pupil.[9]

Throughout the 1880s the Bourbons remained in power by exercising a level of election fraud virtually unmatched in the annals of American politics. In areas controlled by the Democratic party, such as the black-belt cotton parishes in the northern part of the state, ballot boxes were stuffed and votes thrown out or deliberately falsified. "We all admit that when it comes to our elections," declared black-belt Democrat Robert Snyder to the state legislature in 1890, "we suspend the law until the danger is passed" (Kousser 1974, 153). A former Republican governor during Reconstruction lamented that "after the polls are closed" in Louisiana, "the election really begins" (ibid.).

Most egregious was the practice of maintaining blacks on the registration rolls long after they left a parish, or this life. "A dead darkey," as the saying went, "always makes a good Democrat and never ceases to vote" (Hair 1969, 115). The reason for overstating the number of black registrees was that the size of a parish's delegation to the Democratic party's nominating conventions (held for the purpose of filling state-appointed positions, such as local school boards) depended on the Democratic count in prior elections.[10] By inflating the returns, black-belt Democrats ensured their control over the state machine. "Only in the sugar-growing regions of South Louisiana where some influential Republican planters lived, were black men free to vote for more than one party" (113).

The Populist revolt hit Louisiana in the early 1890s, and by 1894 the threat was too large for the Bourbons to ignore. In that year the Bourbon-controlled state legislature passed literacy and property qualifications for the franchise, but the Populist outcry against the restrictions was so vociferous that the Democratic governor decided it was best to settle the issue by a referendum attached to the gubernatorial election in the spring of 1896. By then Louisiana's

Populists had "fused" with the Republican party. The Republican nominee for governor was John Pharr, a wealthy sugar planter.

The Populists were successful in stirring up black support for Pharr. Blacks "who had not attempted to vote in a dozen years" tried to register. In Opelousas, Louisiana, "the registrar . . . kept himself locked in jail to avoid the crowds of blacks who clamored to be added to the rolls." Even in the black belt cotton parishes, wealthy Democratic landlords had "an unusual amount of difficulty . . . discouraging Negro participation in the approaching election" (1969, 237–38, 259).

Despite the surge in black support, Pharr lost by 2,000 votes. Analysis of voting returns shows that the Democrats stole the governor's office. In several predominantly black parishes, Pharr rolled up only a handful of votes, despite his known popularity with black voters (Kousser 1974, 157). Black-belt whites continued the practice of fraudulently stuffing the ballot box for their candidate. Yet the Populist threat had not vanished, for the referendum to restrict the franchise was soundly defeated. The fusion ticket had captured numerous seats in the stage legislature, fraud notwithstanding, and was threatening a recount in the governor's election.

In the end the Democrats prevailed. The recount resolution was repealed and enough legislative support was mustered to enact a new voter registration statute. The effect of the new law was to reduce black voter registration by 90 percent (1974, 163). When a convention was suggested to enshrine the suffrage restrictions in a new state constitution, the voters, now much reduced in number, approved.

In addition to the suffrage restrictions, the state constitution of 1898 contained one other change of significance. For the first time, state law permitted voters in a school district to vote local school property taxes. The joker was that those who would impose the taxes on themselves and others had to meet the new literacy and property requirements for the franchise.

Figure 3.1 shows the trend in public school revenue per pupil enrolled (in constant 1910–14 dollars) in Louisiana from 1886 to 1910. Prior to the 1898 constitution, parish school budgets primarily consisted of state aid that was allocated to them on the basis of the school-age population, independent of race; poll taxes on adult males; and the "police-jury" appropriation, a portion of general parish revenues (derived from a parish-wide property tax) allocated to the schools. The per pupil budget rose from the mid-1880s to 1896, before falling sharply in the wake of a severe agricultural downturn that gripped the state late in the decade. Budgets recovered in the early years of the century to their mid-1890s level, but it was not until after 1904 that school revenues increased substantially. The increase was partly a consequence of higher state allocations, but it was mostly due to an increase in police-jury allocations and, especially, the local property taxes authorized by the 1898 constitution. Between 1898 and 1904, 114 school districts opted for the local tax. By 1910 the number had increased to 1,200.

$ per pupil

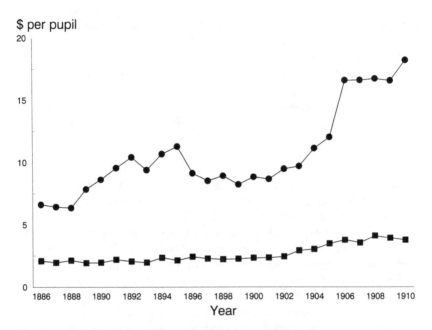

Figure 3.1   Public School Finance in Louisiana, 1886–1910

Notes: A circle indicates the total school budget per pupil enrolled; a square indicates the amount of state educational aid per pupil enrolled. All figures are in 1910–14 dollars; deflator is Warren-Pearson wholesale price index (U.S. Bureau of the Census 1975).
Source: Calculated from state school superintendent's reports (State of Louisiana 1887–1912a).

Figure 3.2 graphs expenditures on teacher salaries per pupil enrolled, by race, over the same period. Unlike the situation in some other states (for example, Alabama or North Carolina), in Louisiana expenditures per white pupil exceeded spending per black pupil throughout the late nineteenth century. Yet it is also clear that expenditures per black pupil were rising prior to 1896 as the per pupil budget was increasing. Furthermore, there was an upturn in the black-white expenditure ratio in 1895–96, at the height of the Populist threat (see Figure 3.3). It was only after the threat had passed that a pronounced decline in the black-to-white ratio of per pupil expenditures would commence. In 1896 the expenditure ratio stood at 0.4 for the state as a whole. In 1902, when the per pupil budget was only slightly higher than in 1896, the expenditure ratio was 0.3. After 1902, school budgets increased substantially, and it is obvious from the graphs that all, or virtually all, of the increase went to the white schools.

But the graphs do not tell the full story. One cannot read off them precisely what the numerical significance of disenfranchisement was. I have therefore estimated a cross-sectional county-level regression of the black-to-white expenditure ratio (BWEXP). The independent variables are the percentage of blacks in the county (%BK), the per pupil budget (PPB), and the percentage

$ per pupil

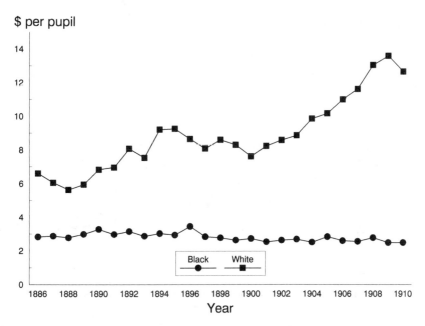

Figure 3.2   Expenditures on Teachers Salaries Per Pupil Enrolled: Louisiana Public Schools, 1886–1910
Notes: Expenditures are in 1910–14 dollars; deflator is Warren-Pearson wholesale price index (U.S. Bureau of the Census 1975). For 1886 to 1903, expenditures were estimated by multiplying the average monthly teacher salary times the length of the school year in months times the number of teachers per pupil enrolled.
Source: See Figure 3.1.

of registered voters who were black interacted with the per pupil budget (%BKV × PPB). The hypothesis is that black political clout ensured that the black schools would receive a share of any increase in school budgets. Thus the coefficient of the interaction term is predicted to be positive, although the coefficient of the per pupil budget could be negative. Data for 1896 were used to estimate the regression because, as the previous discussion suggests, it was in this year that the threat to Democratic rule reached its peak. The variables BWEXP and PPB are in logs; %BK and %BKV are shares between 0 and 1. The results are

$$\text{BWEXP} = 1.21 - 3.60 \text{ \%BK} - 0.72 \text{ PPB} + 0.47 \text{ PPB} \times \text{ \%BKV}$$
$$(2.84) \quad (5.65) \qquad (2.54) \qquad (1.30)$$

$$N = 57, R^2 = 0.55$$

Absolute values of t-statistics are shown in parentheses.

The results support the disenfranchisement hypothesis. The coefficient of the interaction term is positive as predicted and statistically significant at about the 25 percent level. Note, too, the coefficient of the school budget: it is

Black-to-white ratio

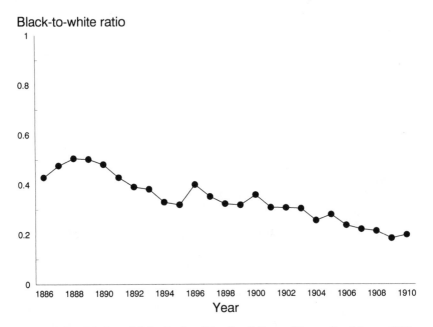

Figure 3.3.   Black-to-White Ratio of Per Pupil Expenditures: Louisiana, 1886–1910
Source: See Figure 3.1.

negative, large, and statistically significant. Were it not for the potential threat the black vote represented, increases in school budgets would have gone much more heavily to the white schools (recall from Fig. 3.2 that expenditures per black pupil rose just prior to 1896).[11]

Between 1896 and 1910 the black share of registered voters in Louisiana declined by 49 percentage points and, in log terms, the per pupil school budget rose by 0.69. According to the regression, these changes would predict a decrease in BWEXP of 0.16 (= 0.47 × 0.69 × 0.49). The actual decrease in BWEXP between 1896 and 1910 was 0.703 (in logs). The disappearance of blacks from the registration rolls accounts for 23 percent (= 0.16/0.70) of the decrease in the black-to-white ratio of per pupil expenditures.

This measure of the impact of disenfranchisement, however, is biased downwards for two reasons. First, because the registration data are known to be measured with error (black-belt fraud), the coefficient of the interaction term is biased towards zero in absolute value.[12] Second, it was after 1904 that school budgets began to rise significantly, yet only 10 percent of the increase in the per pupil budget between 1904 and 1910 was due to a rise in state educational funds. The rest was raised locally, primarily through increased allocations by police juries and the voting of local school taxes. The expan-

Table 3.1   **Regressions of Per Pupil Budgets: Louisiana, 1890 and 1910**

	1890		1910	
	β	*t*-statistic	β	*t*-statistic
Constant	1.30	8.50	2.98	28.40
Percentage black of enrollments	−0.25	−1.24	−0.48	−2.09
Adult males per pupil enrolled	0.76	3.68	0.16	1.05
Assessed wealth per pupil enrolled	0.28	1.59	0.43	3.36
Number of observations	53		54	
R^2	0.77		0.49	

Note: Dependent variable is log of school budget per pupil enrolled.
Sources: School budget and *enrollments:* State of Louisiana (1890, 1910); *adult males:* U.S. Census Office (1895), U.S. Bureau of the Census (1913); *assessed wealth:* State of Louisiana (1892b, 1912b).

sion of local school revenues took place after disenfranchisement in Louisiana.

Further evidence on school revenues is shown in Table 3.1, which contains cross-sectional, county-level regressions of per pupil budgets for 1890 and 1910. In 1890 the number of adult males per child (the poll tax) was the most significant determinant of county-level variation in per pupil budgets. Budgets were lower in the black belt and higher in wealthier parishes, but neither coefficient was statistically significant. In 1910 it was racial composition and wealth that mattered most; both coefficients were large in magnitude and were statistically significant. Predominantly black counties had significantly lower per pupil budgets, and richer counties spent more per pupil. Thus, after disenfranchisement, race and wealth became the dominant determinants of variations in school budgets. Black-belt whites did not need local taxes; they could rely on state aid and the police-jury appropriation. In counties with fewer blacks to exploit, budgets could be raised, provided the whites in question were middle class and interested enough to better their children's schools. In poor counties the white schools fell behind.

In his report for 1926, the state superintendent of education published a lengthy discussion of educational progress in Louisiana since the turn of the century. Page after page recounted the improvements that had been made in the white schools: longer school terms; large, modern structures that had replaced one-room buildings; increases in teacher salaries; better-trained teachers; and a remarkable growth in enrollment in the higher elementary grades and in high schools. When the superintendent got to the schools for black children, there was much less to say. After displaying a table showing how the gap between the average annual salaries of black and white teachers had increased from $99.00 in 1900 to $600.00 in 1925, the superintendent defended the disparity. Black teachers were less qualified, the black schools were open fewer months than the white schools, the vast majority of black children attended the elementary grades, which were cheaper to staff. Why was this the case? "The development of the negro schools," the superintendent explained, "has been as rapid . . . as it should have been, for it has been in keeping with public sentiment. . . . No institution can be developed very much beyond the public opinion on which its success depends" (State of Louisiana 1926, 39).

3.3 Myrdal's Paradox

The disenfranchisement hypothesis is straightforward and persuasive. Stripped of the ballot box, blacks lost a weapon that had previously ensured them a claim on school revenues. Even if blacks had retained the franchise, the Louisiana regressions suggest that the black-to-white spending ratio probably would have declined after the turn of the century, as the demand for better white schools increased. But disenfranchisement was crucial. Without access to the ballot, "appropriations for Negro schools [were] . . . entirely dependent upon the local sentiment of the white school board" (Jones 1917, 28). Disenfranchisement made "progressivism for middle-class whites"—better white schools—cheaper to finance.

The sentiment expressed by Louisiana's state superintendent was typical. Superintendents in black-belt counties knew that the improvements in the white schools had come at the expense of the black children. "The money allocated to the colored children is spent on the education of white children," bragged one local superintendent. "We have twice as many colored children of school age as we have white, and we use their money. Colored children are mighty profitable to us" (Washburne 1942, 111).

In other counties, improvements in the white public schools did not come so cheaply. There, had the question been posed to white middle-class taxpayers, equalizing the level of expenditures in the black schools to the level prevailing in the white schools would have been unthinkable. "The colored race," explained one school official, "is only capable of receiving and profiting by an elementary education, which costs comparatively much less than that suitable for the white race in its more advanced stages of civilization" (U.S. Bureau of Education 1893, 1075). Racist and self-serving as such statements are, they contain a sad grain of truth. School officials kept the black schools open for fewer months than white schools because they reasoned that black parents would not keep their children in school as long as white parents.[13] In cotton counties the black schools might not open until after the harvest and many of these schools were closed during spring planting season. Black families were poorer, on average, than white families. The labor of black children was valuable in agriculture, or at home, or in some other endeavor. This was especially true of older children. Only relatively well-off black parents could afford to send their children to a private high school or to a public one, if available.

Behind this truth lay another. A well-educated black populace was a threat to the social and economic order which placed blacks at the bottom, below poor whites. If blacks had access to good schools, the order might be disrupted. "We must have more money," shrieked a county superintendent in Georgia. "Something is necessarily obliged to be done or the whites will not keep up with the darkey."[14] The Shreveport, Louisiana *Weekly Caucasian* stated that black illiteracy was a problem but (oddly) that "education [was] the most dangerous remedy for the evil yet proposed. That education is a long stride toward social equality no sane man can doubt" (Hair 1969, 127). For every white who believed the black public schools were money down the drain, others could be found who were surprised by the tremendous sacrifices black parents made to send their children to school. "The colored people manifest a great desire to have their children educated," marveled a Georgia school official. "Their schools are overflowing whenever opened" (U.S. Bureau of Education 1893, 1079).

Later I shall demonstrate that there was reason behind the sacrifices of black parents (Chapters 6 and 7). Schooling offered blacks a way out of the rural South. "The old Negroes," as one North Carolina school official explained, "went earnestly to work to learn to read. They failed . . . but they resolved that they would secure education for their children, and with this special end in view, the escape from manual labor" (1893, 1080). Cheap, uneducated black farm labor helped fuel the prosperity of black-belt whites (Mandle 1978; Wright 1986). The labor was cheap because there were few alternatives for blacks in black-belt counties.

At the heart of the matter lay a conflict between the separate-but-equal doctrine (see Chapter 5) and the tax burden of segregated schools. Much attention has been devoted to whether white taxpayers were still subsidizing black schools after disenfranchisement (as most whites believed) or whether blacks were subsidizing white schools (as many blacks believed). Recent studies have not reached a consensus, but none has argued that a subsidy from blacks to whites could have been very large in per capita terms (Smith 1973; Kousser 1980a; Pritchett 1989). But there is no doubt that, had the equal part of separate-but-equal been a reality *and* had the increase in expenditures in the white schools occurred as it did, a massive subsidy from whites to blacks would have been required.[15] According to the letter and spirit of constitutional law, the price of *de jure* segregated schools was supposed to be equal schools, but there was little early in the century to compel southern whites to pay the price.[16] Discriminatory funding of black schools persisted because racial inequality enjoyed widespread political, social, and economic support among whites, there was little southern blacks could do about it at the polls, and the courts were not yet an option.

Yet, as compelling as the disenfranchisement hypothesis is, it has a serious flaw. Once blacks were disenfranchised, why should a school board in Mississippi have spent anything at all on the black schools? Funding of black public schools did not disappear after disenfranchisement; indeed, the black-to-white ratio of per pupil spending remained roughly constant from 1910 to 1940, when real expenditures per white pupil were increasing (Chapter 2). "The great wonder," Gunnar Myrdal pondered, "is that the principle of the Negroes' right to public education was not renounced altogether. But it did not happen" (1944, 888).

It is important to recognize what Myrdal's paradox is *not* about. It is not about the elimination of all black schools per se. Black private schools, particularly above the elementary grades, were substitutes for public schools. Black parents contributed large amounts of money, goods, and services to supplement meager allocations of public school funds; these additional resources were rarely included in official school budgets. The puzzle is why *public* school funds continued to flow to the black population at all. There are several partial solutions to Myrdal's paradox; although each taken separately is inadequate as the sole explanation, together they provide a satisfactory resolution.

The first response to Myrdal's query is his own. However deep the racial prejudice, southern whites still believed in the "American Creed." Access to public schools, which provided the means towards upward mobility in the American economy, were fundamental to the creed. "The American Creed," Myrdal declared, "showed itself strong enough not to allow the sacred principle of public education [for blacks] to succumb in the South" (1944, 889). In evaluating Myrdal's solution, the issue is not whether southern whites believed in "equal" schools. The issue is whether southern whites believed blacks had a "right" to some type of public education.[17] Was adherence to this limited form of the creed really as widespread in the South as Myrdal asserted? Literary evidence can be found on both sides of this question but, to the best of my knowledge, no quantitative surveys of opinion were ever taken. It is true, however, that vocal opposition to black elementary schools declined as the century progressed, which is consistent with Myrdal's creed solution.

But the strongest argument against the creed solution is that it is redundant. Even if school officials were not constrained by guilt, there were other incentives prodding them in the same direction, such as the threat of legal intervention under the separate-but-equal doctrine. Local officials enjoyed wide latitude in interpreting the doctrine as they saw fit (or ignoring it altogether), and the monetary and nonmonetary costs of bringing suit in cases of alleged violations were considerable (Chapter 5). But an utter violation of the doctrine at the elementary school level—a total elimination of public funding—was so obviously unconstitutional that it is doubtful it would have been tolerated for long on a region-wide scale.[18] Not even the state courts of the South, which were hardly partial to black causes, would have winked at this sort of denuding of separate-but-equal.[19]

Yet the argument about court pressure must be made with care. The threat of court action created a lower bound under which funding for the black schools would not have fallen, on average. It is arguable that the lower bound was rising over time, to prevent the racial gap in school quality from becoming too large (and thus vulnerable to court action) as the white schools improved. But, whatever the lower bound was, some school boards were spending more, because there was considerable spatial variation in the resources devoted to black schools (Jones 1917; Bond 1934; Johnson 1941; Pritchett 1986). School boards could have reduced expenditures on the black schools and used the savings to benefit the white schools or to cut school taxes, but some did not.

In addition, there is the Supreme Court case of *Cumming v. Richmond County, Georgia* in 1899 (see Chapter 5). The Court supported the decision of a Georgia school board to shut down a public high school for blacks, ostensibly to ensure adequate funds for black elementary pupils, who were greater in number and (from the Court's perspective) need. In effect, *Cumming* meant that school boards were under no legal obligation to provide black public high schools, because such a defense might always be proffered. And, in the immediate aftermath of *Cumming,* most school boards did not provide them, as Jones's (1917) study demonstrated. Yet the number of black high schools increased steadily after World War One, although *Cumming* was still (ostensibly) the legal precedent.

Contributions by philanthropic foundations are another solution to Myrdal's paradox. Such contributions were made typically on a matching basis, thereby stimulating additional expenditure of state and local funds on the black schools.[20] Among the organizations so dedicated, the Rosenwald and Jeanes Foundations deserve special recognition.[21] The Rosenwald Foundation provided millions of dollars to finance the construction of new school buildings for black children. The Jeanes Foundation paid for specially trained teachers to visit the rural schools, work with teachers to improve the curriculum, and generally upgrade the quality of instruction.

A related solution involves the "bureaucratization" of southern schools. As the century progressed, day-to-day management of southern public schools passed from the hands of local officials to professional educators, many of whom were more liberal than the politicians they replaced (Harris 1985). In North Carolina, greater spatial inequality in white expenditures (and greater racial disparity) after disenfranchisement led to demands in some counties for increased state control over local school boards. State officials used the opportunity to increase their authority and to "coerce local officials into improving [the] Negro schools" (Westin 1966, v). State education departments appointed special agents who served as advocates for greater funding for the black schools, as ombudsmen, and as liaisons to the black community and to philanthropic foundations.[22]

Another answer invokes the potential economic benefits to southern whites from a better-educated black labor force (Freeman 1973). White taxpayers were willing to foot some of the bill for the black schools as long as the sort of education provided raised the return on white-owned capital or was consistent with reigning beliefs about proper roles for blacks in the Southern economy. Literary evidence supporting Freeman's argument is easy to find. "We want [Negroes] to become better cooks, better servants, better washwoman, better workmen in field and farm and shop. We will cheerfully pay taxes to give him that sort of schooling" (1973, 35). A white school official stated that "those in charge of negro education do not lose sight of the environment in which negroes are required to live and work." Yet another explained that "the colored people must not lose sight of the fact that manual labor . . . will be their lot to a larger degree than that of the white people. . . . Let them . . . show that education does not spoil them as laborers. . . and all the help they need . . . will be extended to them" (U.S. Bureau of Education 1893, 1080).

Whether blacks should receive an "industrial" versus a "classical" education was debated within the black community. The debate reached its zenith in the famous confrontation between Booker T. Washington and W. E. B. Du Bois. Washington believed it was in the blacks' best interest to acquiesce to segregation in the short run. By learning the manual arts and industrial skills, blacks could gradually improve their economic lot, at which point they could become a political and social force to be reckoned with. The more radical Du Bois rejected Washington's arguments, claiming that industrial education would merely prepare blacks for a new kind of slavery.

The issue of industrial education, however, has received more attention in the history books than it ever did in real life. Washington's version of industrial education included less true industrial training than he claimed (Spivey 1978). White school officials spoke of the need for industrial education, but devoted relatively few resources to it. In retrospect, the reason is clear—there was a "free-rider" problem. If employers were to support industrial education on a grand scale, they would have to be assured there would be some return on their investment. In the best of circumstances, the return would be delayed into the future when black children entered the labor force. But there was no way to prevent the blacks from leaving the region where they had been educated. An education was a ticket out of the rural South, and everyone knew it. The incentive worked in the opposite direction. By keeping the black schools relatively impoverished, much of the region's labor force could be kept at home, down on the farm.

The goal of maintaining a cheap labor force in the long run, however, was inconsistent with the goal of attracting labor in the short run. The final resolution of Myrdal's paradox is the mobility model (Margo 1990). Black families would leave an area if the provision of schools for their children were seriously threatened. "The white people must not lose sight of the fact," explained one school official, "that it is the labor of a country that makes its wealth and that . . . the education . . . of the children of the laborers is a proper charge upon the property of any country. . . . With good schools . . . there will be less incentive for the country people to crowd into the cities and towns to educate their children" (U.S. Bureau of Education 1893, 1080). Unfortunately for employers, the best workers tended to be those who were most interested in their children's schooling. "Already there has been a considerable emigration of the Negroes," wrote J. W. Joyner, state superintendent of North Carolina's public schools, less than a decade after blacks had been disenfranchised in his state:

> There is no surer way to drive the best of them from the state than by keeping up this continual agitation about withdrawing from them the meager educational opportunities that they now have. Their emigration in large numbers would result in a complication of the labor problem. Some of our Southern farms would be compelled to lie untenanted and untilled. The experience of one district in Wilson county illustrates this. The county school board found it, for various reasons, impossible to purchase a site for a Negro school house. Before the year was out the board received several offers from farmers in the district to donate a site. Upon inquiry by the chairman of the board as to the reason for these generous offers, he was told that when it was learned that no site for the school house could be secured and the Negroes were to have no school in that district, at least one-third of the best Negro tenants and laborers there moved into other districts where they could have the advantages of a school. This is a practical side of this question that our people would do well to consider. What happened in this district will happen in the entire state if we give the best Negroes reason to believe that their public school privileges are to be decreased or withdrawn. (1910, 54)

In the second decade of the twentieth century, a "considerable emigration of Negroes" took place; Joyner's fears were confirmed. Later I shall show that the Great Migration drew its ranks disproportionately from the better-educated segments of the black population (Chapter 7). Black outmigration seems to have prompted the following discussion at a school board meeting in East Feliciana Parish, Louisiana, in 1926:

> That the Negroes are an economic asset would not be challenged. That they have been leaving the parish for the past twenty years has clearly been shown by the data from the census reports. That they emigrate because of meager school conditions cannot be proved, but the consensus of opinion among both white and Negro leaders . . . is that one of the most potent influences that can be brought to bear in retaining them is the provision of reasonably satisfactory school facilities. . . . The parish must provide better schools and longer terms or the exodus of Negroes will continue, perhaps at an increasing rate. (Foote and Robertson 1926, 20–21)

The loss of black labor was not the only loss in this parish. "The continued residence of the Negro population has an important bearing on the school revenues, because the Negro educables now bring into the parish from the state school fund $20,000 more than is now expended for Negro education" (1926, 21).

Meetings like the one in East Feliciana parish took place throughout the

South after the onset of the Great Migration, and similar opinions were voiced. The initial improvements in the black schools, in the form of longer school years and the provision of high schools, occurred in the 1920s, once the permanent nature of the migration became clear. Some firms went so far as to supplement expenditures in the black schools to attract (or keep) a high quality, stable workforce (Bond 1939; Fishback 1989).

Black mobility was a threat in the case of the elementary schools, because the school districts numbered in the thousands, were geographically small, and were dispersed over a large area. School boards might have "colluded" by forming one gigantic governmental unit—an educational cartel—but the usual difficulties of enforcing collusive arrangements when the number of participants was large would have offset any gains from an even lower level of expenditures on the black schools. Collusion would have been difficult across state lines and impossible across the Mason-Dixon line.

When the efficient scale of public funding was large relative to the spatial dispersion of the black population and its per capita demand for education, and when the private sector responded to some extent (as was the case with higher education), the threat of exit was a feeble weapon. The loss of the small number of blacks who left the South to go to law school, for example, did no damage to the southern economy. It was far cheaper to provide out-of-state scholarships to black students rather than open separate-but-equal facilities (Tushnet 1987). Exit, in other words, was no substitute for political voice and adherence to the equal clause of the separate-but-equal doctrine.

Thus, despite the impact of disenfranchisement, the "supply curve" of black public schools was not fixed and unchanging, unresponsive to "market forces." Successive generations of black parents, better educated than previous generations, desired more and better public schools for their children—and the system responded, albeit slowly and grudgingly.

In some states, especially in the Upper South, the various institutions and incentives that make up the solution to Myrdal's paradox were sufficient to cause the black-to-white spending ratio to begin a slight upward trend after World War One (see Tables 2.5–2.7). But, in the region as a whole, the institutions and incentives were not enough to force an equalization of school expenditures. Pressure for equalization finally came from a conjunction of long-term trends, forces outside the South, and events beyond the region's control. In the 1920s the National Association for the Advancement of Colored People (NAACP) began a concerted legal campaign to end educational discrimination in southern schools (Tushnet 1987). In the early 1930s, poor economic conditions forced cutbacks in public school funds in the South, and the black schools bore the brunt of the decline (Westin 1966; Tyack, Lowe, and Hansot 1984). Frustrated by the lack of progress and by the reductions, blacks became increasingly willing to turn to the courts. The initial court battles, focussing on desegregation of higher education and the elimination of separate wage scales for black and white teachers, were fought in the late 1930s and early 1940s (Kluger 1977; Tushnet 1987; Chapter 4). In addition, periodic monitoring of the black schools by the U.S. Office of Education; the various studies by black scholars such as Du Bois, Horace Mann Bond, Charles Johnson, and others; and Gunnar Myrdal's *An American Dilemma* were instrumental in disseminating information about conditions in southern schools to a wide audience. During World War Two the "dilemma" of race relations, including educational discrimination, became a subject of national (and federal) concern (Vatter 1985). By the late 1940s, when it became clear that the legal tide and public opinion were turning against it, the South responded by paying closer attention to the equal part of separate-but-equal, fearing the loss of the separate part (Black and Black 1987). But by then it was too late: the NAACP had switched to a different strategy—*de jure* segregation was morally wrong—a strategy that would culminate successfully in *Brown v. Board of Education* in 1954.

3.4 Summary

In the late nineteenth century the black-to-white ratio of per pupil expenditures in southern public schools declined as a consequence of black disenfranchisement and growing demand for better white schools. Although public school funds continued to flow to the black population after disenfranchisement, the forces that ensured the flow would continue were poor substitutes for voting rights and enforcement of the law. Ultimately it took political weapons (the NAACP, the courts, and public opinion) to fight an injustice that was caused by political upheaval in the first place.

I have focussed in this chapter on racial differences in per pupil expenditures. Chapter 2 suggested, however, that racial differences in wages paid to teachers were an important proximate cause of racial differences in per pupil expenditures. To complete my analysis of the political economy of segregated schools, the next chapter examines the determinants of racial differences in teacher salaries.

4 "Teacher Salaries in Black and White": Pay Discrimination in the Southern Classroom

As Chapter 2 showed, racial differences in teacher salaries in the South were an important proximate cause of racial differences in per pupil expenditures. Analysis of why black teachers received different wages than white teachers provides additional insights into the political economy of resource allocation in segregated schools. Data from 1910 and 1940 reveals that black teachers experienced significant amounts of "wage discrimination," that is, black teachers were paid less than equivalently qualified white teachers. This discrimination was a consequence of demand-side behavior by school boards and of supply-side factors in the labor market causing the supply price of black teachers to be less than that of white teachers. Wage discrimination diminished sharply during the 1940s, as a result of court action, tight labor markets, and changing social attitudes.

4.1 Racial Differences in Teacher Salaries, 1890–1954

In September 1939 the NAACP filed a lawsuit against the Norfolk, Virginia school board, on behalf of Melvin Alston, president of the Norfolk black teachers association. The suit replaced one filed previously on behalf of Aline Black, whose case became moot when the school board fired her. Alston's suit claimed that the Norfolk board discriminated against black teachers by paying them lower salaries for no reason other than race. Black elementary teachers, with no prior experience and a normal school degree, received $226 less per year than similarly qualified white teachers. A white male, hired to teach in the city's segregated white high schools, earned 53 percent more than a black teacher with the same teaching experience and education. There was no subterfuge about the behavior or intentions of the school board: the salary schedules were public knowledge. In February of 1940 Alston's suit was dismissed by a federal district judge on just these grounds. Once Alston had signed the contract offered to him by the board, he had silently acquiesced to the pay inequity.

The U.S. Court of Appeals disagreed. To "arbitrarily [pay] less to Negroes than to white persons," the Court reasoned:

for public services of the same kind and character [by] men and women equally qualified according to standards which the state itself prescribes . . . is as clear a case of discrimination on the ground of race as could well be imagined and falls squarely within the inhibition of both the due process and equal protection clauses of the 14th Amendment. (Tushnet 1987, 79–80)

The school board's appeal to the U.S. Supreme Court was denied without a hearing. The NAACP was delighted with its victory. By refusing to hear the appeal, the Supreme Court had implicitly ruled against racially based salary schedules, thereby easing the burden of proof in subsequent cases.

The inequality in pay in Norfolk was hardly unusual. A 1941 NAACP pamphlet entitled "Teacher Salaries in Black and White" documented enormous racial disparities in teachers' pay in the South. On average, black teachers earned 40 to 50 percent of what white teachers earned. Despite "intimidation, chicanery, and trickery of almost every form imaginable" (1987, 81) by school officials, and the opposition of some black educators, the NAACP persisted in bringing equalization suits. Norfolk wasn't the first, or the last of the victories. The battle had

been an uphill climb, but the fight can be won. It can be won through the persistence, organization, and continued cooperation of the teachers. . . . It can be won through the moral and financial support of all intelligent citizens, Negro and white. And it can be won through the united resolution of all of us to fight until full equality is established within the jurisdiction of every school board in the United States. (1987, 81)

The pay differentials that gave rise to the eloquent pleas of "Teacher Salaries in Black and White" were not always as gross, nor would they stay the same after World War Two. Race-specific data on teacher salaries are given in Table 4.1. The primary sources are the reports of the state superintendents of education for the various southern states. Later in the chapter I shall supplement these with evidence on individual teachers drawn from the public use sample of the 1940 census. The salary estimates do not include board or in-kind payments. Allowing for board and in-kind payments would probably narrow somewhat the racial salary gap early in the century—there is some evidence that black teachers were paid more frequently in kind, particularly by parents—but adjusting for such payments would not change any substantive conclusions (Margo 1984b, 309). It should be noted that, although annual estimates are given, the substantive conclusions are the same for monthly salaries.

In 1890 the average annual salaries of teachers were generally lower for

Table 4.1   **Annual Salaries of Public School Teachers: Selected Southern States, 1890 to 1950 (in 1950 dollars)**

	c. 1890	c. 1910	1936	1950
Alabama				
Black	255	311	643	1,901
White	215	790	1,390	2,214
Ratio	1.19	0.39	0.46	0.86
Florida				
Black	319	312	966	2,643
White	342	676	2,018	3,056
Ratio	0.93	0.46	0.48	0.86
Louisiana				
Black	343	240	790	2,486
White	418	940	1,825	3,222
Ratio	0.82	0.26	0.43	0.77
Mississippi				
Black	251	284	484	760
White	313	639	1,535	1,884
Ratio	0.80	0.45	0.32	0.40
North Carolina				
Black	204	268	1,064	2,721
White	207	506	1,590	2,675
Ratio	0.98	0.53	0.67	1.02
South Carolina				
Black	NA	251	592	1,515
White	NA	694	1,617	2,149
Ratio	NA	0.36	0.37	0.70
Virginia				
Black	466	399	1,019	2,003
White	482	854	1,766	2,080
Ratio	0.97	0.47	0.58	0.96
National average	724	1,102	2,516	3,010

Note: NA: not available.
Source: 1890, 1910, Margo (1985, 46, 48, 52, 54), which gives length of school year (in days) and average daily teacher wage; annual salary is daily wage × average length of school year; 1936, Blose and Caliver (1938); 1950, U.S. Department of Health, Education, and Welfare (1954). NATIONAL AVERAGE: 1890, 1910, U.S. Bureau of Census (1975, 168); 1936, Blose and Caliver (1938); 1950, U.S. Department of Health, Education, and Welfare (1954). Deflator is the wholesale price index of the Bureau of Labor Statistics (U.S. Bureau of Census 1975).

blacks than for whites, but the salary gap was much smaller than it would become soon after the turn of the century. In the Deep South states of Louisiana and Mississippi, black teachers earned about 80 percent of what white teachers earned. The gap was narrower in Florida and North Carolina (2–6 percent). In Alabama, due to a slightly higher concentration of black teachers in counties with above average salaries, the average black salary actually exceeded the average white salary.

By 1910 the black-to-white salary ratio had fallen well below its 1890s

Black-to-white ratio

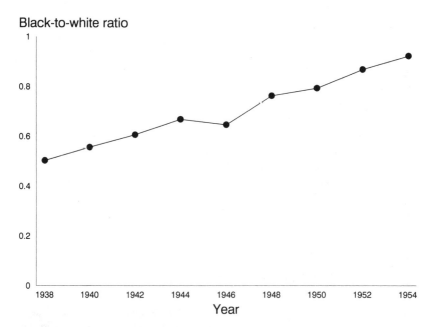

Figure 4.1   Black-to-White Ratio of Average Annual Teacher Salaries: The South, 1938–1954
Source: Calculated from data in Federal Security Agency, U.S. Office of Education (1942, 1947, 1949, 1950, 1951) and U. S. Department of Health, Education and Welfare (1954, 1957, 1959).

level.[1] The proximate cause was a dramatic increase in the pay of white teachers. Average annual salaries of white teachers doubled or tripled in real terms, a rate of growth that exceeded the national average. The experience of black teachers was just the opposite. In three states the salary of black teachers fell, and in no state did black salaries keep pace with white salaries.

Pay differentials on account of race existed in southern schools before the turn of the century, but the racial salary gap widened between 1890 and 1910. In Chapter 3 I argued that the decline in the black-to-white ratio of per pupil expenditures was, in part, caused by disenfranchisement. The rise in the racial salary gap shows that white teachers, as well as middle-class whites and their children, gained from disenfranchisement.

Between 1910 and the mid-1930s, average salaries of black teachers increased in real terms. In most states this growth was sufficient to cause the black-to-white ratio of average salaries to rise somewhat, although in absolute dollars, the gap was larger ca. 1936 than in 1910. And in Mississippi, the black-to-white ratio actually fell, from 0.45 in 1910 to 0.32 in the mid-1930s. Clearly, there was no substantial movement towards equalization of salaries in the South before 1940.

Equalization was the trend, however, during the 1940s. Figure 4.1 shows the black-to-white salary ratio between 1938 and 1954. In 1942 black teachers earned an average annual salary equal to 61 percent of that paid to white teachers. Two years later the ratio had risen to 67 percent, and by 1950 the ratio was 79 percent. In 1954 the average annual salary of black teachers was nearly equal (92 percent) to that of white teachers. Thus between 1944 and 1954 the increase in the black-to-white salary ratio was larger than in the previous three decades combined.

To summarize, the black-to-white ratio of teachers' pay followed a U-shaped pattern over time, as pointed out previously in Chapter 2. It is also apparent that, between 1910 and 1940, the salaries of black teachers fell far below those of white teachers. The next two sections consider whether the racial difference in pay can be attributed to racial differences in the characteristics of teachers or in other variables, or whether the pay gap represented wage discrimination.

4.2   The Determinants of Teacher Salaries: 1910 and 1940

The typical black teacher labored in a poorly equipped classroom, taught larger classes for fewer days per year, and earned less doing it than did her white counterpart. Why were black teachers paid less than white teachers? The principal reason, according to the NAACP, was wage discrimination. School boards simply paid more to a white teacher than a black teacher with equal qualifications. The teacher salary lawsuits would eventually make the differentials illegal. But before the suits were brought, school boards discriminated willfully and flagrantly.

Wage discrimination, however, might not have been the sole cause of the pay gap. Even if black teachers had received "equal pay for equal work," they might have been employed more frequently in school districts that, for any number of reasons, paid low salaries. Even if pay *within* school districts had been equalized, there might still have been an overall pay gap.[2]

Further, the professional qualifications of black teachers were generally not as good as those of white teachers. It is true that racial differences in qualifications were the manifestation of inadequate facilities for training black teachers. Few black teachers held postgraduate degrees, for example, because there were few programs for them to attend. However, if school boards were willing to pay higher salaries to better-educated and more experienced teachers regardless of race, racial differences in qualifications would result in racial differences in salaries.

This section examines the determinants of racial differences in teacher salaries, using ca. 1910 county-level data on monthly teacher salaries, and individual-level data from the 1940 census public use sample on annual and weekly salaries. My investigation is based on regressions of the following form:

(1) $\ln W = X\beta + \varepsilon$

The dependent variable, ln W, is the log of the teacher's salary; the X's are characteristics of teachers or possibly other variables affecting wages; the β's are regression coefficients; and ε is an error term.

Data are analyzed for 1910 from three states, Florida, Louisiana, and North Carolina. For Florida and Louisiana the data are sex specific as well, and in these states the dependent variable is the (sex-specific) log of the average monthly teacher salary.[3] For North Carolina the data are not sex specific, so the dependent variable refers to the log of the monthly salary, averaged over male and female teachers in a county.

In the 1910 regressions the qualifications of teachers are measured by the percentage of teachers holding first grade (or higher level) teaching certificates. First grade (or "state" grade) were generally the highest quality certificates. Commonly they were awarded if the teacher achieved a high enough score on an examination given by local or state officials, or if the teacher had completed a certain level of education (for example, a normal school degree). It is true that certification is a less than perfect indicator of qualifications. Standards varied across school districts, school officials had a great deal of leverage in awarding certificates, and there is evidence that black teachers had greater difficulty acquiring first grade certificates than did white teachers (Kousser 1980a, 185). Precisely for these reasons, I originally limited my analysis to Florida, North Carolina, and Louisiana, where other race-specific information on qualifications was reported, such as the percentage that attended college or normal school, or the percentage with prior teaching experience. However, it turned out that these other measured variables were highly correlated with certification. Because the substantive conclusions were no different, only the regressions with the certification are reported here.[4]

Racial differences may not have been the only basis for wage discrimination. There is considerable evidence that, in the late nineteenth and early twentieth centuries, female teachers were paid less than comparably qualified male teachers (Strober and Best 1979; Margo and Rotella 1981). In the Florida and Louisiana regressions, the variable labelled Female takes on the value of one if the observation refers to female teachers. In the North Carolina regressions, Female refers to the percentage of female teachers in a county. If a gender gap in pay existed, the variable should have a negative coefficient.

The 1910 regressions also include variables measuring the characteristics of the county. Because of the financial incentives to keep expenditures low in the black schools (Chapter 3), heavily black counties might have offered low salaries, thus attracting less able candidates. To control for this effect, the percentage of blacks in the county is included. Per capita assessed wealth and population density are proxies for a variety of factors that may have affected teacher salaries. By offering higher salaries, wealthy counties could attract more able teachers. Teacher salaries may have been higher in more heavily populated areas, because alternative employment opportunities for teachers were more plentiful.[5]

The regression results are shown in Table 4.2.[6] Teachers holding first grade certificates generally received higher salaries. There is no evidence that the marginal returns to holding a first grade certificate were significantly lower for black teachers.[7] In Florida and Louisiana, female teachers received lower monthly salaries than males, and the gender gap was larger among white teachers. Except in North Carolina, the average black salary decreased as the percentage of blacks increased in a county. Wealthier, more densely populated counties paid higher average salaries regardless of race.

I next examine the determinants of racial differences in teacher salaries in 1940. The data base consists of 2,888 teachers from the 1940 census sample, 567 of whom were black.[8]

Compared with the county-level data previously analyzed, there are advantages and disadvantages to the 1940 teacher sample. The sample is large, covers the entire South, contains information on educational attainment, and pertains to individual teachers. A disadvantage is that teachers were identified by the occupation they reported when the census was taken, but the salary data refer to 1939. Some persons in the sample could have worked in a different job in 1939, but I am assuming that they were, in fact, teachers for all of 1939. Others may have been teachers in 1939, but left the profession before the census was taken. Some persons worked multiple jobs, and their wage and salary income would include earnings from all of the jobs, not just teaching. Finally, there is no good way to distinguish public school teachers from other teachers.

The dependent variables are logs of the annual and weekly salaries. The independent variables, taken from among those available in the 1940 sample, are gender, marital status, age, educational attainment, urban status, and region. Separate regressions were estimated for black and white teachers.

The racial salary gap was large in 1940. On an average annual basis, black teachers earned 59 percent of what white teachers earned; on a weekly basis, 63 percent. The greater discrepancy in annual salaries reflects the shorter school year in the black schools. Black teachers worked fewer days than white teachers, so their annual salaries were lower.

The regression coefficients are shown in Table 4.3. Significantly higher salaries were paid to older teachers, presumably because they were more experienced. The gradient between age and salary was slightly steeper among black teachers, at least up to age 55.[9] White teachers who attended fewer than three years of college earned salaries that were no higher, on average, than those with a high school diploma, but three or more years of college did have a significant payoff. For black teachers, college paid dividends as early as the second year. The biggest gains were reserved for teachers with four or more years of college training. In percentage terms, black teachers appeared to ben-

Table 4.2   **Salary Regressions: 1910**

	Florida		Louisiana		North Carolina	
	Mean	β	Mean	β	Mean	β
White Teachers						
Constant		1.96		3.41		2.12
		(5.20)		(29.83)		(7.49)
Female	0.75	−0.18	0.83	−0.36	0.73	−0.01
		(4.64)		(15.61)		(0.11)
% with first grade certificates	0.32	0.45	0.73	0.23	0.80	0.13
		(2.76)		(3.46)		(0.98)
% of blacks in county	0.39	−0.08	0.38	0.08	0.29	0.18
		(0.66)		(1.30)		(1.42)
Per capita wealth	5.40	0.30	5.66	0.11	5.57	0.17
		(4.96)		(5.29)		(2.72)
Population density	2.81	0.11	3.77	0.04	3.88	0.09
		(4.97)		(2.75)		(2.30)
Mean value-dependent variable	3.89		4.11		3.58	
Number of observations		94		122		98
R^2		0.34		0.75		0.32
Black Teachers						
Constant		0.96		3.14		0.66
		(3.20)		(12.78)		(1.88)
Female	0.72	−0.14	0.71	−0.17	0.69	−0.12
		(3.04)		(4.07)		(0.90)
% with first grade certificates	0.09	0.40	0.34	0.18	0.31	0.29
		(1.84)		(1.99)		(3.84)
% of blacks in county	0.47	−0.45	0.47	−0.72	0.38	0.09
		(2.64)		(6.12)		(0.80)
Per capita wealth	5.30	0.43	5.56	0.10	5.62	0.42
		(6.44)		(2.08)		(5.15)
Population density	3.10	0.12	4.03	0.05	3.88	0.02
		(4.46)		(2.40)		(0.38)
Mean value-dependent variable	3.37		3.47		3.19	
Number of observations		91		118		93
R^2		0.46		0.66		0.42

Notes: Dependent variables: Florida, Louisiana—log of (sex-specific) average monthly salary; North Carolina—log of average monthly salary. *Female:* Florida, Louisiana—equals one if observation pertains to female salary, zero otherwise; North Carolina—percentage of female teachers.
Source: Margo (1984b, 313–15).

efit more from graduate or postgraduate training (on an annual if not on a weekly basis).

A gender gap in salaries was still present in 1940. Among black teachers the gap was wider in 1940 than in 1910. Urban teachers were better paid than rural teachers, but the urban-rural gap was larger among black teachers. Re-

Table 4.3   Salary Regressions: 1940

	White Teachers			Black Teachers		
	Mean	Annual β	Weekly β	Mean	Annual β	Weekly β
Constant		6.72	3.08		6.28	2.73
		(125.91)	(62.80)		(64.78)	(34.70)
Female	0.75	−0.22	−0.12	0.80	−0.21	−0.20
		(7.68)	(4.67)		(3.14)	(3.62)
Married	0.43	0.02	0.06	0.53	0.000	0.02
		(0.59)	(2.32)		(0.001)	(0.45)
Age						
< 25	0.16	−0.36	−0.22	0.17	−0.49	−0.25
		(9.12)	(6.61)		(6.07)	(3.82)
25–34	0.42	−0.13	−0.10	0.41	−0.16	−0.11
		(4.14)	(3.44)		(2.44)	(2.13)
45–54	0.11	0.08	0.01	0.11	0.06	0.07
		(1.71)	(0.26)		(0.68)	(0.94)
≥ 55	0.06	0.09	0.08	0.04	−0.16	−0.12
		(1.67)	(1.61)		(1.24)	(1.12)
Years of schooling						
13	0.04	0.01	0.06	0.07	−0.03	−0.02
		(0.07)	(0.88)		(0.26)	(0.25)
14	0.17	0.10	0.15	0.21	0.18	0.24
		(1.91)	(3.16)		(2.29)	(3.84)
15	0.11	0.24	0.27	0.09	0.26	0.26
		(4.34)	(5.33)		(2.53)	(3.13)
16	0.47	0.36	0.35	0.37	0.51	0.41
		(7.90)	(8.49)		(7.18)	(7.18)
> 16	0.12	0.55	0.53	0.03	0.86	0.63
		(8.43)	(10.35)		(5.61)	(5.01)
Urban	0.27	0.24	0.15	0.35	0.33	0.28
		(8.45)	(5.61)		(5.88)	(6.08)
Region						
East South Central	0.25	−0.16	−0.14	0.23	−0.36	−0.29
		(5.31)	(4.99)		(5.53)	(5.56)
West South Central	0.33	−0.05	−0.04	0.25	−0.16	−0.09
		(0.37)	(1.66)		(2.48)	(1.74)
Mean value-dependent variable	6.75	6.75			6.22	
Number of observations		2,321			567	
R^2		0.21	0.14		0.33	0.30

Notes: *Dependent variables:* Annual—log of annual salary, 1939; Weekly—log of weekly salary (annual salary/weeks worked); absolute value of *t*-statistics in parentheses
Source: See text and Perlmann and Margo (1989).

gional differences were considerable. Black teachers in the East South Central region earned 21 percent less per week than their counterparts in the South Atlantic states. Weekly pay among white teachers did not differ significantly between the South Atlantic and West South Central region, but was signifi-cantly lower (by 9 percent) in the East South Central region.[10]

Table 4.4   **Accounting for the Racial Salary Gap**

1910	Florida	Louisiana	North Carolina
Mean racial salary differential	0.52	0.63	0.39
% explained by mean racial difference in:			
% first grade	19 9	14.2	16.3
Total, independent variables	19.8	9.2	9.9
Constant	192.3	42.9	374.3
Total, coefficients	80.2	90.8	90.1

1940		Annual	Weekly
Mean racial salary differential		0.53	0.46
% explained by mean racial difference in:			
Age		0.8	0.7
Years of schooling		16.4	17.5
Total, independent variables		13.9	14.3
Constant		83.0	76.0
Total, coefficients		86.1	85.7

Source: See text and Margo (1984b).

4.3   Explaining the Racial Salary Gap

The regressions reveal the major determinants of teacher salaries, and how they differed between white and black teachers. But the regressions do not show directly which factors explain the racial salary gap. To answer this question, I employ the following equation:

$$(2) \qquad \ln w_w - \ln w_b = \beta_w (X_w - X_b) + X_b (\beta_w - \beta_b)$$

All variables are measured at their sample means, and the β's are the estimated regression coefficients. The first term on the right-hand side ($\beta_w [X_w - X_b]$) measures how much of the racial difference in average salaries was caused by racial differences in the independent variables (e.g., certification or teaching experience). The second term ($X_b [\beta_w - \beta_b]$) measures the importance of racial differences in the regression coefficients. If the second term is positive, it follows that a black teacher with a given set of characteristics (X_b) would have received a higher salary if the teacher had been white. This is what the NAACP meant by wage discrimination, and it is the same definition employed in studies of racial wage differences today (Blinder 1973). The results of the calculation are shown in Table 4.4.

In 1910, racial differences in the proportion of teachers with first grade certificates account for 14–20 percent of the racial salary differential. Although black teachers were less likely to hold a first grade certificate than white teachers, the lower proportion of first grade certificates cannot explain the racial salary gap. Nor can racial differences in the proportion of female teachers or in geographic location. Rather, 80–85 percent of the racial salary gap is attributed to racial differences in the coefficients, the most important being the constant term.

The results for 1940 are similar. Racial differences in average ages and educational attainment accounted for only 18 percent of the mean racial differences in annual teacher salaries and only 19 percent in weekly salaries. Most of the salary gap—in excess of 80 percent—is explained by racial differences in the coefficients; again, in particular, the constant terms.

The calculation suggests that wage discrimination against black teachers was sizable. In percentage terms, the degree of discrimination was approximately the same in 1910 and 1940. As the NAACP recognized, black and white teachers with similar qualifications commanded distinctly different salaries.

The emergence—and persistence—of wage discrimination was brought about by politics, educational change, and the broader labor market. In the late nineteenth century South, teaching was a part-year occupation for many individuals. To attract a candidate into the classroom for, say, a three-month school term, a school board would have to pay at least as much—typically more—than the person could earn elsewhere during the school term. At the time there was relatively little wage discrimination in other occupations, and school budgets were still divided in rough equality between black and white schools (Higgs 1977; Chapter 2). Because the educational system was rudimentary, the demand for well-trained, professional educators was not present and average salaries, white and black, were low.

Disenfranchisement and educational awakening altered the market for teachers. Middle-class white parents were determined to improve schools for their children. The fraction of white children attending higher elementary grades and high school skyrocketed. Expanding school budgets and monies diverted from the black schools went to satisfy needs of the white schools. The demand for white teachers increased and, in the short run, their salaries rose sharply.

Initially, political change created economic rents accruing to white teachers; that is, they were paid an amount in excess of what was necessary to keep them in the job. These rents were maintained as southern school systems underwent "bureaucratization" after the turn of the century. Modern school systems needed professional educators, and hiring standards, set by state education departments, were raised. Teaching became a career, requiring a substantial investment on the teacher's part in training. For white teachers, acquiring the necessary training was facilitated by larger budgets for state normal schools, summer training institutes, teacher training in city high schools, and overall expansion of higher education opportunities. Such programs were not entirely neglected for black teachers (the need for trained personnel in the black schools was acute), but the dollars first went to satisfy the needs of the white schools. It was up to the South's private black colleges and federal land grant institutions to pick up the slack. Ultimately, bureaucratization led to the adoption of rigid salary schedules with pay gradations for certification, experience, and education. Once salaries were formally tied to "qualifications," racial distinctions were a short step away.

It is important to recognize, however, that racial distinctions did *not* take the form of uniformly low average pay for black teachers. White school officials could have simply hired the least qualified (and lowest paid) teachers from the pool of available black candidates. Some did precisely that, such as one delegate to a 1906 meeting of Georgia county superintendents, who spoke proudly of staffing the black schools in his county with the worst teachers he could find (Dittmer 1977, 143). But, as the wage regressions show, some school boards were willing to hire better-educated black teachers, even though they paid a premium to do so. The pay premium for qualified black teachers reinforces the conclusions of Chapter 3. Incentives existed to provide a certain quality of schooling to black children, even though black parents were unable to influence school expenditures directly at the ballot box.

Labor market factors on the supply side, too, were a cause of wage differentials between white and black teachers. According to Horace Mann Bond (1934, 271):

> a much larger number of Negroes will seek employment as teachers, even when as [college] graduates . . . they are offered greatly inferior wages, than would be the case among white candidates.
>
> It is generally true that the number of "white-collar" jobs open to Negro graduates are inferior in variety or in rewards to those open to white men and women. The white college graduate . . . [has] numerous choices— among clerical work, salesmanship in stores, banks, and securities houses, while the Negro . . . graduate is restricted to a few narrow lines of endeavor most promising of which is the teaching profession. It is another question, however, when we come to the opinion that the public educational system should capitalize upon the prejudice which bars Negroes from other occupations by forcing Negro school graduates to seek employment at pitiable wages. Certainly it is a debatable issue whether or not the school system should take shrewd advantage of the extremities of race, and whether or not the individual should, for equal hours of labor, and for equal types of services, be given inferior wages.

Educated blacks had fewer employment opportunities in the southern economy than educated whites did; thus, other things equal, the "supply price" of educated blacks to the teaching profession was lower than the white supply price. School officials took advantage by paying black teachers less than white teachers. When the NAACP filed suit against the Hillsborough County, Florida school board in 1943, the board contended that "lower salaries for Negro teachers were justifiable" because "the principle of supply and demand should be taken into account since more Negro teachers are available" (Guzman 1947, 65). Chapter 6, in which I will show that educated blacks were excluded from white and skilled blue-collar occupations because of their race, provides econometric support for Bond's argument.

Racially based salary schedules could be maintained because school boards were not under the same pressures to minimize costs as were competitive firms. Given the lower supply price of black teachers, school boards could have lowered their costs by employing black teachers in white schools. None did, as far as I can determine. Exactly this point became the undoing of the Nashville, Tennessee school board when it faced a salary equalization suit in 1941. The board argued that black teachers were paid less because they taught in the black schools; had they been employed in the white schools, the board would have paid them the same as white teachers. The school board claimed that "the differential in pay . . . was based solely on an economic condition in that, colored teachers were more numerous than white teachers . . . [so] they could be employed to work at a lower salary than white teachers" (Tushnet 1987, 89). If that were so, the Court asked, why had the school board never employed a black teacher in a white school? Nashville lost the suit in 1942.

Teaching staffs were segregated primarily because white parents did not want black teachers in the white schools. But there is also evidence that black parents (and black teachers) preferred segregated staffs (Rabinowitz 1974). Having black teachers in the classrooms kept some control over what was taught, and, for the teachers, jobs were preserved for an educated elite. When the teaching staffs finally were desegregated after the *Brown* decision, the demand for black teachers declined. This decline was offset, however, by a simultaneous increase in demand resulting from the enfranchisement of the black population (Freeman 1977).

The existence of wage discrimination against black teachers has two further implications. Black teachers, like black children and their parents, were victims of "separate-and-unequal." As pointed out in Chapter 2, not all of the racial difference in per pupil expenditures represented a lower level of real resources in the black schools (Welch 1973; Donohue and Heckman 1989).[11] Second, because the demand for black teachers was a downward-sloping function of the average teacher salary (Margo 1982), the lower supply price of black teachers possibly kept class sizes smaller (and schools open more days per year) than if the black supply price had been higher. A reduction in wage discrimination against black teachers, therefore, might have worsened overcrowding in the black schools. But this did not happen in the 1940s, as the next section relates.

4.4 The Changing Market for Black Teachers, 1940–1950

The 1940s witnessed significant changes in the market for black teachers in the South. In real terms, the average annual salaries of black teachers increased 82 percent between 1940 and 1950, and the black-to-white salary ratio climbed 23 percentage points. The number of black teachers employed, however, grew slowly, at an average annual rate of 1.5 percent per year.

The rise in black teacher salaries might be explained as the outcome of the

NAACP's teacher salary cases (Welch 1973, 63). The cases sought to eliminate racially based salary schedules; that is, to equalize the salaries of equally qualified black and white teachers. More than thirty cases were brought between 1936 and 1950, and the majority were decided in favor of the plaintiff.[12]

The direct effects of equalization suits on average teacher salaries were arguably minimal. Legally, equalization agreements were binding only on the school board being sued (Marshall 1947, 48). The number of successful cases was tiny relative to the number of jurisdictions that practiced wage discrimination. The process of equalizing salaries after an agreement was reached might be spread over several years. Some school boards adopted racially neutral salary schedules, but simply reclassified black teachers into lower pay grades.[13]

Aware of all this, the NAACP hoped for strong spillover effects. Upon the resolution of the Alston suit (see Sec. 4.1), "petitions to obtain the application of benefits of the decision in other communities were filed by the teachers of . . . other cities and counties in Virginia. . . . By the end of 1943 the campaign for teacher pay equalization had reached eleven of the thirteen Southern States and in most of these the local Boards of Education were attempting to follow the mandates of the law as a result of court action" (Guzman 1947, 64). The North Carolina legislature voted to spend $2,700,000 to insure equalization by 1945. School boards in Texas and Arkansas instituted equalization programs in advance of lawsuits. Mississippi, a holdout, threatened retaliatory action against black teachers if a suit was filed, yet promised to raise salaries (1947, 64–65).

The NAACP was aided in its battle to equalize salaries by World War Two. Millions of blacks, including many teachers, left the South during the 1940s, never to return. Between 1942 and 1946 the number of black male elementary teachers in the South fell 53 percent.[14] The reduced supply of black teachers put upward pressure on salaries. "Many capable, properly qualified Negro teachers have failed to return to teaching from military service, war industries, and other types of employment," noted Louisiana's state superintendent of education in 1946. "Improved salaries," he continued, "constitute a basic factor in retaining our present staff of qualified [black] teachers" (State of Louisiana 1946, 59). This sentiment was a far cry from that of the superintendent's counterpart at the turn of the century who, upon noting a "decrease in the roll of colored children," attributed the decline to the "lessened number of the colored population of the state, caused by their drifting away . . . in search of a change of employment under a fancied idea of improvement in their social condition" (1902, 5).

It might be expected that the equalization suits, coupled with the war, would have caused a reduction in the number of teachers demanded in the black schools. The NAACP sought to equalize the *annual* salaries of white and black teachers. A school board could respond by either raising the annual salary, holding constant the number of days worked; or by increasing the number of days worked (that is, lengthen the school year); or some combination of both. To offset the cost, school boards might have reduced the number of black teachers employed, leading to an increase in class sizes. Similarly, by causing the supply of black teachers to decrease (a leftward shift in the supply curve), World War Two could have reduced the number demanded. Despite the sharp rise in black salaries, there is no evidence that class sizes in the black schools rose appreciably. In fact, the pupil-teacher ratio fell from 36 in 1942 to 32 in 1950. The overall decline in average class sizes occurred, in part, because there was an increase in the proportion of black children attending high school, where class sizes were smaller than in the lower grades. In the elementary grades, class sizes remained stable.[15]

A decrease in the number of black teachers demanded did not occur because the demand curve for black teachers was shifting rightward at the same time. To demonstrate this, I use the following supply-demand model:

$$(3) \qquad \dot{T}_d = \dot{D} - e\dot{w}$$
$$\dot{T}_s = \dot{S} + \delta\dot{w}$$

where T_d is the number of black teachers demanded; T_s is the number of black teachers supplied; D is the demand shift term; S is the supply shift term; w is the annual salary; e is the elasticity of demand; and δ is the elasticity of supply. A "dot" over a variable means that what is being represented is change in that variable. Setting the two equations equal, and solving for w and T gives the following:

$$(4) \qquad \dot{w} = (\dot{D} - \dot{S})/(e + \delta)$$
$$\dot{T} = (e\dot{S} + \delta\dot{D})/(e + \delta)$$

To use the model it is necessary to have estimates of e and δ. Freeman (1977) has estimated both parameters for the 1960s: his estimates are $e = 1$ and $\delta = 1.6$. It is possible that desegregation and the civil rights movement affected the demand and supply elasticities. The demand for black teachers may have become more elastic over time as teaching staffs desegregated. The supply of black teachers also may have become more elastic in the aggregate, as more occupations opened up to educated black men and women, and as more blacks left the South.

Table 4.5 presents calculations of $\dot{D}$ and $\dot{S}$ for 1940–50, using Freeman's parameters and assuming $e = 0.75$ and $\delta = 1.25$. The average annual growth in demand for black teachers is estimated to have been 7.7 percent per year. Growth in demand was lower during the first four years of the war (1940–44) than during the decade as a whole. Except for 1940–42, the supply curve of black teachers was shifting left, at a slightly higher rate than the demand curve was shifting rightward. The combination of increasing demand and decreasing supply contributed about equally to raising the wages of black teachers. Given that S was negative, all of the increase in the number of black teachers employed over the decade was due to rising demand.

Table 4.5   **The Changing Market for Black Teachers, 1940–1950:**
Shifts in Demand or Supply?

	$\dot{w}$	$\dot{T}$	$\dot{D}$		$\dot{S}$	
			$e = 1$	$e = 0.75$	$\delta = 1.6$	$\delta = 1.25$
1940–42	−0.078	0.026	−0.052	−0.033	0.151	0.123
1942–44	0.223	0.006	0.229	0.173	−0.354	−0.273
1944–46	0.086	0.013	0.099	0.078	−0.125	−0.095
1946–48	0.143	0.039	0.182	0.146	−0.190	−0.140
1948–50	0.222	0.061	0.293	0.228	−0.294	−0.217
1940–44	0.145	0.031	0.176	0.140	−0.201	−0.150
1940–50	0.595	0.145	0.740	0.591	−0.807	−0.599

Note: Figures are logarithmic changes between years; for example, w = 0.595 (1940–50) means that w increased at an average annual rate of 6.1 percent (exp [0.595/10] − 1) between 1940 and 1950.
Source: Column 1 is calculated from Figure 4.1; Column 2 is calculated from Federal Security Agency, U.S. Office of Education (1947, 1949, 1950, 1951) and U.S. Department of Health, Education, and Welfare (1954).

Part of the increase in the demand for black teachers can be attributed to an increase in black high school attendance and in the length of the school year. High school teachers were more expensive and class sizes were smaller. A longer school year meant a higher annual salary.[16]

But another factor causing demand to grow was the general social and political climate. Assuming a salary elasticity of 1, had school boards simply reacted to the rise in black salaries by cutting the number of teachers employed, the average class size in black schools might have almost doubled.[17] Not only would this have been unacceptable to teachers and parents, it was unacceptable politically. There was growing pressure on the South to improve its black public schools, to conform more closely to the separate-but-equal doctrine. Drastic reductions in the length of the black school year or in teacher-pupil ratios were not feasible options. Thus, as brilliantly executed as it was, the NAACP's campaign to end educational discrimination was helped by broader changes in the social, economic, and political spheres.

4.5 Summary

This chapter has examined racial differences in teacher salaries in southern public schools between 1890 and 1950. Regression analysis showed that wage discrimination against black teachers accounted for most of the racial salary gap. Discrimination was a consequence of behavior by school boards and employment segregation outside of teaching. The racial salary gap declined during the 1940s, due to shifts in teacher supply and demand. Shifts in supply put upward pressure on salaries. Responding to legal, social, and political pressure, shifts in demand kept class sizes in the black schools from increasing, leading to an erosion of the racial salary gap.

5   The Impact of Separate-but-Equal

During the first half of the twentieth century, southern black children attended public schools that received fewer resources per pupil than public schools attended by white children. The schools were racially "separate" but were not "equal." This chapter will demonstrate that racial inequality in school resources led to racial differences in educational outcomes: school attendance, literacy rates, and standardized test scores. Had the equal part of the separate-but-equal doctrine been adhered to, racial differences in educational outcomes would have been smaller. But "equal" schools were not enough to compensate for various aspects of family background that hindered the average educational achievement of black children.

5.1   The Moral Dilemma of Separate-but-Equal

In 1890 the Louisiana state legislature passed the Separate Car Act requiring "equal, but separate" accommodations for blacks and whites travelling within the state on all passenger railways, except for streetcars. Violations, a misdemeanor, were punishable by a maximum fine of $25 or twenty days in jail. In 1891 a "Citizens Committee to Test the Constitutionality of the Separate Car Law" was formed in New Orleans, under the general direction of Louis Martinet, a prominent black lawyer and doctor. The committee arranged a test case in 1892. Daniel Desdunes, a black man who had purchased a first-class ticket on the Louisiana and Nashville Railroad, was arrested on February 24 after sitting in a whites-only car bound from New Orleans to Mobile, Alabama. The out-of-state destination was chosen deliberately. The Committee rested its case on the belief that the Separate Car Act, because it appeared to apply to interstate travel, violated the interstate commerce clause of the U.S. Constitution. The case never came to trial. On May 25 the Louisiana Supreme Court decided (in the unrelated case of *Abbott v. Hicks*) that the Separate Car Act did not apply to interstate passengers.

A second test case was then arranged involving travel within the state. Homer Plessy was arrested on June 7,[1] upon insisting he be allowed to board a whites-only car of the East Louisiana Railway Company, which was bound from New Orleans to Covington, Louisiana. At Plessy's arraignment in New Orleans, Judge John Ferguson rejected the arguments of James Walker, Plessy's lawyer. Walker asserted that the Separate Car Act, amongst other flaws, "establishe[d] an invidious distinction . . . based on race which . . . abridges the privileges and immunities of citizens of the United States, and the rights secured by the XIIIth and XIVth amendments to the Federal Constitution" (Lofgren 1987, 48–49). Walker then petitioned the Louisiana Supreme Court, and District Attorney Lionel Adams responded on behalf of Judge Ferguson. In December the state court handed down its ruling: the Separate Car Act did not violate the Thirteenth or Fourteenth Amendments. Plessy's trial could proceed.

The stage shifted next to the U.S. Supreme Court. In January 1893 Walker filed a brief citing "manifest error" in the Louisiana proceedings. By perpetuating a racial distinction derived from slavery, the Separate Car Act violated the Thirteenth Amendment. Because railways could simply refuse to carry noncomplying passengers, and train officials were exempted from suits for damages from refusal to carry, Walker argued that the Act violated the equal protection and due process clauses of the Fourteenth Amendment. The brief also challenged Louisiana's claim that the Act was a valid expression of police power. Rather, the Act was "not in the interest of public order, peace, and comfort," but was "manifestly directed against citizens of the colored race" with the purpose "to assort and classify all passengers . . . according to race, and to make the rights and privileges of all cities of the United States dependent on said classification" (1987, 48).

After a long delay, the Supreme Court reached a verdict in May 1896. Writing for the majority was Justice Henry Billings Brown. Derided by one scholar as a "compound of bad logic, bad history, bad sociology, and bad constitutional law" (Harris 1960, 101), Brown's opinion rejected Walker's brief. "Legislation is powerless to eradicate racial instincts," Brown averred, "and the attempt to do so can only result in accentuating . . . difficulties" (Lofgren 1987, 178). Brown cited several pre-*Plessy* cases upholding racial segregation in the public schools to establish the "reasonableness" of the Separate Car Act. The lone dissenter was Justice John Marshall Harlan who, consistent with his earlier dissents in civil rights cases, sharply criticized the Louisiana law and Brown's opinion.

The import of *Plessy* was to establish firmly that "separate-but-equal was unambiguously a part of the law of the Constitution" (1987, 207).[2] In the case of public education, the legal interpretation of separate was relatively straightforward. Every ex-Confederate state, along with Missouri, Maryland and the District of Columbia, compelled separate schools by constitutional fiat or statutory authority.[3] Children who fit the legal definition of "Negro" were required to attend the schools for their race—which is not to say that various legal definitions of Negro were without controversy. *De jure* segregation in education frequently extended beyond classroom walls, for example, to the race of school personnel. Perhaps the height of absurdity was reached when Florida school law required that "school textbooks used by one race were to be stored separately from those used by the other race" (1987, 202).

The meaning of "equal" was less clear-cut. An early definition was provided by the U.S. Supreme Court in its 1899 decision, *Cumming v. Richmond County, Georgia*.[4] Prior to 1897 the Richmond County school board had operated a black public high school in Augusta, Georgia. When faced with rapidly growing demand for the county's black elementary schools, the board closed the high school, ostensibly to shift funds to the elementary schools. Justice Harlan ruled in favor of the school board; inexplicably so, to many scholars, in light of his dissent in *Plessy* and his opinions in other nineteenth century civil rights cases. It is possible to rationalize Harlan's opinion by appealing to what one legal scholar has called "the defense of compensating inequalities" (Tushnet 1987, 24). The needs of the many younger children outweighed the needs of the few older black children who wished to go to a public high school.[5] But the Court was reluctant to interfere with "the management of [public] schools . . . except in the case of a clear and unmistakable disregard of rights secured by the supreme law of the land" (1987, 23). Further, a plaintiff would have to show that a school board had acted out of "hostility to the colored population because of their race," which, Harlan judged, was not the intent of the Richmond school board (ibid.). While the import of *Cumming* was perhaps less extreme than a literal interpretation would suggest, it was far from negligible.[6] Where they existed, schools for blacks had to be separate, but their mere existence was sometimes precarious.

From a legal point of view the defense of compensating inequalities would seem to have been rendered unavailable by the Supreme Court's 1914 decision, *McCabe v. Atchinson, Topeka, and Sante Fe Railroad*. Oklahoma's separate car statute explicitly allowed railways to deny sleeping or dining cars to black travellers, on the grounds that the demand was too small to justify the costs. If the railway had to incur the cost of providing separate cars, it would have to reduce its services elsewhere to all passengers, including whites. In rejecting Oklahoma's argument the Supreme Court established the "personal rights" doctrine: *individuals* were entitled to equal protection under the law of the land. Economic considerations might figure in the decision to provide a particular type of service, but once the service was provided, "substantial equality of treatment of persons . . . under like facilities cannot be refused" (Tushnet 1987, 24).[7] When applied to public education, *McCabe* apparently undercut the defense proferred in *Cumming*. If a black student wished to enroll in high school, the school board could not argue that it provided a vocational school instead or that the elementary schools were more important. In effect, *McCabe* compelled equal facilities to be provided "for both races, no matter what the demand for the special facilities may be" (Mangum 1940, 193).

McCabe notwithstanding, the law evolved in a way to make loopholes readily available and challenges to violations difficult. Mississippi's school code of 1930 specified that any separate school could be discontinued if the average monthly attendance was less than five pupils. West Virginia law required a minimum of ten pupils, except if "circumstances render[ed] it practicable to establish a separate school for a smaller number" (1940, 93–95). Problems might be resolved by permitting children to enroll in a nearby district, at the home district's expense. But what if the schools were so bad or inaccessible that fewer than five or ten pupils attended? Worse, the fact that a black child might have to travel a much longer distance to get to school (without the benefit of a school bus) would not have necessarily violated the separate-but-equal doctrine as it was commonly understood, unless the distance was "unreasonable" or the trip was physically dangerous (Risen 1935, 73).

Separate-but-nonexistent schools for blacks was a big issue at the high school level and beyond. Black teenagers wishing to attend a high school might have to travel or move to a nearby city. The gross absence of professional or postgraduate training for blacks in the South led to a celebrated set of cases brought by the NAACP, such as *Gaines v. Missouri* in 1939. In *Gaines* the Supreme Court outlawed the widespread use of state scholarships for black students to attend universities outside the South, what had been the solution for higher education analogous to the practice of permitting elementary enrollments in nearby districts. *Gaines* also provided for three remedies when blacks sought to be enrolled in state facilities: the state could close down the white school, it could integrate, or it could establish a separate black school. But if it chose the third course, the school had to have substantially equivalent facilities, and the court made it clear that makeshift arrangements would violate the separate-but-equal doctrine.[8]

Nonexistence was not the only, or even quantitatively the most important violation of separate-but-equal. The equal clause was the law when facilities were provided. If southern school boards had attempted to abide by the spirit of the law, a defense of compensating inequalities might still have been available (despite *McCabe*) because, as a practical matter, "no two facilities will be exactly the same, and the courts will inevitably recognize some defense that inequalities are reasonable" (Tushnet 1987, 25). But the point is moot because the violations of separate-but-equal were not marginal ones. Black people knew it, black newspapers reported it widely, published statistics were available.[9] Why, then, was it so long before *Brown?*

The question is one of the deepest, and most tragic, of modern American history, and I could not pretend to answer it here. The superb histories of the NAACP struggle to end *de jure* segregation make it plain that the task was immense (Kluger 1977; Tushnet 1987). Society was racist, and the legal climate was hostile. Potential plaintiffs (teachers, children and their parents) numbered in the millions, a huge geographic area was involved, the NAACP was hardly wealthy, and its staff was small. In many states the appropriate legal remedy was a *writ of mandamus,* compelling state officials to abide by state constitutions which required equal facilities in some manner (for example, in the length of the school year). Obtaining such writs was a costly and arcane process; further, they might have to be obtained year in and year out (Tushnet 1987, 27). In most cases the information required to litigate equalization suits was enormously expensive to collect, even when the inequalities were obvious. Potential plaintiffs lost their jobs or risked bodily harm by participating. If the goal was readily identifiable, the means to achieve it were not.

From the very beginning the core of the NAACP's legal strategy was to link *de jure* segregation with discrimination, and get rid of the former by making the latter too costly to maintain. The strategy had three principal advantages *ex ante:* it was legally sound, it fit the ideology of the major NAACP participants (if not always their clients), and it was much cheaper than bringing a large number of equalization suits.[10] The opposition, of course, did not stand still. The road to *Brown* was strewn with losses as well as some unexpected victories. But the solution to the "endgame"—that *de jure* segregation imposed psychological harm on black children—was brilliant, because it made *Brown,* or a decision like it, inevitable as long as the Court was receptive to such evidence, which it was by the late 1940s.[11]

In its eventual acceptance of the NAACP's arguments, the Court laid the basis for a moral indictment of separate-but-equal in public education. Separate-but-equal was not only bad logic, bad history, bad sociology, and bad constitutional law, it was bad. Not because the equal part of separate-but-equal was poorly enforced, but because *de jure* segregation was immoral. Separate-but-equal, the Court ruled in *Brown,* is inherently unequal. For Tushnet, the struggle to end segregated schools is important in the large for what it says about the history (good and bad) of America's commitment to the values expressed in its Constitution, and it is important in the small for the blueprint it provides to public interest law and advocacy groups seeking to redress civil rights injustices of the past (1987).

While I have no disagreement with this point of view, I believe there is a further historical basis for a moral indictment of separate-but-equal. That basis is a fundamental counterfactual, put succinctly by Morgan Kousser (1980b, 40): How much would the economic "lives of black people in America" have improved "if the court had enforced equal benefits even if the schools were segregated[?]"[12] If the answer to Kousser's query is "a great deal of difference," then the failure to enforce the equal part of the separate-but-equal decision was deeply immoral, too. If the answer is "little difference," there is the added question of why, and possibly the implication that the equal part of separate-but-equal was not enough to advance black economic progress.

Previous claims that the violations of separate-but-equal affected educational and labor market outcomes rest heavily on indirect evidence and inherent plausibility (see, for example, Welch 1974). Modern studies, beginning with Coleman's (1966) famous report, have shown how difficult it is to consistently document positive links between the characteristics of schools (e.g., per pupil expenditures) and school achievement (e.g., test scores).[13] In the 1970s the pendulum swung so far in one direction that two leading scholars in the field entitled one their articles, "Do Schools Make a Difference?" (Summers and Wolfe 1977).

But, no matter how uncertain the answer to that question may be today, it does not follow that the answer was equally uncertain in the past. By historical standards, the modern spatial variation in *measured* school characteristics is relatively small, and ferreting out the partial effect of that variation on achievement is a difficult statistical problem.[14] Compensatory and mandated programs make the problem harder, in that per pupil expenditures may be highest in areas where achievement is lowest. Given these obstacles, it is not surprising that intangible or difficult to measure aspects of schools seem much more important than interdistrict variability in per pupil expenditures. Yet the violations of separate-but-equal were so large, as was the eventual improvement over time in the quality of black schools, that "it is hard to believe that differences in school effectiveness did not narrow along with the convergence in school resources" (U.S. Commission on Civil Rights 1986, 72).

Empirical plausibility, however, is no substitute for empirical evidence. It has been suggested that differences in black-to-white earnings ratios across birth cohorts are evidence that the violations of separate-but-equal had significant consequences. Blacks born in recent decades were educated in higher quality schools; consequently the black-to-white earnings ratio should be higher initially for these cohorts, and the ratio should stay roughly constant throughout their working lives (Smith and Welch 1989). For the most part, the earnings ratios do evolve as the hypothesis predicts.[15] But the evolution of earnings ratios does not *prove* the point, because it is impossible to use aggregate data to distinguish the effects of school quality from other factors associated with particular cohorts. Other tactics have been to include a dummy variable for southern birth or measures of school characteristics in the state of birth in an earnings regression, but on the whole these attempts have not been successful.[16] Direct evidence from the pre-*Brown* era on the impact of separate-but-equal has been little studied.[17]

The remainder of the chapter presents such evidence from three case studies. The first uses data from the public use sample of the 1900 census to demonstrate that, had the black and white schools been "equal," black children would have attended school more frequently than they actually did. The second uses county-level data to show that better schools would have raised black literacy rates. The third case study also uses county-level data to show that enforcement of separate-but-equal would have improved black childrens' performance on standardized tests.

The lax enforcement of the equal part of the separate-but-equal doctrine thus had disastrous consequences for black Americans. But the case studies also show that, even if equality in school resources had prevailed, there would still have been a racial gap in school attendance, literacy, and test scores. The likelihood that a black child attended school, for example, was not only a function of school characteristics but also depended on aspects of family background—parental literacy, for example. Early in the postbellum period, many of these aspects were direct legacies of slavery, and later on, were indirect legacies.

In his recent book, *Without Consent or Contract: The Rise and Fall of American Slavery,* Robert Fogel (1989) puts forth a moral indictment of slavery. By denying economic mobility to individuals and their children, slaveowners violated a basic human right. For the children freed by the Emancipation Proclamation, the withholding of literacy (among other skills) from parents created an intergenerational drag on economic progress that lasted well into the twentieth century. By itself, enforcement of the separate-but-equal doctrine would not have been enough to loosen the chains of illiteracy linking one generation to the next: a compensatory doctrine—"separate-plus-redistribution"—would have been necessary but, needless to say, was not possible at the time. In this way, the moral indictment of separate-but-equal forms a continuum with the moral indictment of slavery.

5.2   Separate-but-Equal and the Racial Gap in School Attendance

Chapter 2 demonstrated that black children in the early twentieth century South attended school less frequently at every age than did white children. Compounded over childhood, the age-specific differences in school attendance led to significant racial differences in educational attainment. In this section I examine the hypothesis that the racial attendance gap was a consequence of racial inequality in the provision of school facilities (Du Bois and Dill 1911, 137; Ransom and Sutch 1977, 28–30). Had the equal part of separate-but-equal been enforced, in other words, the racial attendance gap would have been smaller.

To investigate the hypothesis I use an econometric model of school attendance:

(1) $$A = \beta_0 + \beta_h X_h + \beta_c X_c + \beta_s X_s + \beta_g X_g + e$$

The dependent variable, A, measures the frequency of school attendance by a child; X_h is a set of family background variables; X_c is various characteristics of the child; X_s is a set of characteristics of the public schools; X_g is geographic characteristics; and β's are coefficients; and e is a random error term.

Equation (1) can be thought of as the outcome of a bargaining problem between the parents (or head of the household) and the children, resulting in an allocation of children's time between school and other activities, such as work in the market or at home. The frequency of school attendance is a function of certain characteristics of the parent and of the child; the characteristics

Table 5.1   **Sample Means and Standard Deviations: Southern Families in 1900**

	Black		White	
	Mean	Standard Deviation	Mean	Standard Deviation
Head of household:				
Occupational status	11.9	5.6	18.3	17.1
Percentage literate	0.49	0.50	0.84	0.37
Age	44.0	10.7	43.8	8.1
Percentage homeowner	0.27	0.44	0.61	0.49
Spouse:				
Percentage literate	0.38	0.48	0.78	0.41
Age	35.8	11.7	36.5	11.7
Child:				
Months of schooling	1.3	2.2	2.4	3.0
Age	10.0	3.4	10.3	3.4
Percentage female	0.48	0.50	0.49	0.50
Percentage households with child				
under age 5	0.25	0.42	0.32	0.46
School:				
Schools per 1,000 children (ages				
5–20)	6.9	2.9	11.9	4.9
Length of school year (in months)	4.1	1.0	4.4	1.0
Teachers per 100 pupils	2.7	0.8	3.6	0.9
Average monthly teacher salary				
(in 1900 dollars)	22.83	4.5	29.41	6.3
Geographic:				
Cotton acreage/improved acreage	0.28	0.16	0.20	0.15
Percentage living in plantation				
county	0.60	0.49	0.46	0.50
Percentage living in or near an				
urban area	0.21	0.41	0.15	0.36

Source: Margo (1987).

of the local school; and the economic returns to schooling compared with other uses of the child's time (which may vary with the household's location). Given that most schooling during the period was at the elementary level, completed before the child left home, a household model is appropriate.[18]

To estimate equation (1) I required information on children and their parents. The sample I used consists of 2,020 southern children between the ages of 5 and 16, and was drawn from the public use sample of the 1900 census. Frequency of attendance, the dependent variable, is measured by the number of months of school the child attended in the census year.[19] Child and family background variables were constructed from the information contained in the census sample. The family's county of residence was reported, so for each family it was possible to make a link to county-level data on various school and geographic variables constructed from other sources.

The average characteristics of the sample are displayed in Table 5.1. Because the percent of children attending school at all was far less than 100, the average months attended, calculated over all children, was rather small. Black children attended fewer months of school than white children, and there were large racial differences in the characteristics of families, schools, and place of residence. Black parents were less literate than white parents, their occupational status was lower, and they had less wealth, as indicated by lower rates of homeownership.[20] Compared with the white schools, there were fewer black schools, black school terms were shorter, class sizes larger, and teacher salaries were lower. Black children were more likely to live where cotton was grown and where a form of agriculture known as the plantation system was practiced (U.S. Bureau of the Census 1916), or in or close to an urban area.

For children in the sample who did not attend school, the dependent variable equals zero. Because the frequency of zeros is large, an econometric technique known as Tobit analysis is preferable to ordinary least squares (see Maddala 1983). The Tobit coefficients are shown in Table 5.2.

Children's school attendance was a positive function of the family's economic status, as indicated by the occupational status of the head of household and by homeownership. Consistent with the findings of Chapter 2, literate parents were more likely to send their children to school. The positive effect of parent's literacy may capture variations in economic status not fully reflected by occupation and homeownership; alternatively, better-educated parents may have placed a higher value on educating their offspring. A similar explanation may account for the positive effect of mother's age on black school attendance.

As one would expect from the evidence in Chapter 2, the age of the child significantly affected the probability of school attendance. It turned out that months attended among those in school did not vary by age; thus the positive coefficient of age and the negative coefficient of age squared reflects variations in the ages of entering and leaving school. After accounting for other factors, the child's gender had no significant impact on school attendance. The presence of a child under age 5 in black families lowered school attendance among older children, possibly by increasing the amount of time they were required to spend at home watching their younger siblings.

The school variables—the number of schools per 1,000 children, the length of the school year, the teacher-pupil ratio, and the average teacher salary—measure aspects of the quality of the public schools in the family's county of residence.[21] The greater the number of schools per 1,000 children, the lower are the costs of getting to school, and school attendance should rise. Similarly, the more months schools were open, the longer a child could attend. Smaller class sizes meant that the classrooms were less crowded (seats were available), and teachers could spend more time on instruction and less on discipline. Chapter 4 showed that, within race, higher salaries were associated with better-trained teachers. Hence, within race, the average salary is a proxy for the quality of instruction. Because black teachers suffered from wage dis-

Table 5.2   **The Determinants of Months of School Attendance: Southern Children in 1900**

Variable	Black β	Black t-statistic	White β	White t-statistic
Constant	− 34.50	10.15	− 30.09	14.18
Head of household:				
Occupational status × 10⁻¹	0.62	2.03	0.60	7.62
Literate	1.58	3.82	1.46	3.21
Age	− 0.01	− 0.50	0.03	1.63
Homeowner	0.73	1.70	1.23	3.97
Spouse:				
Literate	1.31	3.15	1.17	2.77
Age	0.04	2.14	− 0.02	− 1.22
Child:				
Age	4.31	9.46	3.97	12.28
Age squared	− 0.18	8.66	− 0.16	11.01
Female	0.12	0.32	0.09	0.74
Under age 5	− 1.33	− 2.97	− 0.17	− 0.58
School:				
Schools per 1,000 children	− 0.03	− 0.34	0.05	1.40
Length of school year (in months)	0.86	4.08	0.28	1.46
Teachers per 100 pupils	0.76	2.84	0.44	2.44
Average monthly teacher salary (in 1900 dollars)	0.07	1.54	0.02	0.40
Geographic:				
Cotton/improved acreage	− 2.53	− 1.23	− 1.71	− 1.20
Plantation county	− 0.24	− 0.37	− 0.07	− 0.16
In urban area	1.86	3.43	0.75	1.52
σ	4.17	92.48	4.18	134.86
Log likelihood	1,054.9		1,974.0	
Number of observations	868		1,152	

Source: Margo (1987).

crimination, however, the mean racial difference in average teacher salaries overstates the true difference in the quality of instruction (see below).

The coefficients of the school variables are expected to be positive, and as Table 5.2 shows, this expectation is confirmed by seven of the eight coefficients.[22] Longer school terms and smaller class sizes would have encouraged children of both races to attend school more frequently, and these effects were larger among blacks.[23] A better-trained teaching force also would have increased black school attendance.

The geographic variables, which also refer to the family's county of residence in 1900, control for variations in the returns to schooling compared with other uses of the child's time. The share of improved acreage devoted to cotton and whether plantation agriculture was dominant in the county should have been negatively related to school attendance. Prior to mechanization, child labor was especially productive in cotton agriculture; as one school superintendent from Georgia explained, "Whole families are reared without ever seeing the inside of a school. They are kept at work in the cotton fields" (State of Georgia 1907, 113). Cotton cultivation was frequently associated with plantation agriculture, in which tenant farmers operated small plots under the supervision of a single landlord. According to Charles Johnson (1934, 129) "literacy was not an asset in the plantation economy." By contrast, in urban counties children had fewer productive employment opportunities (compared with cotton cultivation); additionally, nonfarm jobs that urban children might aspire to frequently required some schooling (see Chapter 6).

Cotton cultivation or residence in a plantation county was negatively associated with school attendance, but the effects were small in magnitude and statistically insignificant for both races. If, however, children between the ages of 17 and 20 are added to the sample, the coefficients of the cotton variable are much larger for both races, which suggests that the effects were concentrated among older children. Urban children attended school significantly longer than rural children, and the effect was larger among blacks.[24]

Table 5.3 gives the percentage of the mean racial difference in school attendance explained by the mean racial differences in the independent variables. The figures shown for school characteristics answer the question posed at the beginning of this section: how much smaller the racial attendance gap would have been if separate-but-equal had been enforced. Enforcement of separate-but-equal is defined to be equal average school characteristics. Figures are shown assuming equalization of all school characteristics, and of all school characteristics *except* the average teacher salary. Equalizing all school characteristics overstates the effect of separate-but-equal because, as Chapter 4 showed, most of the racial difference in average teacher salaries reflected wage discrimination against black teachers. On the other hand, equalizing all school characteristics except the average teacher salary understates the impact of separate-but-equal, because some of the racial salary gap was a consequence of racial differences in the training and experience of teachers. Thus excluding teacher salaries from the calculation produces a lower bound on the effect of separate-but-equal.

There are two ways to perform the calculations, one using the Tobit coefficients for whites, the other using the coefficients for blacks. Both are shown, but I would argue that, from an historical point of view, the calculations using the black coefficients are more appropriate ones.[25] Any hypothetical equalization would have brought the characteristics in the black schools up to the level in the white schools, and the black coefficients show how such an equalization would have affected black school attendance.[26]

Racial differences in school characteristics account for 40–77 percent of the racial attendance gap, depending on how the effect of separate-but-equal is calculated. Had the equal part of separate-but-equal been enforced, the racial

Table 5.3   The Impact of Separate-But-Equal on School Attendance

	Predicted Difference in Months Attended (white minus black)	% Explained
At sample means	0.93	
If adult literacy equalized:		
Black	0.41	55.7
White	0.38	59.1
If literacy, occupational status, homeownership equalized:		
Black	0.24	74.2
White	0.16	82.8
If all school characteristics equalized:		
Black	0.22	76.3
White	0.44	52.7
If all school characteristics equalized excluding teacher salary:		
Black	0.56	39.9
White	0.51	45.2
If all independent variables equalized:		
Black	−0.73	
White	−0.39	
If all independent variables equalized excluding teacher salary:		
Black	−0.54	
White	−0.33	

Note: Predicted differences are calculated using the Tobit coefficients and the following formula (Maddala 1983, 159): $E(m) = F(X\beta/\sigma)X\beta + f(X\beta/\sigma)\sigma$, where $E(m)$ is the predicted months attended; F is the standard normal cumulative distribution; and f is the standard normal density function. *Black:* calculation performed using black coefficients; *White:* calculation performed using white coefficients. *Equalized:* black sample mean equals the white sample mean; *Excluding teacher salary:* black and white sample mean teacher salaries are not equalized in the calculation (see text).

attendance gap would have been much smaller. But even if it had been enforced, black children still would have attended less frequently than white children, because of racial differences in family background. Inadequate educational opportunities were not the sole, or even quantitatively the most important reason for the racial attendance gap. Racial differences in adult literacy, occupational status, and homeownership account for 74–83 percent of the racial attendance gap; adult literacy, by itself, explains over half of the gap.[27]

The final four rows of Table 5.3 show the predicted mean racial difference in months attended (white minus black) equalizing *all* variables in the regression (that is, except for race). The predicted differences are *negative:* under these hypothetical circumstances, the black child would have attended more months of school than the white child. Thus the lower average attendance of black children cannot be attributed to a lack of interest on the part of their parents; indeed exactly the opposite was true—black parents had a deep desire to see their children educated (Anderson 1987). It follows that the long-term narrowing of the racial gap in school attendance rates (Chapter 2) was accomplished with the aid of pure "catch-up," that is, the willingness of black parents to send their children to school despite adverse circumstances—poverty, adult illiteracy, and bad schools.

5.3 Separate-but-Equal and the Racial Literacy Gap in Alabama

The vast majority of southern blacks learned to read and write in separate-and-unequal public schools. It is no small matter historically if the failure to enforce the separate-but-equal doctrine slowed the long-term decline of black illiteracy in the South. I examine this question by analyzing the impact of separate-but-equal on child literacy rates in Alabama from 1920 to 1940. The Alabama data were collected as part of a state school census. To the best of my knowledge, no other southern state reported similar information between these dates. It is unclear if the data are specific to public school students, but any bias is probably small, as private school enrollments for both races were but a fraction (no more than 5 percent) of public school enrollments during the period (see Margo 1986a, 794).

Table 5.4 documents racial differences in literacy and school characteristics in Alabama between 1920 and 1940. Black children in Alabama lagged behind their white counterparts in learning to read and write. In 1920 the literacy rate of black children (ages 7–20) was 68 percent, compared with 88 percent among white children. By 1940 the black literacy rate had risen to 88 percent and the literacy gap had fallen to 8 percentage points. In 1920, instructional expenditures per pupil in the black schools equalled 29 percent of expenditures per pupil in the white schools. For every dollar of school capital per white child, black children received 34 cents. The length of the school year in the black schools averaged 93 days, two months less than the white average. A majority of black students—84 percent—attended schools taught by a single teacher, a figure 31 percentage points higher than that for whites.

By 1940, conditions in the black schools had improved for the most part. In real terms, instructional expenditures per pupil in the black schools had quadrupled since 1920 and the black-white ratio of per pupil expenditures rose to 0.47. The length of the black school year averaged 141 days, an increase of 48 days over the 1920 figure. Although the proportion of black schools with one teacher fell over the period, the decline in one-teacher schools was proportionately greater for whites. Despite a tripling in the real value of school capital per black pupil between 1920 and 1940, the increase in the value of school capital was far greater in the white schools, and the black-to-white ratio of the school capital stock was smaller by a half.

Throughout the period, black children lagged behind white children in literacy rates, but over time the racial difference in illiteracy diminished sharply. Judging by the evidence in Table 5.4, the black schools were distinctly in-

Table 5.4   **Racial Differences in Child Literacy and Public School**
                       Characteristics: Alabama Counties, 1920–1940

Percentage literate, ages 7–20			
White	0.88	0.93	0.96
Black	0.68	0.77	0.88
Difference	0.20	0.16	0.08
Length of school year (in days)			
Black	93	119	141
White	130	151	148
Ratio	0.72	0.79	0.95
Expenditures per pupil, per day (in 1930 dollars)			
Black	0.02	0.05	0.08
White	0.07	0.12	0.17
Ratio	0.29	0.42	0.47
Value of school capital per pupil $\times\ 10^{-2}$ (in 1930 dollars)			
Black	0.08	0.21	0.25
White	0.23	1.07	1.43
Ratio	0.35	0.20	0.17
Percentage one-teacher schools			
Black	84	61	53
White	53	32	20
Ratio	1.58	1.91	2.65

Source: Margo (1986a).

ferior to the white schools. How large was the effect of the racial inequality in school characteristics on the racial literacy gap?

To answer this question, I use an econometric model of literacy rates. The unit of observation is the county, the dependent variable is the proportion literate (ages 7–20) in the county, and the explanatory variables are county averages. The model is

$$(2) \qquad L_{it} = \beta_0 + \beta_1 E_{it} + \beta_2 X_{it} + \beta_3 F_{it} + e_{it}$$

L is the literacy rate in county i in year t (t = 1920, 1930, 1940); E is a measure of student effort; X is a set of public school characteristics; F is a set of family background variables; the β's are regression coefficients; and e is a random error term.

Equation (2) is an "educational production function" relating educational achievement to a set of inputs. Achievement (here the average literacy rate) depends on a combination of factors: student effort, the characteristics of schools, and family background. Achievement will be higher if, holding X and F constant, the student puts in more effort. Holding E and F constant, an improvement in some aspect of school quality (e.g., a longer school year) will result in higher achievement. But achievement depends on more than student effort and school attributes; it depends, as in the analysis of school attendance, on family background. Modern studies have demonstrated conclusively that many factors, such as family income, the educational attainment of parents, and the stability of family life, affect how well children do in school, no matter how good the schools are (Summers and Wolfe 1977; Hanushek 1986).

Effort is measured by the average daily attendance rate of pupils in grades one through six. The idea is that the literacy rate will be higher if, other things equal, students attend class more frequently, so the coefficient of the attendance rate should be positive. The school characteristics are those listed in Table 5.4. All of these should have positive coefficients, except the proportion of one-teacher schools. According to Welch (1973, 59), "discipline would have consumed a significant proportion of instructional time and energy" in one-teacher schools, which implies a negative coefficient for this variable.

The family background variables are race (separate equations were estimated by race), per capita income, and the proportion of families who owned their home. Race-specific, county-level data on incomes are not available for the period and must be estimated.[28]

The fact that the data are county averages creates certain problems. Use of county averages obscures the effects of the independent variables within counties. The large age span (7–20) covered by the literacy rate means that some children would have been out of school, and the current value of characteristics might be only weakly correlated with conditions when they did attend (if they attended at all). In this case, school characteristics are measured with error, and thus their impact on literacy rates may be understated. Because the data from the different years are pooled, a final issue concerns the method of estimating equation (2). Two methods are available, the random effects estimator and the fixed effects estimator, and the results of both are reported in Table 5.5.[29]

The most important school characteristics were the length of the school year and the amount of instructional expenditures. Both variables were economically and statistically significant determinants of literary rates, regardless of race. The value of the school capital and the percentage one-teacher schools, however, had no significant impact on literacy rates.[30] The absence of a relation between the percentage one-teacher schools and literacy is surprising in light of Welch's conjecture, but it may be that any negative effects of one-teacher schools were offset by a positive impact on younger children of mixing them with older children at higher grade levels.

Family background variables—race, per capita income, and homeownership—were important determinants of literacy rates, independent of school characteristics. The per capita income and homeownership coefficients were positive, and were larger for blacks than for whites, again indicating (as in Sec. 5.2) the close link between family background and educational outcomes in black families.

The remaining step is to calculate the impact of separate-but-equal. As in Section 5.2, I interpret enforcement of separate-but-equal as a counterfactual in which the racial gap in mean school characteristics is reduced to zero.[31] I use the coefficients to calculate what the average white and black literacy rates

Table 5.5   Determinants of Literacy: Alabama Counties, 1920–1940

	White		Black	
Variable	RE	FE	RE	FE
Constant	−0.53	−0.43	−1.29	−1.23
	(4.10)	(2.62)	(6.17)	(5.03)
Attendance rate	0.02	0.01	0.15	0.13
	(1.03)	(0.21)	(2.93)	(2.09)
Length of school year (in days)	0.10	0.07	0.25	0.18
	(4.25)	(2.40)	(6.62)	(3.54)
Expenditures per pupil, per day $\times$ 10^{-2} (in 1930 dollars)	0.33	0.17	0.48	0.12
	(3.52)	(1.35)	(2.32)	(0.40)
Value of school capital per pupil $\times$ 10^{-1} (in 1930 dollars)	0.01	−0.03	−0.04	−0.16
	(0.17)	(0.55)	(0.38)	(1.53)
Percentage one-teacher schools	0.003	0.01	−0.03	0.03
	(0.16)	(0.68)	(0.74)	(0.52)
Per capita income	0.02	0.04	0.05	0.03
	(1.98)	(1.32)	(2.10)	(0.40)
Percentage own home	0.03	−0.06	0.30	0.26
	(1.02)	(0.95)	(3.05)	(0.76)
Number of observations	201		180	
Mean squared error	0.007	0.008	0.006	0.006

Notes: RE = random effects estimates; FE = fixed effects estimates. Absolute values of *t*-statistics in parentheses.
Source: Margo (1986a).

would be under such conditions, and compare the counterfactual literacy gap to the actual literacy gap. Because some of the racial difference in instructional expenditures reflected wage discrimination against black teachers, the effect of equalizing school terms is calculated separately. The calculations are shown in Table 5.6. The rows labelled White use the white coefficients and the rows labelled Black use the black coefficients.

Equalization of school term lengths and instructional expenditures would have had a significant effect on the racial literacy gap. Using the random effects coefficients, had the average length of the term in the black and white schools been the same in both years, other things equal, the racial literacy gap would have been smaller by 5–31 percent. Had separate-but-equal also been enforced with respect to instructional expenditures, the racial literacy gap would have been smaller in total by 15–55 percent. The larger reductions occur when the black coefficients are used to perform the calculations which, as previously argued, is the better way to specify the counterfactual. The fixed effects coefficients yield a smaller impact, but also support the conclusion that enforcement of separate-but-equal would have narrowed the racial literacy gap.

Table 5.6   The Impact of Separate-But-Equal on Literacy Rates

| | % Explained of Racial Literacy Gap | | |
	1920	1930	1940
Equalize school terms			
White			
Random effects	12.3	12.5	5.2
Fixed effects	8.6	8.8	3.6
Black			
Random effects	30.7	31.3	13.0
Fixed effects	22.1	22.6	9.4
Equalize school terms and instructional expenditures			
White			
Random effects	24.0	26.6	33.8
Fixed effects	14.6	16.1	18.3
Black			
Random effects	47.7	51.8	54.6
Fixed effects	26.3	27.7	19.8
Equalize per capita income and homeownership			
White			
Random effects	9.3	13.2	25.1
Fixed effects	9.4	13.8	27.0
Black			
Random effects	40.6	57.3	106.4
Fixed effects	30.5	42.5	79.3

Source: Margo (1986a, 798).

The Alabama data suggest that racial inequality in the length of the school year and instructional expenditures kept the racial literacy gap higher than it would have been had the equal part of separate-but-equal been reality instead of myth. But, by itself, separate-but-equal was not enough: a significant portion of the remainder of the racial literacy gap can be attributed to family background variables (per capita income and homeownership). Had incomes and wealth been equalized, the racial literacy gap would have been narrowed by even more than if separate-but-equal had been enforced.

It is likely that some of the effect of the income and wealth variables is a reflection of racial differences in adult literacy, which could not be included in the regressions due to data limitations. Illiterate parents could not substitute for inadequate schools and teach their children to read and write. A high rate of adult illiteracy hindered the spread of literacy in the next generation of black children, independent of racial inequality in school resources.[32]

5.4   Separate-but-Equal and Test Scores: Maryland Public Schools

Strict enforcement of the equal part of separate-but-equal would have narrowed racial differences in school attendance and in literacy rates. These educational outcomes are important to study because, as Chapters 6 and 7 will demonstrate, school attendance and literacy significantly affected labor market outcomes for black men. The modern literature on educational achievement, however, studies only the effect of school inputs on standardized test scores (see, e.g., Summers and Wolfe 1977). In theory, a standardized test measures the "output" of the educational process. School attendance is an input, not an output. Literacy is an output, but quite a crude one in comparison with a carefully designed standardized test.

Peter Orazem (1987) has recently investigated the impact of separate-but-equal on standardized test scores. For several years between 1924 and 1938, Maryland's state board of education reported county averages of test scores for its racially separate schools. Orazem analyzed the variation in test scores in the context of an econometric model of educational production similar to the one employed in the previous section. During this period the average test score in the black schools fell below the average score in the white schools, but the racial gap in test scores narrowed over time. Orazem also calculated how much higher black test scores would have been had school inputs been equalized between the races (that is, the effect of separate-but-equal).

The achievement measure used in Orazem's study is the race-specific proportion of students in the county "taking a nationally standardized test of reading skills who meet or exceed the national norm for the test" (1987, 716). The variable refers solely to children in the elementary schools. School characteristics are the length of the school year, measures of teachers' education and experience, class size, the value of the school capital stock, and the proportion of one-teacher schools. The average test score was assumed to be a linear function of the average daily attendance rate and the school inputs. Separate equations were estimated for black and white schools.[33]

An advantage of the Maryland data is that, unlike the Alabama literacy rates, the test scores are solely for children currently in school. The relation between school characteristics and educational output, thus, is apt to be closer than in my study of Alabama. It is fortunate the test was nationally normed, although without access to the actual questions, it is hard to say whether any cultural or regional bias crept in. We cannot be certain if success on the test translated into economic success but, because the test measured reading skills (literacy), it must have had some bearing. A problem with Orazem's study is the absence of any family background variables other than race (his equations are race specific).[34]

Equalizing school characteristics would have narrowed the racial gap in test scores by between 24 and 57 percent, depending on whether the white or black coefficients are used for the calculation and whether dummy variables for counties are included in Orazem's regressions.[35] The average reduction, taken over all of Orazem's regressions, is 37 percent. The average reduction in the literacy gap in Alabama (using the random effects figures in Table 5.6) is 38 percent.[36] Given the differences between Orazem's and my study, it is significant that both yield similar conclusions about the impact of separate-but-equal. It is significant, too, that Orazem found that the length of the school year had a strong positive effect on test scores, consistent with my findings on school attendance and literacy rates.

5.5   Conclusion

Strict enforcement of the equal part of separate-but-equal would have narrowed racial differences in school attendance, literacy rates, and test scores. In the next two chapters I shall show that education improved the labor market outcomes of black men in the early twentieth century South. Thus the violations of separate-but-equal hindered the long-term economic progress of black Americans. However, separate-but-equal was not enough to fully equalize educational outcomes. Only a radical redistribution of school board budgets in favor of black children might have compensated for the family background effects that kept black children out of school, slowed the spread of literacy, and caused the test scores of black children to be lower than those of whites.

6   The Competitive Dynamics of
     Racial Exclusion: Employment
     Segregation in the South,
     1900 to 1950

Previous chapters have shown that there were large racial differences in schooling in the South before 1950. This chapter and the next consider the implications of these differences for labor market outcomes. Chapter 6 focuses primarily on employment (industry and occupation) in the South, while Chapter 7 examines migration from the South. The results suggest that an eclectic mixture of the human capital and institutionalist models does a better job of explaining racial differences in labor market outcomes than either model taken separately.

6.1 Race and Employment in the South, 1900–1950: An Overview

This section reviews quantitative evidence on racial differences in employment in the South (industry and occupation) from 1900 to 1950. Its purpose is to put forth a set of basic facts to be examined in greater detail later in the chapter.

Panel A of Table 6.1 gives agricultural participation rates (the percentage of the labor force engaged in agriculture) for southern males from 1900 to 1950. The figures for ages 10 and over were derived from the published census volumes, while those for adults (ages 20–64) were calculated from the public use samples. Because the definition of the labor force in terms of ages changed in 1940 (to ages 14 and over), only figures for adult males are given for 1940 and 1950. No figures for adult males are given for 1920 or 1930 because census sample data are currently unavailable for those years.[1]

The South began the twentieth century as an agricultural economy—a majority of male workers, black and white, worked in farming. Agricultural participation rates were slightly lower for adult males than for all males in the labor force, but were still substantial. Importantly, racial differences in agricultural participation rates were relatively small at the turn of the century—4

Table 6.1   The Shift of Labor Out of Southern Agriculture, 1900–1950

A. Percentage of Male Labor Force in Agriculture: The South

	Ages 10 and Over			Ages 20–64		
	Black	White	Dif	Black	White	Dif
1900	64.2	59.9	4.3	60.7	58.7	2.0
1910	64.6	56.5	8.1	61.7	52.1	9.6
1920	57.7	46.8	10.9			
1930	52.8	39.9	12.9			
1940				46.5	32.5	14.0
1950				34.2	21.3	12.9

B. Percentage of Adult Male Labor Force in Agriculture, By Race and Age Group

	1900	1910	1940	1950
Black				
20–24	62.7	57.0	53.1	27.9
25–34	55.0	53.4	40.1	25.7
35–44	57.9	58.1	39.8	24.4
45–54	65.5	65.3	51.3	29.5
55–64	64.5	71.9	58.7	37.3
White				
20–24	63.1	51.6	34.5	17.9
25–34	54.2	47.6	22.7	15.1
35–44	55.4	48.1	28.0	17.6
45–54	61.8	54.7	35.6	19.0
55–64	66.8	61.4	50.9	29.7

Note: In Panel A, Dif means black minus white percentages.
Sources: **Ages 10 and over:** *1900,* U.S. Census Office (1904, 220–410); *1910, Black,* U.S. Bureau of the Census (1918, 503); *1910, White,* U.S. Bureau of the Census (1914, 434–529); *1920,* U.S. Bureau of the Census (1923, 874–1039); *1930, Black,* U.S. Bureau of the Census (1935, 303–9); *1930, White,* U.S. Bureau of the Census (1933, 105–1741). **Ages 20–64:** Author's calculations from census public use samples; 1940 figures exclude persons with emergency work relief jobs.

percentage points for males ages 10 and over, and 2 percentage points for adult males.

Over the next fifty years the southern economy "modernized," that is, labor shifted out of agriculture. In 1930, 40 percent of the white male labor force (ages 10 and over) was agricultural, a decrease of 20 percentage points from 1900. Black labor, too, shifted out of agriculture, but at a slower pace than white labor, with a decline of 13.4 percentage points between 1900 and 1930. Among adult males, agricultural participation rates declined from 1900 to 1940 for both races, but the decline was greater for whites. During the 1940s, however, black labor shifted out of southern agriculture more quickly than white labor did. Still, the racial gap in agricultural participation rates among adult males was larger in 1950 than in 1900.

Panel B of Table 6.1 gives agricultural participation rates among adult males by race and age group. Prior to World War Two, the shift of labor out of southern agriculture was a "cohort" phenomenon. That is, successive generations of younger males had lower agricultural participation rates, while older cohorts remained in agriculture as they aged. Consider the 25–34 age group in 1910: 53 percent of blacks and 48 percent of whites were in farming. Among those in the age group still in the South in 1940 (now between the ages of 55 and 64), 59 percent of the blacks and 51 percent of the whites were engaged in agriculture. But agricultural participation rates of 25 to 34-year-olds in 1940 were lower than in 1910 (the same was true of 20 to 24-year-olds). During the 1940s, however, the outflow from agriculture occurred in *every* age group, blacks to a greater extent than whites.

More detailed evidence is given in Panels A and B of Table 6.2, which show the distribution of employment by broad (one-digit) industrial and occupational categories. In 1910 blacks were relatively more numerous than whites in durable goods manufacturing, transportation-communications-public utilities, and personal services. Black labor was underrepresented in the other nonfarm industries, especially wholesale and retail trade (by 7 percentage points). In 1940 blacks continued to be overrepresented in durable goods manufacturing and personal services, and were underrepresented in mining-construction, nondurables manufacturing, trade, finance, and business services, professional services, and government jobs. In six of nine nonfarm industries, the degree of over- or underrepresentation of black labor was higher in 1940 than in 1910.

During the 1940s the migration of black labor off the farm found its way into the South's nondurable goods manufacturing plants, reducing the underrepresentation of black labor in that industry. Black labor also flowed into durable goods manufacturing, increasing its overrepresentation there. The proportion of black men employed in trade and professional services also rose over the decade. Black employment in personal services fell (the white share did not), suggesting the relatively high share of black employment in services in 1940 may have been a consequence of the Great Depression. The racial gap in employment increased in mining-construction, financial and business services, and government.

The distribution of employment across occupations in the South was more racially dissimilar than the distribution of employment across industries. At the turn of the century, black men were severely underrepresented in white-collar jobs. Sixteen percent of white men held white-collar jobs, compared with 2.7 percent of black men, or a racial gap of 13.6 percentage points. In the next several decades, black men entered white-collar occupations, increasing the percentage so employed to 3.7 percent in 1940 and to 5.5 percent in 1950. But the fraction of white men with white-collar jobs rose even faster. By 1940 the racial gap in white-collar employment was 22 percentage points, increasing to 24 percentage points within a decade. Disaggregation of the data

Table 6.2   **Distribution of Employment in the South: Males, Ages 20–64 (in percentages)**

	1900	1910	1940	1950
A. Occupation				
White collar				
Black	2.7	2.3	3.7	5.5
White	16.3	20.0	25.8	29.1
Professional/technical				
Black			1.5	
White			4.8	
Managers				
Black			1.2	
White			9.8	
Clerical/sales				
Black			1.0	
White			11.2	
Skilled blue collar				
Black	3.8	5.2	4.3	6.7
White	9.5	12.4	14.1	20.0
Semi-skilled blue collar				
Black	4.9	6.3	10.8	20.7
White	5.7	7.5	18.1	20.8
Service				
Black	4.2	5.7	10.9	10.3
White	1.5	2.5	4.1	3.5
Domestic				
Black			2.9	
White			0.1	
Protective				
Black			0.3	
White			2.3	
Other (includes personal)				
Black			7.7	
White			1.7	
Unskilled nonfarm laborer				
Black	23.8	18.8	23.8	22.6
White	8.1	5.7	5.8	5.3
Farm operator				
Black	37.6	39.9	26.2	20.7
White	44.2	39.4	22.2	15.2
Farm laborer				
Black	23.1	21.8	20.3	13.5
White	14.5	12.7	10.0	6.1
Segregation index	26.7	26.1	39.2	37.0
Sample size				
Black	2,065	6,011	4,767	5,346
White	4,921	18,956	20,237	20,445

Table 6.2   **(continued)**

B. Industry	1910	1940	1950
Agriculture			
Black	62.4	45.8	32.8
White	52.1	31.8	21.0
Mining-construction			
Black	6.7	8.4	11.2
White	7.8	12.2	15.7
Nondurables manufacturing			
Black	2.6	5.8	7.5
White	4.7	11.2	11.2
Durables manufacturing			
Black	9.8	11.0	13.7
White	7.5	8.6	9.5
Transportation-communications-public utilities			
Black	8.7	7.4	8.7
White	8.2	7.4	8.7
Wholesale-retail trade			
Black	3.7	7.9	11.0
White	10.9	14.7	16.3
Financial-business services			
Black	0.8	2.2	2.8
White	2.7	4.5	5.4
Personal services			
Black	3.6	8.1	6.3
White	1.7	2.8	2.8
Professional services			
Black	1.4	2.5	3.8
White	3.2	3.3	4.2
Government			
Black	0.3	1.0	2.3
White	1.2	3.6	5.3
Segregation index	15.0	21.7	19.5
Sample size			
Black	6,012	4,693	5,352
White	18,963	15,106	20,467

Sources: 1900, 1910, census public use sample; *1940, 1950,* 20 percent random sample of census public use tapes; 1940 sample excludes persons with emergency work relief jobs. Farm laborer category includes unskilled laborers, industry not specified, but living on a farm.

on white-collar employment further reveals that, throughout the period, a majority of black professionals in the South were found in just two occupations, teaching and preaching.[2] Cross classifications of industry and occupation show that blacks holding managerial positions were mostly self-employed businessmen, in wholesale and retail trade, financial and business services (e.g., real estate agencies), or personal services.[3]

If black employment in white-collar work lagged behind white employment, a skilled blue-collar job was another means of upward mobility. But blacks were underrepresented in skilled blue-collar jobs, and their underrepresentation increased over time. In the 1900 sample, 3.8 percent of black men held skilled blue-collar jobs, compared with 9.5 of white men. The black proportion increased to 4.8 percent in 1910, but the increase in the white proportion was larger, so that the racial gap in skilled blue-collar employment rose to 7 percentage points. The fraction of adult black men in 1940 with skilled blue-collar jobs was actually lower than in 1910. Black employment in the skilled trades expanded during the war decade, but growth in white employment was greater, and the racial gap rose to 13 percentage points by 1950.

In the semi-skilled operative category, blacks were underrepresented slightly in 1900. About 5 percent of black men in the 1900 sample held such jobs, compared with 5.7 percent of white men. In the next forty years, the fraction of adult black men in semi-skilled occupations increased, but white employment in semi-skilled jobs rose even faster, to 7.3 percentage points in 1940. But the racial gap closed abruptly during the 1940s, as black men filled newly created jobs in southern factories.

If they had problems finding white-collar and skilled blue-collar employment, black men had much less trouble getting a low-paying service job or a job as an unskilled laborer. The proportion of black men in service occupations (such as domestic, personal services, or protective services) more than doubled over the first half of the twentieth century. In the 1950 sample, 10.3 percent of black men held service jobs, compared with only 3.5 percent of white men. The racial gap in domestic employment—6.8 percentage points— was nearly three times as large as in 1900. The proportion of black men working as unskilled nonfarm laborers remained roughly constant between 1900 and 1950, at about 23 percent. The proportion of white men in such jobs, however, declined consistently, from 8.1 percent in 1900 to 5.3 percent in 1950. Consequently, the racial gap in unskilled nonfarm employment increased, from 15.7 percentage points in 1900 to 17.3 percentage points in 1950.

A summary statistic of racial dissimilarities in employment is a "segregation index." The index I use is[4]

$$(1) \qquad SI = \left(\sum_i |b_i - w_i|/2 \right) \times 100$$

where b_i is the share of the black labor force in industry or occupation i; w_i and is the share of the white labor force in industry or occupation i. The segregation index ranges from zero to 100. Complete integration (a value of zero) would occur if the black proportion equalled the white proportion in every industry or occupation. Complete segregation (a value of 100) would occur if industries and occupations were either all white or all black; that is, for every industry or occupation in which w_i was positive, b_i would be zero, and vice versa.

Values of the segregation index are shown in Table 6.2. It is important to keep in mind that the values are *not* invariant to the number of industry and occupational categories. Were a larger number of categories used, the indices would take on larger values, indicating greater racial dissimilarity.[5] This is particularly true in the case of industrial segregation. It is unlikely, however, that substantive conclusions would change if the number of categories were expanded.

The results show that employment segregation in southern industry increased from 1910 to 1940: the value of the index in 1940 (21.7) was 45 percent higher than in 1910. Occupational segregation, too, rose in this period. During the 1940s, employment segregation declined in the South. Despite the decline, however, both the industry and occupation indices show that segregation was greater in 1950 than in 1910.

In summary, labor shifted out of southern agriculture between 1900 and 1950. Prior to World War Two, this shift was primarily a cohort phenomenon and in overall magnitude was greater for whites than for blacks. Black men were underrepresented in the expansion of nonfarm employment in particular industries in the South, and in the expansion of white-collar and blue-collar employment. Overall, employment segregation in the South worsened between 1900 and 1940. Employment segregation declined in the 1940s as blacks left farming for semi-skilled nonfarm jobs. Despite this decline, industries and occupations in the South were more highly segregated by race in 1950 than in 1900.

6.2   The Southern Economy and Black Progress

The human capital and institutionalist models discussed in Chapter 1 offer very different explanations of the evolution of racial differences in employment in the South. The human capital explanation has several parts. On average, real incomes in southern agriculture were lower than real incomes in the nonfarm sector, South or North. The odds of entering the nonfarm economy in the South were a positive function of schooling (Ransom and Sutch 1977; Higgs 1989). As each successive birth cohort came of age and entered the labor force, better-educated members of the cohort, black or white, were more likely to find a nonfarm job. But, because racial differences in the quantity and quality of schooling were persistently large—and, in the case of racial differences in school quality, were increasing early in the century—the black shift into the nonfarm economy lagged behind the white shift, particularly in the expansion of blue- and white-collar employment. The lag produced the increase in employment segregation in the South after 1900, which, in turn, was a key proximate cause of failure of the aggregate black-to-white earnings ratio to rise before World War Two. Region-specific indices of relative (black-to-white) occupational status (a proxy for the earnings ratio) show a decline in the South during the first half of the twentieth century (Becker 1957).[6]

In addition to the effects of schooling, the shift of black labor out of southern agriculture may have been slowed initially by "spatial mismatch" (Higgs 1989). Early in the century the southern black population was concentrated in rural black-belt counties, where nonfarm jobs were few and far between. Finding a nonfarm job frequently required leaving the black belt for a distant town or city. Spatial mismatch diminished in importance, however, as industrialization spread throughout the South, leading to a more uniform geographic distribution of people and jobs.

The institutionalist view is well expressed by Gavin Wright (1986) in his recent book, *Old South, New South* (see also Mandle 1978). According to Wright, a dualistic labor market emerged in the South before 1950 in which white and black workers were "noncompeting groups" in the nonfarm labor market. Wright (1986, 196) rejects the argument that this dualism can be attributed to racial differences in schooling, because "schooling had little to do with job requirements" in most of the South's expanding nonfarm industries. Consider, as Wright does, the case of cotton textiles. Prior to the 1960s few blacks were employed in textiles, but not because of inadequate schooling; textile jobs have never required much in the way of formal education (Heckman and Payner 1989). Rather than being causally related, racial differences in employment and in schooling were the joint outcomes of a "larger historical process of creating a segregated society" (Wright 1986, 197).

Wright also rejects the claim that racial differences in employment can be explained by differences in the geographic distribution of white and black labor within the South. Location was irrelevant because:

> segregation followed industry lines rather than geography. The state of North Carolina contained all-white cotton mills and nearly all white furniture factories, along with heavy tobacco factories and mixed saw and planing mills. Tobacco manufacturing was a major black employer even though it was concentrated in white-majority states like North Carolina. . . . This regularity held down to the level of particular towns. . . . In Birmingham, where two-thirds of the iron and steel workers were black, the Avondale cotton mill was 98.1 percent white. (1986, 178)

Rather, Wright argues, employment segregation in industry was a consequence of historical accident and fixed costs. Cotton textiles are again a prime example. The textile industry developed in the Northeast before the Civil War. After the war the industry moved to North and South Carolina in search of cheaper labor, which it found by employing whites, primarily in family groups. Once the racial pattern was established, however, it became unprofitable for mill owners to substitute "inexperienced" blacks for "whites who had been born and raised in a mill village," even if blacks could be paid a lower wage (1986, 189). Black labor predominated in such industries as tobacco processing and lumber milling, but the same had been true under slavery.

Within industries occupational segregation was a matter of racial prejudice and privilege. There were "black" jobs, primarily menial, and "white" jobs. Whites simply refused to work for a black foreman. Black access to apprenticeship and training programs in the skilled blue-collar trades was jealously restricted by prejudiced employees, employers, and trade unions. White employers did not hire blacks in retail sales or office work because white customers or clients would be offended.[7] The "old" black middle class (Landry 1987), composed of black merchants and professionals (including clergy and teachers), serviced a segregated clientele, but the number and average size of black-owned establishments was too small to provide a significant alternative source of nonfarm employment for blacks (Greene and Woodson 1930).

In normal times, most *individual* southern firms, owned or managed by whites, had few or no incentives to deviate from these social norms; and once the norms were in place, individual blacks could overcome them only by enormous effort and, not infrequently, at great personal risk.[8] To dislodge the competitive dynamics of racial exclusion, the South had to be "shocked" out of regional isolation and segregationist ideology. World War One was an initial shock; while it ushered in the beginnings of an exodus of black labor from the South (Chapter 7), for a variety of reasons it did not fundamentally alter racial hiring patterns in southern nonfarm industries (Mandle 1978; Wright 1986; Whatley 1990). World War Two had a much bigger impact. In the early 1940s, labor markets were extremely tight and the demand for nonfarm labor skyrocketed. As shortages of semi-skilled and skilled white labor intensified, pressure to overcome social norms mounted. Although the South was slow to respond initially, a black breakthrough in nonfarm employment, concentrated in semi-skilled operative jobs, had occurred there as well by 1944. The expansion of black nonfarm employment was also aided by Roosevelt's Executive Order 8802, which outlawed racial discrimination in hiring in defense plants (Vatter 1985, 132–34).[9]

The effects of World War Two were, first, to reduce employment segregation in the South; and second, to permanently raise wage levels in southern agriculture, which provided the impetus for agricultural mechanization and further displacement of farm labor in the late 1940s and throughout the 1950s (Day 1967; Wright 1986). But, by itself, World War Two was not enough; the southern economy was still highly segregated in 1950. Further progress awaited an additional shock, the civil rights movement and its associated antidiscrimination legislation.

6.3 Employment Segregation in the South: An Econometric Analysis

In this section I use the census samples to distinguish between the human capital and institutionalist interpretations of the history of employment segregation in the South. The analysis is based on least squares regressions of the form

(2) $p = X\beta + \varepsilon$

where p is the probability an individual would be employed in a particular industry or occupation; the X's are personal characteristics (for example, age and years of schooling); the β's are coefficients to be estimated; and ε is a random error term.[10]

Industry and occupation categories are those shown in Table 6.1. It is important to stress that the dependent variable is *not* an industry-occupation cell (e.g., semi-skilled operatives in durable goods manufacturing). Unfortunately, the sample sizes are too small to permit disaggregation of that sort. The independent variables are taken from the census samples: age, literacy (1900, 1910), years of schooling (1940, 1950), census region, degree of urbanization, marital status, and an indicator of geographic mobility.[11]

The mobility variable indicates whether the person's state of residence differed from his state of birth. The hypothesis is that, if spatial mismatch were important, black interstate migrants should have been employed more frequently in nonfarm occupations and industries. The mobility variable has obvious limitations. The number of moves across state lines vastly understates total moves, and certainly state boundaries were not coincident with well-defined labor markets. Unfortunately, there is no good way to distinguish rural-to-urban migration in the census samples. While I can (and do) control for the degree of urbanization of the person's residence, I cannot tell whether (except for moves across state lines) an urban resident grew up in a particular town or city, or moved there from the countryside. To the extent that rural-urban moves were associated with shifts in jobs (which, of course, to at least some extent they were), the regressions understate the significance of spatial mismatch.

Two sets of estimations were performed. In the first set the white and black samples were pooled, and a dummy variable indicating race was included among the independent variables.[12] The signs and magnitudes of the coefficients of the race variable measure the extent to which black labor was over- (a positive coefficient) or underrepresented (a negative coefficient) in a given industry or occupation, controlling for other factors. It is straightforward to aggregate the race coefficients into a segregation index.[13]

Although the pooled regressions reveal the importance of race per se in determining the distribution of employment, the regression specification constrains the coefficients to be the same for blacks and whites. The second set of estimations, therefore, is race specific. Later in the chapter I use the race-specific coefficients to calculate segregation indices under various assumptions about racial differences in schooling.[14]

The full set of regression coefficients reveals an enormous amount of detail about employment in the South, but is too complex and unwieldy to discuss here. Instead, attention is focused on the race, schooling, and migration coefficients.

Panel A of Table 6.3 shows the race coefficients from the occupation regressions. The principal finding of Panel A is that race per se (that is, holding other factors constant) was an economically significant determinant of the distribution of occupations in the South. The importance of "pure" racial over- or underrepresentation, however, varied across occupations, as can be seen by comparing the race coefficients with the racial differences in the sample mean occupation shares (Tables 6.1 and 6.2). Much of the overrepresentation of blacks in the farm laborer category can be explained by factors other than race. It is also noteworthy that, in 1940 and 1950, black underrepresentation in white-collar employment—and, to a much lesser extent, in the semi-skilled category in 1940—was considerably less once factors other than race are controlled for. However, blacks were still overrepresented among unskilled nonfarm laborers and in domestic and personal service. Factors other than race cannot explain this overrepresentation.

Panel B of the table reveals the effect of schooling on occupations. Among blacks, schooling had a large, negative effect on the probability of employment as a farm laborer; and, as the century progressed, a negative effect on the probability of employment as a farm operator or unskilled nonfarm laborer. Schooling improved the chances a black man would be employed in service jobs (primarily personal service), skilled blue-collar and white-collar occupations and—in 1940 but *not* 1950 (see Sec. 6.5)—as a semi-skilled operative. Education reduced the probability a white man would be employed in agriculture or as an unskilled nonfarm laborer, but (except in 1940) had little effect on employment chances in services. Early in the century, better-educated whites were more likely to be employed in the skilled blue-collar trades, but as the century progressed, increasingly opted for white-collar employment. It is important to note that the positive effects of schooling on white-collar employment (and skilled blue-collar employment in 1900 and 1910) were higher for whites than for blacks.

The migration coefficients shown in Panel C demonstrate that the distribution of occupations in the South was not neutral with respect to migrant status. Interstate migrants, black or white, were far more likely to be employed in the nonfarm sector. In terms of upward mobility in the nonfarm economy, however, interstate migration had a bigger impact on whites. Among blacks, interstate migrants were significantly more likely to be employed as unskilled nonfarm laborers or in service occupations, but any positive effects of migration on blue- or white-collar employment were small and generally statistically insignificant. White interstate migrants, by contrast, were more likely than blacks to find employment in skilled blue-collar or white-collar occupations. The impact of migration, however, was much smaller in 1950 than earlier in the century, suggesting that any spatial mismatch between jobs and people diminished over time as the South industrialized.

The results of the industry regressions broadly confirm those from the occupation regressions. As Panel A of Table 6.4 demonstrates, race per se

Table 6.3   **Coefficients from Occupation Regressions**

	1900	1910	1940	1950
A. Coefficients of Race (= 1 if black)				
Farm operator	−0.088*	−0.027*	−0.022	−0.001
Farm laborer	0.039*	0.046*	0.042*	0.033*
Unskilled nonfarm laborer	0.155*	0.154*	0.151*	0.172*
Services	0.036*	0.041*	0.077*	0.067*
Domestic			0.028*	
Protective			−0.018*	
Other			0.067*	
Semi-skilled blue collar	−0.011	−0.007	−0.106*	−0.064*
Skilled blue collar	−0.034*	−0.055*	−0.095*	−0.149*
White collar	−0.097*	−0.138	−0.046*	−0.084*
Professional/technical			0.034*	
Managers			−0.036*	
Clerical/sales			−0.044*	

B. Schooling Coefficients (= 1 if literate, 1900 and 1910; years of schooling completed, 1940 and 1950)

	1900	1910	1940	1950
Farm operator				
Black	−0.014	0.004	−0.012*	−0.012*
White	−0.073*	−0.028*	−0.016*	−0.010*
Farm laborer				
Black	−0.099*	−0.061*	−0.017*	−0.011*
White	−0.069*	−0.082*	−0.015*	−0.009*
Unskilled nonfarm laborer				
Black	0.009	−0.019	−0.010*	−0.012*
White	−0.053*	−0.051*	−0.009*	−0.009*
Services				
Black	0.036*	0.033*	0.014*	0.008*
White	0.003	0.007	−0.001*	−0.001
Domestic				
Black			0.001	
White			−0.0002*	
Protective				
Black			0.0005	
White			0.00005	
Other				
Black			0.013*	
White			−0.001*	
Semi-skilled blue collar				
Black	−0.007	0.011	0.003**	−0.005
White	−0.003	0.010	−0.012*	−0.021*
Skilled blue collar				
Black	0.029*	0.022*	0.003*	0.009*
White	0.068*	0.048*	−0.001	−0.007*
White collar				
Black	0.045*	0.024*	0.019*	0.021*
White	0.127*	0.125*	0.054*	0.057*

Table 6.3 **(continued)**

	1900	1910	1940	1950
B. Schooling Coefficients (= 1 if literate, 1900 and 1910; years of schooling completed, 1940 and 1950)				
Professional/technical				
Black			0.013*	
White			0.020*	
Managers				
Black			0.003*	
White			0.015*	
Clerical/sales				
Black			0.003*	
White			0.019*	
C. Migration Coefficients (= 1 if interstate migrant in the South)				
Farm operator				
Black	−0.042	−0.074*	−0.087*	−0.062*
White	−0.073*	−0.096*	−0.094*	−0.059*
Farm laborer				
Black	−0.081*	−0.077*	−0.042*	−0.019
White	−0.033*	−0.019*	−0.003	0.005
Unskilled nonfarm laborer				
Black	0.071*	0.091*	0.061*	0.009
White	0.021**	0.027*	0.004	0.004
Services				
Black	0.015	0.014**	0.022**	0.026
White	0.0002	0.002	0.03*	0.002
Domestic				
Black			−0.006	
White			−0.0004	
Protective				
Black			0.004**	
White			0.026*	
Other				
Black			0.024*	
White			0.004	
Semi-skilled blue collar				
Black	0.015	0.005	0.024*	0.030
White	0.037*	0.026*	0.006	−0.010
Skilled blue collar				
Black	0.005	0.023*	0.002	−0.003
White	0.028*	0.037*	0.026*	0.008
White collar				
Black	0.015	0.012*	0.020*	0.011
White	0.053*	0.023*	0.031*	0.050*
Professional/technical				
Black			0.013*	
White			0.018*	

(continued)

Table 6.3 **(continued)**

	1900	1910	1940	1950
C. Migration Coefficients (= 1 if interstate migrant in the South)				
Managers				
Black			0.005	
White			0.016*	
Clerical/sales				
Black			0.002	
White			−0.002	

Notes: An asterisk means significant at 1 percent level or better, and a double asterisk means significant at 5 percent level or better. Significance tests were based on least-squares *t-* statistics.
Source: See Table 6.2 and text.

influenced the distribution of employment across industries. Controlling for factors other than race, blacks were overrepresented to a significant extent in agriculture, durable goods manufacturing (except in 1940), and personal services. Blacks were underrepresented in mining-construction, wholesale and retail trade, nondurable goods manufacturing (which includes textiles), and government.[15] Educated men of both races were more likely to work outside of agriculture, and schooling had its biggest positive impact on employment in services, not in manufacturing. Interstate migrants were more likely to be employed in the nonfarm sector, particularly mining-construction and durable goods manufacturing. Consistent with the occupation results, the impact of interstate migration declined over time.

6.4   Accounting for Employment Segregation

In this section I use the regression coefficients to calculate counterfactual segregation indices under various assumptions about racial differences in the independent variables. The occupation indices are shown in Panel A, and the industry indices in Panel B, of Table 6.5.

The indices in the rows labelled Race were calculated from the race coefficients in Tables 6.3 and 6.4. They reveal levels and trends in employment segregation, adjusting for all factors (in the regressions) other than race. Because these factors did affect the extent of employment segregation, the indices are smaller in value than those based on the sample mean occupational and industrial employment shares in Table 6.2. Controlling for factors other than race lowers occupational segregation by 10 to 14 percent in the early twentieth century; the reductions are larger for 1940 and 1950, but the 1940 and 1950 regressions use a much better measure of educational attainment (years of schooling instead of literacy). Controlling for factors other than race lowers industrial segregation by about a third in 1910 and 1940. However, after adjusting for other factors, employment segregation in the South was

Table 6.4   Coefficients from Industry Regressions

	1910	1940	1950
A. Coefficients of Race (= 1 if black)			
Agriculture	0.031*	0.021*	0.030*
Mining-construction	−0.002	−0.050*	−0.041*
Nondurables manufacturing	−0.020*	−0.057*	−0.048*
Durables manufacturing	0.027*	0.006	0.027*
Transportation-communications-public utilities	0.019*	0.007	−0.011
Wholesale-retail trade	−0.052*	−0.022*	−0.027**
Financial-business services	−0.013*	−0.003	−0.001
Personal services	0.027*	0.064*	0.048*
Professional services	−0.009	0.040*	0.041*
Government	−0.007*	−0.006**	−0.018*
B. Schooling Coefficients (= 1 if literate, 1910; years of schooling completed, 1940 and 1950)			
Agriculture			
Black	−0.064*	−0.029*	−0.024*
White	−0.147*	−0.031*	−0.018*
Mining-construction			
Black	0.005	−0.001	0.0003
White	0.011	−0.005	−0.007
Nondurables manufacturing			
Black	−0.0003	−0.0004	−0.004
White	0.003	−0.0005	−0.001
Durables manufacturing			
Black	0.001	−0.006*	−0.005*
White	−0.002	−0.005*	−0.007*
Transportation-communications-public utilities			
Black	−0.002	−0.001	0.002
White	0.024*	0.002*	−0.003*
Wholesale-retail trade			
Black	0.015*	0.006*	0.002
White	0.055*	0.013*	0.010*
Financial-business services			
Black	0.008*	0.004*	0.005*
White	0.020*	0.005*	0.007*
Personal services			
Black	0.021*	0.010*	0.007*
White	0.007**	0.001*	0.0002
Professional services			
Black	0.017*	0.014*	0.012*
White	0.023*	0.013*	0.013*
Government			
Black	−0.0003	0.002*	0.005*
White	0.006**	0.006*	0.006*

(continued)

Table 6.4   **Coefficients from Industry Regressions**

	1910	1940	1950
C. Migration Coefficients (= 1 if interstate migrant in the South)			
Agriculture			
Black	−0.127*	−0.118*	−0.072*
White	−0.116*	−0.086*	−0.060*
Mining-construction			
Black	0.056*	0.054*	0.029
White	0.049*	0.042*	0.020
Nondurables manufacturing			
Black	−0.011**	0.004	−0.012
White	0.020*	0.0004	0.002
Durables manufacturing			
Black	0.040*	0.053*	0.031
White	0.025*	0.013*	0.010
Transportation-communications-public utilities			
Black	0.033*	−0.001	0.028
White	0.014*	0.0006	−0.016
Wholesale-retail trade			
Black	−0.008	0.003	−0.029
White	−0.002	0.006	0.009
Financial-business services			
Black	−0.002	−0.007	−0.010
White	−0.005	0.006	−0.005
Personal services			
Black	0.001	−0.005	0.044
White	0.007*	0.008	0.010**
Professional services			
Black	0.017*	0.008	0.028
White	0.009*	0.005	0.016*
Government			
Black	0.001	0.002	0.007
White	−0.002	0.006	0.014*

Notes: An asterisk means significant at 1 percent level or better, and a double asterisk means significant at 5 percent level or better. Significance test based on least-squares *t*-statistics.
Source: See Table 6.2 and text.

higher in 1950 than earlier in the century.[16] It is noteworthy that pure racial segregation continued to worsen during the 1940s, despite the large shift of black labor out of agriculture.

The next several rows in Panels A and B give values of the segregation indices under various assumptions about racial differences in schooling. The calculations are based on employment distributions predicted from the occupation and industry regressions. Racial differences in educational attainment (literacy and years of schooling) contributed to employment segregation, but the impact was modest. A small fraction of occupational segregation around the turn of the century can be attributed to racial differences in literacy. The percent of occupational segregation explained by racial differences in years of

Table 6.5   **Segregation Indices**

	1900	1910	1940	1950
A. Occupation				
Sample means	26.7	26.1	39.2	37.9
Race	23.1	23.4	26.9	28.4
Percentage explained	13.5	10.3	31.4	25.1
Equal literacy	24.5	24.1		
Percentage explained	8.2	7.9		
Equal years of schooling			30.8	31.4
Percentage explained			21.4	17.2
Equal years of schooling, adjusted for school quality			27.9	27.0
Percentage explained			28.8	28.8
B. Industry				
Sample means		15.0	21.7	18.5
Race		10.4	13.7	14.5
Percentage explained		32.0	36.9	20.8
Equal literacy		13.6		
Percentage explained		9.3		
Equal years of schooling			17.2	15.0
Percentage explained			20.7	18.0
Equal interstate migration rates		15.8	21.1	18.1
Percentage explained		–	2.8	2.2

Notes: "Equal": white mean = black mean; "–": percentage explained was less than zero.
Source: See text. Sample means: segregation index calculated from regression sample mean occupational and industrial employment shares.

schooling was 21 percent in 1940 and 17 percent in 1950. Had black and white literacy rates been the same in 1910, the industry segregation index would have been 13.6 instead of 15.0, a decline of 9.3 percent. If mean years of schooling in 1940 had been the same for both races, the industrial segregation index would have equalled 17.2 instead of 21.7, a 20.7 percent decrease. Controlling for racial differences in educational attainment does not alter the fundamental finding that employment segregation in the South was worse in 1950 than in 1900 or 1910.

The adjustments for schooling can be criticized, however, because they do not take into account racial differences in the quality of schooling. The final rows in Panel A show the results of an adjustment for school quality. The assumption is that for the quantity and quality of schooling to be considered truly equal for blacks and whites, mean years of schooling for blacks had to equal the white mean plus three additional years. Thus, for example, a black man completing nine years of schooling is assumed to have been as well educated as a white completing 6 years of school. The basis for such an adjustment is that black scores on standardized tests were lower than white test scores (Bond 1939; Orazem 1987).[17]

Racial differences in the quality of schooling certainly were a factor in employment segregation. The indices of occupational segregation in 1940 and 1950 would have been 29 percent smaller had both school quantity and quality been equalized. Nevertheless, much of employment segregation in the South is not explained by racial differences in the quantity and quality of schooling. Race, not schooling, was the principal factor limiting the participation of black labor in certain industries and occupations.

The final row in Panel B gives the industry segregation indices under the assumption that the black and white interstate migration rates were equal. Industrial segregation would have been little changed had blacks been as mobile across state lines as were whites.[18] Similar results (not shown) were obtained for occupational segregation. Spatial mismatch limited the participation of black labor in the nonfarm economy, but it was not a major factor behind employment segregation in the South.

6.5   Black-White Earnings Ratios in the South: 1940–1950

Prior to World War Two the shift of labor out of southern agriculture was a cohort phenomenon. Schooling and migration—"human capital"—were integral to this shift. Better-educated, geographically mobile blacks (and whites) left farming; the illiterate and immobile stayed behind. The quantitative significance of illiteracy and immobility can be revealed by using the agricultural industry regressions to calculate the probability that an uneducated, immobile (i.e., did not migrate across state lines), young black male (ages 20 to 24) would be employed in agriculture. This probability exceeded 70 percent in 1910 and 1940, but the probability fell to below 50 percent in 1950. The best explanation of the decline is the one offered by Wright (1986), that is, an increase in the nonfarm demand for black labor, coupled with rising agricultural wages leading to displacement of farm workers. I have already shown that many blacks who left agriculture in the 1940s found employment as semi-skilled operatives. Before World War Two, schooling and semi-skilled employment for blacks were positively related, but the influx of rural, less educated blacks reversed the sign of the relationship during the 1940s.

Data from the 1940 and 1950 public use samples reveal that the black-to-white ratio of average weekly earnings of adult males rose in the South by about 17 percent between 1940 and 1950 (Table 6.6).[19] Because agricultural wages were lower than nonfarm wages (including wages in semi-skilled occupations), the greater relative (black minus white) shift of black labor out of agriculture may have raised the earnings ratio.[20] But it is also true that racial differences in educational attainment were smaller in 1950 than in 1940, as better-educated blacks entered the southern labor force (Chapter 2). This decline in racial differences in years of schooling might also have increased the earnings ratio.

To distinguish between the two hypotheses, I estimated race-specific earnings regressions for southern males ages 25 to 64, using samples from the

Table 6.6   **Regressions of Weekly Wages: The South, 1940 and 1950**

	1940			1950		
	Mean	β	t-statistic	Mean	β	t-statistic
A. Black Males						
Constant		2.34	40.43		3.08	39.86
Age						
25–34	0.39	−0.15	−4.00	0.35	−0.01	−0.21
45–54	0.19	−0.01	−0.30	0.22	−0.06	−1.05
55–64	0.09	−0.10	−1.62	0.12	0.05	0.74
Years of schooling com-pleted × 10^{-1}	0.493	0.32	5.88	0.582	0.33	5.13
Married	0.80	0.03	0.77	0.77	0.09	1.85
Sector:						
Agricultural	0.25	−0.90	−21.08	0.16	−0.69	10.40
Service	0.36	−0.12	−2.97	0.44	−0.003	−0.06
SMSA resident	0.39	0.11	2.98	0.51	0.23	5.09
Region:						
East South Central	0.24	−0.21	5.15	0.23	−0.06	−1.10
West South Central	0.22	−0.14	3.38	0.24	0.02	0.35
Dependent variable	2.14			3.33		
Number of observations		1,352			746	
R^2		0.35			0.28	
B. White Males						
Constant		2.32	41.31		3.40	54.60
Age						
25–34	0.41	−0.16	−4.73	0.36	−0.07	−2.00
45–54	0.20	0.10	2.41	0.22	0.11	2.75
55–64	0.10	0.05	0.44	0.13	0.04	0.94
Years of schooling × 10^{-1}	0.848	0.69	18.22	0.911	0.50	11.98
Married	0.84	0.15	4.09	0.88	0.16	3.66
Sector						
Agricultural	0.11	−0.97	−20.78	0.08	−0.78	−14.10
Service	0.44	−0.03	−1.00	0.48	−0.11	−3.62
SMSA resident	0.40	0.24	8.19	0.52	0.17	5.86
Region						
East South Central	0.19	−0.13	−3.46	0.17	−0.05	−1.17
West South Central	0.36	−0.006	−0.18	0.38	−0.004	−0.12
Dependent variable	2.94			3.96		
Number of observations		2,270			1,627	
R^2		0.39			0.25	

(continued)

Table 6.6   **(continued)**

C. The Increase in the Black-to-White Wage Ratio (% of increase explained)

	Black		White	
	1940	1950	1940	1950
Racial differences in sectoral shift	30.8	25.8	35.6	26.5
Shift out of agriculture	33.8	26.9	36.4	30.0
Narrowing of racial differences in years of schooling	5.0	5.4	11.3	8.1

Notes: **Panel C:** Percentage explained is $\beta^i_j (dx^w - dx^b)$, i = black, white, j = 1940, 1950, where the β's are the regression coefficients and dx's are the changes between 1940 and 1950 in sample means (from Panels A and B); "sectoral shift": total effect of all sectoral shifts.
Sources: **Panels A, B:** 10 percent random samples from 1940 and 1950 public use tapes. Dependent variable is log of weekly earnings.

1940 and 1950 public use tapes.[21] The dependent variable is the log of weekly earnings, and the independent variables are dummy variables for age group, years of schooling, location in the South (region and an urban dummy), marital status, and dummy variables for economic sector (agricultural and service; the manufacturing sector was omitted).

Sample means and regression coefficients are shown in Panels A and B of Table 6.6. Better-educated men of both races earned higher weekly wages, although the rate of return to schooling was higher for whites. Among whites, earnings rose with age through the age group 45–54, but the age-earnings profile was much flatter for blacks. Married white men earned more than single men; the premium for married black men was much smaller and statistically insignificant. The results confirm that agricultural wages were far below nonfarm wages in both years, but that the wage gap between agriculture and manufacturing diminished during the 1940s. Earnings were higher in urban than in rural areas in both years; regional differences were substantial in 1940 (especially for blacks), but diminished over the decade.

Panel C of Table 6.6 uses the sample means and the regression coefficients to calculate how much of the increase in the mean earnings ratio between 1940 and 1950 can be explained by sectoral shifts in employment versus changes in years of schooling. Between 27 and 36 percent of the increase in the earnings ratio can be attributed to the greater relative shift of black labor out of agriculture. Declining racial differences in years of schooling were less important, accounting for 5 to 11 percent of the increase in the earnings ratio.[22]

It has been argued in recent studies that the civil rights movement and its associated antidiscrimination legislation played a minor role in raising the national earnings ratio in the 1960s and 1970s (Smith 1984; Smith and Welch 1989). The earnings ratio increased during the 1940s (also in the 1950s) *before* social change had occurred and civil rights legislation fully enacted. According to Smith and Welch (1989, 55) the pre–civil rights increase in the earnings ratio "suggests that . . . slowly moving historical forces [e.g., education] . . . were the primary determinants of the long-term black economic improvement." But, as I have shown, the increase in the earnings ratio in the South during the 1940s was not a consequence of "slowly moving historical forces" but of abrupt changes in labor demand in the context of large sectoral differences in wages. The experience of the 1940s supports the institutionalist argument that, historically, black economic progress and labor demand were closely linked.

6.6 Summary

Analysis of the census samples reveals much about the determinants of employment in the South during the first half of the twentieth century. Racial differences in the quantity and quality of schooling limited the participation of blacks in the nonfarm southern economy. In the words of Roger Ransom and Richard Sutch (1977, 31), illiteracy "helped to trap the black farmer in southern agriculture." Educational discrimination in the South was worse in the upper elementary and high school grades, but it was precisely this level of education that would have led to greater black employment in blue- and white-collar occupations. Consistent with the human capital model, a narrower racial gap in the quantity and quality of schooling would have improved the employment prospects of southern blacks, leading to a higher earnings ratio before World War Two.

But the quantitative impact of racial differences in schooling was modest, and it was concentrated in certain occupations and industries. More and better schooling would have increased the number of *self-employed* blacks in white-collar occupations.[23] The expansion of black employment in managerial positions in corporations, in clerical and sales jobs in large firms, and in the government would be the product of a later era.

Race, not schooling or spatial mismatch, was the principal factor behind employment segregation in the South. Overall, employment segregation in the South was worse on the eve of World War Two than at the turn of the century. The finding that employment segregation increased over time is not new; in the early 1950s Donald Dewey (1952, 282) noted:

> In the fifty years before World War II the relative position of Negro workers in Southern industry actually deteriorated; they did not share proportionately the expansion of urban employment and they were not upgraded as individuals into jobs previously held by whites.

What *is* new is the finding that employment segregation increased *after* controlling for racial differences in schooling and other factors.[24] The rise in employment segregation was not, primarily, a consequence of racial differences in human capital. Rather, it seems that black participation in the southern economy was constrained by discrimination and social norms.[25] During the

1940s, employment segregation declined and the black-to-white earnings ratio rose, as black labor left southern agriculture in response to an increase in nonfarm labor demand. But World War Two did not fundamentally alter the social norms that supported racial discriminations. Controlling for factors other than race, employment segregation in the South was higher in 1950 than in 1940.

In the 1950s and 1960s the dualism of southern labor markets finally came into conflict with the long-term increase in black schooling. Recent histories have emphasized the grass roots character of the early civil rights movement (Morris 1984; Branch 1988). The brilliance and courage of the principal protagonists notwithstanding, the boycotts, sit-ins, and freedom marches could not have succeeded without the broad-based support of blacks who had suffered mightily under *de jure* and customary segregation. Blacks entering the southern labor force in the 1950s and 1960s were better educated than previous generations. For them, and their parents, the wait to end segregation had been long enough. Eventually the new generations would have a new ally in the federal government, whose enforcement of antidiscrimination legislation helped facilitate the expansion of black employment in nontraditional occupations and industries in the South in the late 1960s and early 1970s (Donohue and Heckman 1989).

7   "To the Promised Land":
Education and the Black Exodus

The probability that a black male held a nonfarm job in the South has been shown to be a positive function of schooling. This chapter demonstrates that schooling and leaving the South were also positively related, and that changes over time in schooling explain a significant fraction of black migration. The economic status of black migrants compared favorably with that of non-southern blacks, but fell well below the economic status of non-southern whites.

7.1 Schooling and the Great Migration

Table 7.1 shows the percentage of the black population residing in the South and the percentage of southern-born blacks residing outside the South, from 1900 to 1950. At the turn of the century, fully 90 percent of the black population lived in the South and only a tiny proportion (4.3 percent) of those born in the region were living elsewhere. The proportion of black migrants increased to 8 percent in 1920 and to 13 percent in 1930. Migration came to a halt during the Great Depression, but resumed with fervor during the 1940s. By 1950 the proportion of blacks living in the South had declined to 68 percent, and 20 percent of those born in the region had left it.

Historians have thoroughly investigated the broad social and economic forces at work behind the movement of black people from the South, the so-called Great Migration.[1] Less attention has been paid to the migrants themselves, however. It is known that young, single men and women predominated (although many families, too, participated); that migrants were drawn disproportionately from areas of the South with ready geographic access to, and information about, the North; and that the migrants clustered in a small number of large metropolitan areas with established black communities. For many migrants, a big northern city like Pittsburgh or Chicago was the final destination of a carefully plotted, lengthy trip, one with many intermediate sojourns.

Table 7.1   **The Great Migration, 1900–1950**

	% of Blacks Residing in the South	% of Blacks Born in the South but Residing Elsewhere
1900	89.7	4.3
1910	89.0	4.9
1920	85.2	8.1
1930	78.7	13.3
1940	77.0	13.5
1950	68.0	20.4

Sources: Percentage residing in the South was calculated from U.S. Bureau of the Census (1975). Percentage born in South but residing elsewhere was calculated from the following: *1900, 1910:* U.S. Bureau of the Census (1918, 65); *1920:* U.S. Bureau of the Census (1922, 636); *1930:* U.S. Bureau of Census (1935, 27); *1940:* U.S. Bureau of the Census (1944, 30, 35); *1950:* U.S. Bureau of the Census (1953, 12).

For others the flight was unplanned and nonstop all the way. By the deed itself the migrants sought a higher standard of living and to be rid of Jim Crow's daily indignities. "To the ambitious men and women venturing North," writes historian James Grossman (1989, 37), "the Great Migration represented a new strategy in the struggle for the full rights of American citizenship."

The idea that schooling and black migration might be related is not novel. Bowles (1970) used published census data to show that between 1955 and 1960, better-educated blacks were more likely to have left the South. Earlier published census have proven to be less informative.[2] Either the characteristics of migrants were never compiled separately from those of nonmigrants or the cross classifications were too limited to support detailed analyses (Vickery 1969, 144–47). Here I surmount the problem by relying on samples of individuals drawn from the public use tapes of the 1900, 1910, 1940, and 1950 censuses.

Migrant status is inferred if a person was born in the South but lived outside the region when the census was taken. Although this way of measuring migration is far from perfect—in general, multiple or return migration cannot be identified—the defects are outweighed by that fact that the variable can be constructed in a consistent manner across the census samples.

Table 7.2 reports the basic findings on schooling and black migration from the sample. Separate figures are given for all persons who in principle could have been in the labor force as conventionally measured (ages 10 and over in 1900 and 1910, and ages 14 and over in 1940 and 1950); and for adult males, ages 20 to 64.

The probability of migration rose sharply over time, but at any point in time, the chances of having left the South were higher among the better educated. In 1900, for example, literate adult males were three times as likely to have migrated than were illiterate ones. In 1940, persons who had attended high school were twice as likely to have migrated than persons with no or

Table 7.2   **Schooling and Black Migration from the South**

	Full Sample		Adult Males (Ages 20–64)	
	% All	% Migrants	% All	% Migrants
1900				
Illiterate	53.4	2.5	47.7	3.9
Literate	46.6	8.5	52.3	12.3
Total		5.3		8.3
1910				
Illiterate	38.8	2.8	38.2	3.2
Literate	61.3	8.9	61.8	12.3
Total		6.5		8.9
1940: Years of schooling completed				
0–1	10.9	7.7	12.3	8.7
2–4	29.1	8.4	33.7	8.3
5–8	43.3	17.1	40.6	23.2
9–12	14.2	23.3	10.8	29.8
≥13	2.5	23.2	2.6	31.7
Total		14.6		17.4
1950: Years of schooling				
0–1	8.4	13.9	8.7	14.6
2–4	20.9	18.3	23.5	20.7
5–8	43.7	28.4	43.2	34.8
9–12	23.1	40.6	21.0	47.4
≥13	3.9	29.4	3.6	36.2
Total		27.9		32.4
Number of observations	5,224		1,897	

Note: % Migrants: born in South but residing elsewhere. In the full sample, data for 1900 and 1910 are for ages 10 and over; for 1940 and 1950, ages 14 and over.
Sources: 1900, 1910: census public use tape; *1940, 1950:* 20% random sample of census public use tape.

limited schooling (0–4 years). In 1950 there is some evidence that the relationship followed an inverted U-shaped pattern. A possible explanation is that the "black elite" (lawyers, doctors, teachers) had an established segregated clientele in the South by midcentury, and for them the economic benefits of migrating may have been smaller.

Although I know of no other sources with which to check the general reliability of the estimates in Table 7.2, there is some independent evidence to verify the figures for grades 13 and above. According to Johnson (1938, 41), who collected a national sample of college-educated blacks, the outmigration rate of the southern born was 25 percent, quite close to the 1940 figure reported in the table.

As clear as Table 7.2 seems to be, there are a number of reasons why the schooling-migration relationship might be more apparent than real. The relationship could be confounded with age, family, cohort, and distance effects on

Table 7.3   Coefficients of Schooling: Logit Analysis of Migration

	β	t-statistic	dp/dx
1900: Literate	1.221	6.512	0.093
1910: Literate	1.115	8.199	0.090
1940: Years of schooling			
2–4	0.671	2.314	0.084
5–8	1.991	7.214	0.248
9–12	2.596	8.653	0.324
≥13	2.330	5.854	0.291
1950: Years of schooling			
2–4	0.464	1.826	0.102
5–8	1.280	5.311	0.280
9–12	1.926	7.494	0.422
≥13	1.415	4.067	0.310

Note: dp/dx evaluated at sample mean probability.
Source: See text.

migration. Older youths and young adults who had completed their schooling would be more likely to migrate than children living at home. Persons in large families were less likely to migrate than persons in smaller families. Average schooling levels rose over time, but so did the probability of outmigration. Schooling levels were lower in the Deep South, but one might expect migration to the North to vary with distance.[3]

Yet another issue is that some persons migrated from the South as children and attended school in the North. Because schools were better in the North, such children would have completed more grades, on average, than did their counterparts in the South. But the pattern was not typical, because the migration rate of black children was much lower than the sample average. In 1940, for example, only 8 percent of southern-born black children, ages 14 and under *and* enrolled in school, were migrants.[4]

Given these various points, a multivariate analysis of schooling and migration is in order. Column 1 of Table 7.3 reports schooling coefficients derived from logit regressions, in which the independent variables were constructed from the information available in the samples.[5] The results in the table pertain to adult males, but similar findings were obtained for the full samples. A more detailed discussion of the determinants of migration appears in Section 7.3. Here the issue is simply whether the positive effect of schooling is still apparent once other factors are controlled for simultaneously.

In all of the regressions the schooling coefficients are positive, large, and statistically significant. Schooling was positively associated with the probability a southern black would migrate from the region, independent of other factors that affected the probability of moving.

A subtler problem is that schooling may be an indicator of some unobserved background characteristic that positively influenced the probability of migra-

Table 7.4   Schooling and White Migration from the South

	%	% Migrants
1900		
Illiterate	12.2	6.1
Literate	87.8	10.8
Total		10.3
1910		
Illiterate	9.3	4.4
Literate	90.7	12.2
Total		11.5
1940: Years of schooling		
0–1	3.4	5.3
2–4	11.7	7.2
5–8	43.8	14.8
9–12	30.8	14.1
≥13	10.4	18.7
Total		13.8
1950: Years of schooling		
0–1	2.5	5.3
2–4	8.2	9.8
5–8	37.7	16.6
9–12	37.0	18.3
≥13	14.6	21.3
Total		17.1

Sources: See Table 7.2.

tion.[6] Of particular concern is that schooling might be positively correlated with an urban residence prior to migration, which was not reported in the census samples. Urban blacks had better access to information about economic opportunities outside the South than did rural blacks, but urban schooling levels were higher than rural schooling levels. However, the appendix to the chapter demonstrates that, even under the most favorable assumptions, such a bias cannot explain the schooling-migration relationship.

Given that schooling had a positive effect on the probability of migration from the South and that the effect apparently cannot be attributed to biases in the census data, it is important to ask if a similar relationship existed between schooling and white migration from the South. Table 7.4 shows the relationship between schooling and white migration. Better-educated whites were more likely to have left the South then their less-educated counterparts; and there was an increase in white outmigration over time.

Racial differences in schooling, however, cannot possibly explain racial differences in migration. It is true that early in the century the white outmigration rate exceeded the black rate. But had blacks had the same literacy rate as whites, black migration would have exceeded white migration. On the eve of World War Two, the white migration rate was less than the black migration rate, even though white schooling levels were far higher. Clearly, race was an overriding factor in determining who left the South, and its explanatory power increased over time.

7.2 Accounting for Changes in Black Migration: The Role of Schooling

What "caused" the Great Migration? Widely noticed and reported on, the initial wave of the movement occasioned a number of informed studies by contemporaries, whose methodology and findings have largely framed the debate down to the present day (Epstein 1918; U.S. Department of Labor 1919). Most of these early students concluded that short-run "push-pull" factors, exogenous to individuals, explained why black people left when they did. At the turn of the century, real wages in the South were below the average in the rest of the United States. But the lure of higher wages failed to "pull" significant numbers of southern blacks into the North, because a competing group—European immigrants—filled the jobs that might have gone to southern blacks (or, for that matter, to southern whites).

The supply of immigrants was reduced with the outbreak of World War One. At the first the reduced supply had little effect, because business was slack. Eventually the insatiable labor demands of a wartime economy made northern employers willing to try someone new, and they turned to southern black men (Whatley 1990). The news got through in a number of ways. Northern employers, willing to foot the bill for transportation, sent labor agents south looking for workers. Word of mouth travelled down the tracks, carried by black railroad workers. The North was advertised to be a wondrous "promised land" where black people could find jobs at unheard-of rates of pay; where they could sit next to white folks on public transportation; where they did not have to defer or look down when spoken to; where they could spend their money as they pleased; and where they could be upwardly mobile without the threat of lynching. Conditions in southern agriculture were poor at the time. An insect with a voracious appetite for cotton, the boll weevil, had infested large parts of the region, wreaking havoc on the cotton economy and the blacks' incomes.

Stories of a promised land were exaggerated. The North was not prepared for the black influx. Housing conditions in migrant neighborhoods were deplorable. High rents sapped some of the higher pay. The North had its own brand of racial etiquette, and race relations turned sour when riots broke out in several cities. Some southern whites were ecstatic when the migration took hold, imagining their "race problem" could finally be solved by exporting it. Others (and some black leaders) pleaded with potential migrants, urging them to stay put. The South, as the saying went, was the "Negro's Natural Home." But the black masses did not listen. Once the flow started, they continued to stream north, literally depopulating whole areas of the South in their wake.

Chicago's black population increased 248 percent between 1910 and 1920; Detroit's, by a factor of seven (Grossman 1989, 4).

Nativist legislation, nonfarm economic growth, and a comparatively weak farm economy helped sustain further black outmigration in the 1920s. The flow slowed during the Great Depression. But soon the trickle became a tidal wave when, once again, war broke out. Millions of black people left the rural South for jobs in northern cities, never to return. Agricultural wages in the South rose to unprecedented levels by the late 1940s, leading to widespread mechanization in the 1950s, and further outmigration (Cogan 1982; Wright 1986).

In view of the widespread acceptance of the "push-pull" framework, it is worth pointing out that some scholars have disagreed with parts of it, downplaying the causal importance of shocks. Writing during World War One, at the height of the first wave of migration, Francis Tyson, advisor to the Division of Negro Economics in the Department of Labor, argued:

> The Negro migration is neither an isolated nor a temporary phenomenon, but the logical result of a long series of linked causes beginning with the landing of the first slave ship and extending to the present day. . . . The intelligent Negro has long believed that his only escape . . . is to go to the North. . . . [The] basic causes for his migration are inherent in the social and economic system which has retarded his progress for years. (U.S. Department of Labor 1919, 155)

Statistical analysis of county-level data led Robert Higgs (1976) to question whether the boll weevil was a significant push factor.[7] According to William Vickery (1969), the world wars have been overrated as pull factors. Regional income differences compelled the migration; except through a temporary stimulation of labor demand, World War One had no independent effect. Vickery also claimed that some of the migration during the 1940s would have occurred anyway, having been postponed because of the Great Depression.

The relationship between schooling and migration would seem to support a long-run, supply-side explanation of the Great Migration, one associated with long-run changes in black schooling. An individual characteristic—in this case, schooling—is positively associated with the probability of an event occurring—in this case, migration from the South. Why the association existed is discussed in Section 7.3; for the moment, simply assume that the relationship was a causal one. As the average value of the characteristic increases, so too does the proportion of the population experiencing the event. Chapter 2 demonstrated that average schooling levels of southern blacks increased over the first half of the twentieth century, which is prima facie evidence that the supply-side explanation could be quantitatively significant. There is the related implication that, if black schooling levels had equalled white schooling levels, the black migration rate would have been higher than it was.

Column 1 of Table 7.5 shows the change over time in the black migration

Table 7.5   **Effects of Schooling on Black Migration**

	Predicted Increase (in percentage points)	% Explained	Equal Schooling	% Increase
1900–10				
Full sample	1.20	100.0		
Adult males	0.80	133.3	11.3	26.9
1910–20				
Full sample	0.43	13.4		
1910–30				
Full sample	0.83	9.9		
1910–40				
Full sample	1.24	14.4		
Adult males	1.86	21.9	23.9	37.3
1910–50				
Full sample	1.39	9.0		
Adult males	2.07	8.8	38.0	17.3
1940–50				
Full sample	1.59	12.0		
Adult males	2.79	18.6		

Autoregression of State-level Outmigration, 1910–1930 (*t*-statistics in parentheses):

$$M_t = 0.034 + 0.832\,M_{t-1} + 0.027\ (\text{Yr}=1920) + 0.043\ (\text{Yr}=1930)$$
$$\quad\ \ (0.594)\quad (3.851)\qquad\ \ (4.140)\qquad\qquad\ (3.938)$$

Number of observations = 51
$R^2 = 0.96$

Notes: Full sample: ages 10 and over. *Predicted Increase:* predicted change in black migration rate, assuming black schooling level in the terminal year (e.g., 1920) equalled the level in the base year (e.g., 1910). Predicted migration rates are based on the cross-tabulations from Table 7.2. *% Explained:* predicted change in migration rate/actual change in migration rate (actual change from Tables 7.1 and 7.2). Calculations of percentage explained for full sample assume that the actual change in the black migration rate for ages 10 and over equalled the actual change for the entire population. Because the actual change in migration for ages 10 and over was greater than for all ages, the full sample calculations are biased upwards. *Equal schooling:* predicted black migration rate if mean black schooling equalled mean white schooling level; mean white schooling levels are from Table 7.4. *% Increase:* percentage increase in black migration rate if mean black schooling level equalled mean white schooling level. *Autoregression:* dependent variable is percentage migrants (born in South but living elsewhere); regression includes state dummies (not shown).

rate (in percentage points) predicted by the change in black schooling; Column 2 gives the percentage explained by the change in schooling. For example, the row labelled 1930 shows the impact on migration from increasing the black literacy rate in 1910 to its 1930s value. The predicted changes are based on the schooling effects in Table 7.2. Separate calculations are performed for the overall population and for adult males.

Prior to World War One, changes in black literacy rates can account fully for changes in black migration, which supports the "talented tenth" hypothesis. The percentage explained is much lower between 1910 and 1920, the decade of the First World War. Slightly less than one-sixth of the change in black migration between 1910 and 1940 could have been predicted had the black literacy rate in 1910 equalled its level in 1940. A similar conclusion applies to the migration during World War Two. The proportion explained is higher for adult males than for the general population.

Column 3 of Table 7.5 shows the predicted black migration rate for adult males under the assumption that the average schooling levels of blacks and white were the same (e.g., they had the same literacy rate). Column 4 shows the ratio of the predicted rate to the actual rate. Had black and white schooling levels been equal, a significantly larger fraction of southern-born blacks would have left the region. The predicted-to-actual ratios would be even larger if an adjustment were made for quality of schooling, as was done in Chapter 6.[8]

The supply-side explanation deserves more credit than it has previously received. Had America not been involved in the two world wars nor the boll weevil infested southern cotton fields, a steady fraction of blacks would nevertheless have left the South. A numerically significant portion of the Great Migration, as Tyson believed, was the "logical" outcome of a "long series of linked causes" and not an "isolated" or "temporary phenomenon." Further, racial inequality in schooling contributed to keeping the black migration rate lower than it would have been in the absence of that inequality.

Yet it is also clear that the bulk of the movement and its particular timing cannot be explained by changes in schooling, and that exogenous shocks were crucial. Table 7.5 reports a regression of the percentage of black migrants on its lagged (by ten years) value. The data are state aggregates from the 1910, 1920, and 1930 censuses, and the regression includes a full set of state and year dummies.[9] The autoregressive parameter (the coefficient of the lagged dependent variable) is about 0.8, and is highly significant statistically.[60] Examining the constant term, its value is insignificantly different from zero.[11] If a state, say Alabama, began the twentieth century with a very low proportion of black migrants (which it did), the percentage of migrants would be expected to remain very low, unless jolted upward by a positive "innovation," an unexpected shock causing more blacks to leave the region.[12] Without the intervention of such shocks (e.g., the world wars) the southern share of the black population at midcentury would have been larger than it actually was.[13]

The strong dependence of the current migration rate on its lagged value is consistent with the notion of a "family and friends" effect—migration begets more migration.[14] The importance of the "family and friends" effect in encouraging southern blacks to migrate has long been emphasized by scholars of the Great Migration (Vickery 1969; Kirby 1983; Wright 1986). The existence of an established base of black migrants facilitated the transmission of information back to the South about conditions outside the region.

7.3 Explaining the Schooling-Migration Relationship

Economic analyses of migration typically begin with Larry Sjaastad's (1962) formulation of the problem. In Sjaastad's model, an individual migrates from one area to another if the expected benefits of doing so exceed the costs. The benefits may be pecuniary (e.g., higher earnings) and/or nonpecuniary (e.g., freedom from Jim Crow). The costs, too, are pecuniary (transportation costs) and/or nonpecuniary (the psychic costs of leaving a familiar environment).

Within the context of the Sjaastad model, the simplest explanation of the schooling-migration relationship would be that the economic benefits of leaving the South were greater for better-educated blacks. Previous studies have shown that black migration was motivated by the promise of higher earnings in the North (Vickery 1969; Bowles 1970). If the potential earnings gains from migration rose with education, the schooling-migration relationship could be rationalized.

Table 7.6 presents evidence from the 1940 census sample on the annual earnings differential between black migrants and nonmigrants. The differentials pertain to adult males, ages 20 to 64. The census data—nominal wage and salary earnings in 1939—have been adjusted for regional differences in the cost of living, but I make no claim that the adjustments are complete.[15] Black men who were not wage and salary workers (e.g., farm owners or tenants, self-employed professionals) do not figure in the table. It would clearly be better if the data came from a more representative year in the business cycle, but I know of no other relevant pre–World War Two data that do. No adjustment has been made for the possibility that, because migrants may have been more ambitious or hard working than nonmigrants, their earnings gains may have exceeded the gains that would have been experienced by stayers had the stayers migrated.[16] It is likely, however, that adjusting for selectivity bias would not affect the substantive conclusions reached below.[17]

Overall, the wage evidence seems supportive of an economic explanation of the schooling-migration relationship. The earnings differential was positive: there were, as pointed out earlier, real wage gains associated with migration. The earnings differential was smaller for the group with 0–4 years of schooling than for the group with 5–8 years of schooling, but the latter had a higher migration rate than the former. The same conclusion holds if the comparison is based on a regression analysis of earnings rather than sample means.

Yet there are limits to a purely economic explanation. The migration rate for the 5–8 schooling group was nearly three times as large as the 0–4 group, but the earnings differential was only twice as large. Blacks with more than a grade school education were more likely to be migrants, despite the fact that the earnings differential was far smaller at the high school level and beyond.[18]

One reason why the better educated might have higher migration rates in-

Table 7.6   **The North-South Wage Gap in 1939: Migrants vs. Nonmigrants
(black males, ages 20 to 64)**

	Unadjusted ($)	% Difference	Adjusted ($)	% Migrants
Annual Earnings				
Years of schooling				
0–4	198.20	42.5	116.43	8.5
5–8	256.38	46.4	173.63	23.2
≥9	57.55	8.2	52.10	30.2
Weekly wages				
Years of schooling				
0–4	4.94	40.7	3.58	
5–8	6.13	45.9	4.84	
≥9	2.25	13.7	2.04	

Notes: Unadjusted ($): mean difference in annual wage and salary earnings in 1939 between southern-born blacks who left the South and southern-born blacks who stayed in the South; *% Difference:* Unadjusted ($) as a percentage of mean earnings of nonmigrants; *Adjusted ($):* difference in earnings derived from a regression, including age, marital status, and SMSA residence; *% Migrants:* from Table 7.2. Persons employed on work relief jobs (e.g., the WPA) are excluded). Earnings data are adjusted for regional differences in the cost of living by assuming that state-level cost-of-living (COL) indices for 1939 were the same as in 1929; see Williamson and Lindert (1980, 323–25). Williamson and Lindert also give COL indices for 1949, which could be averaged with the 1929 indices; the resulting indices would show slightly larger North-South wage gaps. Separate rural and urban indices were calculated assuming that the urban COL = (1.27 × rural COL) (see 1980, 325). If the person lived in an SMSA, the urban index was used to deflate wages; otherwise, the rural index was used.
Source: 1940 public use sample.

volves financing the costs of migration. Within the South the earnings of black men rose, on average, with schooling (Chapter 6). Because better-educated blacks had higher earnings, they could more easily afford the pecuniary costs of migration.[19]

Yet another reason involves the relationship between schooling and non-farm employment. Chapter 6 showed that better-educated black men were more likely to hold nonfarm jobs in the South. The vast majority of jobs held by black migrants in the North were also nonfarm jobs. Thus, schooling increased the likelihood a black person would enter the nonfarm sector, whether the job was in the South or in the North.

Schooling was beneficial to migrants for another reason: it facilitated information flows between North and South. Black newspapers such as the *Chicago Defender,* which circulated widely throughout the urban South, and letters from black migrants were critical conduits through which knowledge about job opportunities and living conditions was communicated to potential migrants (Grossman 1989). A fully literate population was not an absolute necessity for an efficient flow of labor market information between South and North; literate family members or friends could, and did, assist those who were illiterate in acquiring knowledge about job opportunities. When the *Defender* arrived in small southern towns, people gathered at local shops to listen to the latest news. Nonetheless, it seems hard to deny that the spread of literacy among southern blacks facilitated the flow of information. The ability to read and write lowered an important cost of migration, that of acquiring accurate knowledge about the region of destination.

The responses to help-wanted advertisements appearing in the *Defender* are revealing on this point.[20] "Some time ago down this side," wrote a Miami man in response to an ad that appeared in 1917, "it was a rumour about the great work going on in the north. But at the present time every thing is quite there, people saying that all we have been hearing was false until I caught hold of the Chicago Defender I see where its more positions are still open." A Memphis man noted he was "a constant reader of your paper [the *Defender*] which can be purchased here," continuing on to request information on "average salaries paid there [Chicago] for unskilled labor and . . . board and room rent." A young woman from Alabama stated she was "a reader of the Chicago Defender I think it is one of the Most Wonderful Papers of our race printed. . . . I am writeing to see if You all will please get me a job."

Potential migrants, too, perceived a link between schooling and their chances of finding employment. "I am a college graduate," wrote a man from Georgia in 1917, "and understand Bookeeping." A Texas man wrote that he was "desiring work in New York or some of the adjoining states. . . . I have a little education too if it can be used to any advantage." Yet another claimed he was "willing to do most eny kind of earnest work. I am 36 years old and can read end write the english language." A woman from Louisiana stated she "read the Defender every week. . . . I am honest and neat and refined, with a fairly good education." Schooling—along with such attributes as sobriety, churchgoing, and a stable, married family life, which the applicants carefully noted—was a signal of reliability and of adaptability to a different (and distant) social and economic environment.

Above all, schooling was what distinguished younger blacks from older blacks, particularly older blacks who grew up during slavery or its immediate aftermath. "My father," wrote a black minister in the early twentieth century:

> was born and brought up a slave. He was taught his place and was content to keep it. . . . I know there are certain things that I must do, and I do them . . . [but my son] has been through the eighth grade; he reads easily. For a year I have been keeping him from going to Chicago; but he tells me . . . that in the fall he's going. He says, "When a young white man talks rough to me, I can't talk rough to him. You can stand that; I can't. I have some education, and inside I have the feelin's of a white man. I'm goin." (U.S. Department of Labor 1919, 33)

In the literature on the Great Migration there has yet to be a consensus on the effects of Jim Crow on the propensity to leave the South. While some scholars (Grossman 1989) argue that discrimination was a big "push" factor, others (Vickery 1969) disagree, claiming that changes in discrimination over time were not large enough to explain the magnitude of the movement. The effect of discrimination on the propensity to migrate, however, may have varied with schooling. For younger blacks, an unwillingness to acquiesce to Jim Crow seemed to be a consequence of being better educated. Dissatisfaction with the status quo prompted the "talented tenth" to leave. As schooling spread deeper into the black community, so did the dissatisfaction; and with it, the willingness and wherewithal to go North.

7.4   Black Migrants and the Northern Economy: Assimilation and Schooling

When he got off the train in Chicago, the world the black migrant confronted was very different from the one he left behind. Even if he had previously lived in a southern town or city, there was little in his prior experience to prepare him for life in the urban North. Throughout the Great Migration, contemporary observers attributed the poverty, irregular employment, and slow economic progress among blacks in northern cities to difficulties faced by black migrants in acclimating themselves. It was this slowness to assimilate, to adapt to a different and constantly changing economic environment, that limited racial economic progress, not solely (or simply) racial discrimination. As Edward Banfield (1968, 68) wrote in the 1960s,

> the Negro's main disadvantage is . . . that he is the most recently unskilled, and hence relatively low-income, migrant to reach the city from a backward rural area. The city is not the end of his journey but the start of it. He came to it not because he was lured by a cruel and greedy master but because he was attracted by job, housing, school and other opportunities that, bad as they were, were nevertheless better by far than any he had known before. Like earlier immigrants, the Negro has reason to expect that his children will have increases of opportunity even greater than his.

The assimilationist hypothesis is important because it offers another explanation of the stability of the black-to-white earnings ratio before World War Two. The results of the chapter thus far, however, might seem at odds with the assimilationist hypothesis, since it was the better-educated blacks who migrated. Yet the assimilationist hypothesis could still be true. Southern black migrants were better educated than nonmigrants, but "they were still poorly educated by northern standards. Inadequately educated and inappropriately trained, most migrants had few options" in the northern economy (Grossman 1989, 183). The Great Migration lowered the average educational attainment of the black labor force in the North.[21] If the assimilationist hypothesis were true, one would expect to find that, in economic status, southern black migrants lagged behind their northern-born counterparts.

The most careful prior investigation of the assimilationist hypothesis is a well-known study by Stanley Masters (1975). Using a sample drawn from the public use tape of the 1960 census, Masters showed that black migrants who had arrived in the North before 1955 (whom Masters called "Lifetime" migrants) had higher earnings than comparable non-southern-born blacks, but those who arrived after 1955 (whom Masters called "Recent" migrants) did worse. But, no matter where they were from, black incomes fell far below white incomes. Masters (1975, 51) concluded that the "low income of blacks in the . . . North" was mainly a consequence of "white discrimination and not just a relatively short-run problem of dynamic adjustment resulting from migration difficulties." A limitation of Masters' study is that it pertains to a single year, 1960, towards the end of the Great Migration. Persistent adjustment difficulties might still have characterized the experience of southern blacks during the earlier part of the Great Migration.

This section extends Masters' study by examining the economic status of black migrants using data from the 1900 to 1950 census samples. The results confirm Masters' findings for the earlier period. In terms of their earnings and occupations, southern black migrants did not lag behind non-southern-born blacks—far from it, they did better. The gap between southern- and non-southern-born blacks' economic status did decline with schooling, but even better-educated southern black migrants did comparatively well.

Panel A of Table 7.7 shows occupational distributions of southern-born black migrants and non-southern-born blacks in 1900–1910, 1940, and 1950. The occupational distributions support the claim made earlier in the chapter: the vast majority of southern black migrants held nonfarm jobs. Most northern blacks, regardless of where they came from, held low-paying service jobs or were unskilled laborers. Some improvement in occupational status occurred during the 1940s, as many blacks moved into semi-skilled jobs in northern manufacturing. The proportion in white-collar occupations, too, increased over time.[22]

Overall, there was little difference in the occupations held by southern black migrants or non-southern-born blacks. An index of occupational dissimilarity between the two groups ranged between 7 and 10 between 1900 and 1950 (recall from Chapter 6 that the maximum value the index can equal is 100). The slight rise in the index between 1910 and 1940 is consistent with the assimilationist hypothesis, but might also be due to the impact of the Great Depression on black employment.

Panel B of Table 7.7 gives evidence on unemployment by migrant status. The annual frequency of unemployment is the proportion of blacks who experienced unemployment during the census year; the unemployment rate is the usual concept (the proportion unemployed at a point in time). Early in the century black migrants were *less* likely than non-southern blacks to become unemployed in a year's time, and there is no evidence that black migrants had higher unemployment rates than non-southern blacks.

The early twentieth century censuses did not investigate when someone migrated to the North, but the 1940 census did: a person's location in 1935 was reported, so it is possible to distinguish migrants who arrived before 1935

Table 7.7   **The Economic Status of Black Migrants**

A. Occupational Distributions, Adult Black Males (in percentages)

	1900/1910	1940	1950
White collar			
Southern born	5.2	11.8	11.3
Non-southern-born	4.8	15.7	17.6
Skilled blue collar			
Southern born	7.2	7.4	12.7
Non-southern-born	7.9	10.3	11.4
Semi-skilled blue collar			
Southern born	13.8	16.7	28.0
Non-southern-born	13.0	17.9	27.0
Service			
Southern born	32.2	27.3	16.3
Non-southern-born	29.4	27.3	19.4
Unskilled nonfarm labor			
Southern born	32.4	32.8	29.4
Non-southern-born	29.2	21.6	22.2
Farm operator			
Southern born	3.4	1.6	0.3
Non-southern-born	5.9	1.5	0.9
Farm laborer			
Southern born	5.9	2.4	1.7
Non-southern-born	9.7	5.7	1.5
Segregation index			
Southern-born/Non-southern-born blacks	7.1	11.3	10.0
Blacks/whites	51.7	45.2	44.4

B. Unemployment (in percentage points)

	1900	1910	1940	1950
Frequency	−4.7	−3.7		
Rate		−1.1		−0.2
Definition 1				
Lifetime			−2.5	
Recent			1.0	
Definition 2				
Lifetime			1.0	
Recent			−1.6	

C. Earnings and Weekly Wages, 1939 (in percentages)

	Lifetime		Recent	
	Unadjusted	Adjusted	Unadjusted	Adjusted
Annual earnings	10.5*	5.8*	−21.3*	−7.1
Weekly wages	8.3*	5.1*	−12.2*	−3.5
Ratio × 100, black/white				
Annual earnings = 62.5				
Weekly wages = 68.0				

(continued)

Table 7.7   **(continued)**

D. Interactions of Migrant Dummy with Schooling (Panel C, row 1)

	Lifetime	Recent
Annual earnings		
Migrant	0.291*	0.119
Migrant × years of schooling	− 0.029	− 0.017
Weekly wages		
Migrant	0.191*	0.280*
Migrant × years of schooling	− 0.017*	− 0.041*

Notes: **Panel B:** *1900, 1910, 1950,* figures are differences in sample means (in percentage points) between southern-born and non-southern-born black males (ages 20–64) residing outside the South; *1940,* all black males in labor force (see text). FREQUENCY: *1900,* proportion experiencing unemployment in census year (May 1899–April 1900); *1910,* proportion experiencing unemployment in calendar year 1909. RATE: proportion unemployed on census date. DEFINITION 1: counts WPA workers as employed. DEFINITION 2: counts WPA workers as unemployed; see Margo (1988a). LIFETIME: migrated from South before 1935. RECENT: migrated from South between 1935 and 1940. **Panel C:** Rows 1 AND 2, figures are exp (*r*) − 1, where *r* is the mean difference between migrants and non-southern-born blacks in log earnings and log weekly wages. UNADJUSTED: difference in sample log means. ADJUSTED: calculated from coefficients of migrant dummies. Other independent variables are age, age squared, years of schooling, marital status, census region, and SMSA location. Row 3, ratio = exp (*r*) − 1, where *r* is the mean difference in log earnings and log weekly wages between non-southern blacks (including southern black migrants) and non-southern whites.
*Statistically significant at 5% level or better.
Sources: **Panel A:** *1900/1910,* census public use sample; *1940, 1950:* 20% random sample of census public use tape. **Panel B:** *1900, 1910, 1950,* see Panel A; *1940,* Margo (1989). **Panel C:** Rows 1 and 2, Margo (1989); Row 3, 20% random sample of 1940 census public use tape. **Panel D:** Margo (1989).

from those who arrived after. Following Masters' terminology, I refer to pre-1935 migrants as Lifetime and post-1935 as Recent.

Panel C of Table 7.7 shows differences in average annual earnings and weekly wages between Lifetime and Recent migrants and non-southern-born blacks.[23] In 1940 the annual earnings of Lifetime migrants exceeded those of non-southern-born blacks by 11 percent; the gap for weekly earnings was slightly smaller (8 percent).[24] Recent migrants earned less than non-southern-born blacks and, therefore, less than Lifetime migrants.

None of the comparisons thus far has controlled for factors other than migrant status. The Adjusted columns in Panel C are derived from regression coefficients of migrant status. Holding constant factors other than migrant status, economic differences between migrants and non-southern-born blacks were small (particularly for Recent migrants), but the differences were still positive and large for Lifetime migrants. Panel D reports regression coefficients of the migrant status dummies interacted with years of schooling. Among Lifetime migrants with little or no schooling, annual earnings and weekly wages were much higher than among non-southern blacks. The economic differences between migrants and non-southern-blacks, however, were much smaller at higher schooling levels. A similar pattern emerges in comparing the weekly earnings of Recent migrants and non-southern-born blacks.

Masters (1975) explained the relative success of black migrants by appealing to "selectivity bias," the idea that migrants were not a random sample of the southern black population. His reasoning would appear to apply equally well to the earlier years of the Great Migration. Poorly educated blacks were unlikely to go North, but the ones who did were rewarded, perhaps because they were more ambitious and hardworking.[25] For the better educated the prospect of migrating to the North was less daunting, because they were already likely to enter the nonfarm economy at some point.

Better-educated migrants were atypical of the population, but relatively less so within their education group. Black migrants, however, suffered from the lower quality of southern schools, and these disadvantages were greatest at the high school level or beyond. The result was a decline in the earnings of black migrants relative to the earnings of non-southern blacks, as schooling levels increased. Most non-southern blacks themselves were only a generation or two removed from the South. Faced with limited opportunities for upward mobility, "succeeding generations" might not have been "willing to work as hard as the migrants" (Masters 1975, 60).

The opportunities *were* limited, compared with those available to non-southern whites. Panel C of Table 7.7 also shows that the earnings of black migrants were far below those of non-southern whites.[26] Indices of dissimilarity (Panel A, Table 7.7) reveal that the distribution of occupations among whites differed far more from the distribution of occupations among black migrants, than did the occupations of migrants with those of non-southern blacks. Yet, in clear contrast with southern trends, racial employment segregation in the North appears to have been falling over time.[27] The North was not a promised land, but its labor market offered the migrant higher wages, a way out of the rural South, and the prospect of a better life for their children.

7.5 Summary

Chapter 6 documented that long-run increases in black schooling were associated with shifts in the distribution of occupations among southern blacks, in particular the shift of black labor out of agriculture. This chapter has documented a positive association between schooling and the probability a southern black would leave the South. A complex, interrelated set of factors encouraged better-educated blacks to migrate. The earnings gains from migration rose with schooling; the better-educated could more easily finance any costs of migration; the jobs migrants took were nonfarm jobs; the ability to read and write lowered the costs of acquiring accurate information about the North; and blacks who had been to school were generally more dissatisfied with life in the South.

Recent research by economic historians has emphasized the regional character of southern labor markets before World War Two (Mandle 1978; Wright 1986). "The defining economic feature of the South prior to World War Two was not poor performance or failure," according to Gavin Wright (1986, 64), "but [the] isolation . . . of the southern labor market from national and international flows." When the northern economy expanded, jobs went to European immigrants, not southern blacks (or whites). The exclusion of southern blacks, argues Wright, cannot be explained by "ignorance and poverty" or "poor education and general unsuitability for . . . industrial jobs" because "millions of Europeans with equally poor qualifications were coming much longer distances . . . to take the very jobs [blacks] were supposedly ignorant of" (1986, 73). Europeans succeeded because they got there first. Once established, "kinship networks" sustained labor flows in both directions, creating an international labor market the South was utterly excluded from.

The South, according to Wright, was left out because of slavery and bad timing. Before the Civil War the Peculiar Institution "insulated the South from outside labor flows." After the war the region was "consumed by the turbulence . . . of Reconstruction" precisely when "mass immigration was becoming an established part of the northern social fabric" (1986, 74).

The results of this chapter do not challenge the notion that southern labor markets were "isolated," but they do identify a different cause. Contrary to Wright's assertion, European immigrants and southern blacks who stayed behind did not have "equally poor qualifications," at least as far as literacy was concerned. Immigrants from most countries had far higher literacy rates than did southern blacks.[28] Immigrants who could read and write, *in any language,* had higher earnings than those who could not (Higgs 1971).[29] The similarity of the relationships between schooling and nonfarm employment in the South and schooling and migration in the North demonstrates that ignorance, poverty, and poor education *were* root causes of southern isolation. Southern and non-southern labor markets were always linked, for those who could afford to move and who could fit in.

The explanatory power of schooling should not be overstated, however. "Shocks" were critical to getting the Great Migration started. If the isolation of southern blacks from non-southern labor markets was not fully predetermined by historical circumstances, neither was it solely an individual's affair. Poor schooling cannot explain why blacks were more likely to leave the South than were whites.

Recent research has documented the importance of the Great Migration in raising the national black-to-white earnings ratio prior to 1960 (U.S. Commission on Civil Rights, 1986; Smith and Welch, 1989). This research, however, has not addressed a fundamental question: if leaving the South was so profitable, why wasn't the Great Migration greater early on? The answer to this question involves elements of supply and demand. The long-term trends in black schooling and migration were causally related, and changes over time in black schooling explain a numerically significant share of black migration from the South. But if the nonfarm demand for black labor outside the South had not increased during the world wars, fewer blacks would have left the South. The results of the chapter, therefore, support a selective combination of the human capital and institutionalist models, as did the results of Chapter 6.

By the early twentieth century, disenfranchisement had led to racial inequality in educational opportunity, and these inequalities measurably reduced black schooling levels. By limiting the flow of black labor from the rural South, educational discrimination helped perpetuate the traditional existence of a supply of low-wage labor well into the twentieth century, a fact that the southern white elite was keenly aware of (Wright 1986). In the final analysis the Great Migration could not be stopped; the white elite could not prevent successive generations of black children from becoming better-educated than previous generations. Schooling, in turn, helped each new generation of black children enter a world of wider opportunities.

Appendix
Migration and Prior Urban Residence

This appendix evaluates the hypothesis that the schooling-migration relationship is merely a proxy for a positive relationship between migration and prior urban residence. Urban blacks were more likely to leave the South than were rural blacks. But, because urban schooling levels were higher than rural schooling levels, the effect of schooling on migration could be overstated. The logit regressions in Table 7.3 do not control for prior urban residence, because prior urban residence was not reported in the census samples.

I begin by examining the possible bias in 1900. Suppose that (a) the true effect of literacy on the probability of outmigration is zero; (b) the outmigration rate of rural blacks is zero (only urban residents migrate); and (c) urban residence prior to migration is unobserved. Under these assumptions, what would the *observed* difference be in outmigration rates between literate and illiterate blacks?

The following two equations can be used to answer this question:

(1) $$m_L\alpha + m_{IL}(1 - \alpha) = m$$

(2) $$m_L/m = \beta$$

where m_L = observed migration rate of literates; m_{IL} = observed migration rate of illiterates; m = overall migration rate; α = overall proportion literate; and β = observed proportion of migrants who were literate. Note that the observed effect of literacy on migration is simply $m_L - m_{IL}$. The parameters α and m can be calculated from the 1900 census sample: $\alpha = 0.47$ and $m = 0.053$. From assumption (b) it follows that β is the literacy rate of urban residents who migrated. Assumption (a) implies that literates and illiterates have the same probability of migration; thus an estimate of β is the proportion of urban blacks in the South in 1900 who were literate: $\beta = 0.61$ (calculated from the 1900 census tape). Inserting the values of α, β, and m into equations (1) and (2) gives $m_L - m_{IL} = 0.03$, or 50 percent of the difference in the outmigration rates of literates and illiterates (0.06) (see Table 7.2). It is clear that 50 percent is an upper bound, even if assumptions (a), (b), and (c) were true, because urban literacy rates were lower than 0.61 before 1900 (the literacy rate of those who migrated would have been less than the rate in 1900).

The procedure can be repeated for 1940 and 1950, and the results indicate that the bias in those years is at most equal to 25 percent of the effect of schooling on migration reported in Table 7.2. Hence the conclusion in the text: the schooling-migration relationship among southern blacks cannot merely be a proxy for an unobserved relationship between migration and prior urban residence.

8   Conclusion: Race, Social Change, and the Labor Market

In the forty years after World War Two the black-to-white earnings ratio increased and a "new" black middle class emerged. These changes stand in stark contrast to the half century before 1940, which witnessed little improvement in the relative economic status of black Americans.

I have discussed two frameworks for interpreting long-term trends in racial income differences: a supply-side, "human capital" model, and a demand-side, "institutionalist" model. The human capital model emphasizes racial differences in the quantity and quality of schooling, arguing that once these differences narrowed after World War Two, relative black status improved. In the institutionalist model, by contrast, improvements in the relative economic status of blacks were dependent on "shocks" to the economy that increased the nonfarm demand for black labor. Using a variety of econometric techniques and previously unexploited data sources, I have then critically examined the empirical validity of the two models.

Focussing on the South, I considered the historical evidence on racial differences in the quantity and quality of schooling. Each successive generation of black children attended school more frequently than had their predecessors and, as a result, achieved higher child literacy rates. The racial gaps in school attendance and child literacy rates, which were huge in 1880, had essentially disappeared by 1950. Census data revealed, however, that racial differences in average educational attainment (or "years of schooling") among adults remained persistently large until after World War Two. The gap for adults was mainly a result of the fact that, prior to 1954, the majority of southern black children attended *de jure* segregated schools. The relative "quality" of these schools—as measured by the black-to-white ratio of per pupil expenditures—followed a U-shaped pattern over time. That is, from an initial position of similarity, relative quality declined in the late nineteenth and early twentieth centuries, remained roughly stable from 1910 to 1940, and then increased in the 1940s.

The decline in relative quality around the turn of the century was found to be the consequence of black disenfranchisement and growing white demand for better schools. On the eve of World War One, expenditures per pupil in southern black schools fell far below expenditures per pupil in southern white schools. A portion of this difference reflected pure "wage discrimination" against black teachers. Although southern blacks were disenfranchised, various institutions and incentives existed that ensured public school funds would continue to be allocated to the southern black population. These institutions and incentives were reasonably successful in keeping the black schools from progressively falling further behind as the white schools improved, but they were not enough to force an equalization of school expenditures. The trend towards equalization, especially in teacher salaries, was the outcome of a concerted political and legal effort. Success was achieved in part by the timing of the effort during the 1940s, when labor markets were tight and social attitudes had begun to change.

During the first half of the twentieth century, the South failed to abide by the equal part of the separate-but-equal doctrine, as established in the Supreme Court's 1896 case, *Plessy v. Ferguson.* It was demonstrated that separate-but-unequal provision of public schools in the South retarded black educational achievement. Had the schools been separate-but-*equal,* southern black children would have attended school more frequently, achieved higher literacy rates earlier in the century, and had higher scores on standardized tests. However, separate-but-equal would not have compensated for aspects of family background—poverty and adult illiteracy—that hindered black educational achievement. This "intergenerational drag" was a major factor behind the persistence of racial differences in schooling before World War Two.

The consequences of racial differences in schooling for labor market outcomes were also studied. Before World War Two the shift of labor out of southern agriculture, black and white, was a cohort phenomenon. Better-educated, geographically mobile southerners were more likely to enter the nonfarm economy as young adults, where earnings were higher than in agriculture. But blacks were underrepresented in the expansion of nonfarm employment in the South before the Second World War. Employment segregation in the South increased over time, and this increase cannot be explained by racial differences in the quantity or quality of schooling. During the 1940s, southern blacks of all ages left farming for nonfarm jobs created during the war, and this sectoral shift led to an increase in the black-to-white earnings ratio in the South between 1940 and 1950.

Schooling and black migration to the North, like schooling and nonfarm employment in the South, were shown to be positively related. Better-educated blacks were more likely to take part in the "Great Migration." Yet secular trends in black schooling could not fully explain the magnitude or timing of the flow of black labor from the South; increases in the nonfarm demand for black labor during the world wars were crucial. Various indicators revealed that the economic status of black migrants compared favorably with that of nonsouthern blacks. The stability of relative black status before World War Two could not be blamed on difficulties black migrants had in adjusting to a different social and economic environment, insofar as employment segregation outside the South was actually decreasing during the first half of the twentieth century.

Considered separately, the human capital and institutionalist framework proved too simple to explain the absence of improvement in relative black status during the first half of the twentieth century. Human capital, intergenerational, and institutionalist factors were involved, and these factors were intertwined in complex ways. If black people had been better educated earlier in the century, more would have been able to enter blue- and white-collar occupations in the South, more would have migrated to the North, and relative black status would have been higher. But the shift of black labor out of southern agriculture would have been much smaller than it actually was had it not been for "shocks" like the world wars.

Although I have focussed on the period before 1950, my findings have important implications for understanding events after 1950 and, more broadly, the relationship between social change and economic development. In 1954 the Supreme Court outlawed *de jure* segregated public schools, but the *Brown* decision did little to stop the post-1950 emergence of *de facto* segregated schools, a consequence of black migration into central cities coupled with massive suburbanization of the white population. Unlike their counterparts in the early twentieth century South, black children after *Brown* could legally attend the same schools as white children, provided they lived in the same school district; but, because of extraordinarily high levels of residential segregation, few blacks were able to do so. In the face of *de facto* segregation and continued racial inequality in school resources, court-ordered busing plans have frequently been imposed; very recently the Supreme Court has upheld the right of federal district judges to require school boards to levy taxes to pay for desegregation plans.

Another implication concerns the historical origins of post-1950 gains in relative black status. Successive generations of black parents in the South made sacrifices to send their children to school. Faced with many constraints—government and labor market discrimination, poverty, adult illiteracy—their efforts were frequently thwarted. Eventually, however, the sacrifices paid off, and racial differences in schooling narrowed. Blacks who entered the labor market in the decades after 1950 were, on average, much better educated than earlier cohorts. Unwilling to submit any longer to segregationist ideology, these new generations were an important catalyst for social activism. The South became the major battleground: the civil rights movement began there, it was the South that was targeted for federal civil rights enforcement, and it was in the South that the greatest gains in relative black status occurred in the late 1960s and early 1970s (Jaynes and Williams 1989;

Heckman 1990). "The purpose of outlawing employment discrimination," according to three recent members of the U.S. Commission on Civil Rights, "was to increase the opportunities for *qualified* blacks to gain better paid employment. The programs have done that" (U.S. Commission on Civil Rights 1986, 122; emphasis added). The history of the modern civil rights movement has been told in terms of its major events and protagonists (Branch 1988). It is time to add past generations of black parents to that history. They are the unsung heroes of the civil rights movement.

Postwar gains have not been distributed equally throughout the black community. Along with the new black middle class, there emerged the black "underclass"—poor, primarily inner-city blacks who, as a group, are likely to grow up in single-parent families, are undereducated, and are much more likely to be unemployed or out of the labor force as adults than other Americans. Some scholars have attributed the existence of the underclass to postwar government welfare policies that allegedly subsidize nonparticipation in the labor market and lead to dissolution of traditional, two-parent families (Murray 1984). Others argue that welfare policy does not explain joblessness and family structure in the ghetto (Ellwood 1988). Although I would not pretend to evaluate the substance of this debate here, I would suggest that contemporary economic inequality within the black community cannot be understood independently of historical forces. Blacks displaced by agricultural mechanization were among the last to leave the rural South. With limited education and few job skills, they faced many difficulties in competing successfully in an urban economy that by the late 1960s was already much different than its pre-1960s predecessor (Wright 1986). Given the short period of time since then (about a generation), and in light of the evidence of intergenerational drag earlier in the century, it is plausible that economic inequality in the black community would have increased anyway, whether or not government policies played a role. The historical roots of the underclass deserve further investigation.

It is frequently said that the growth of competitive, market economies and social progress go hand in hand. Freely mobile workers can always leave if they are treated unfairly; discrimination is unprofitable for private firms (and sometimes for governments). Competition ultimately makes it costly for societies to maintain rigid social norms in the face of long-run economic growth and structural change. The economic history of black Americans, however, offers little evidence in support of these claims. Before the Civil War the southern economy grew at about the same rate as the rest of the country; there is no evidence that slavery was incompatible with industrialization (Fogel 1989; Goldin 1976). From the end of the Civil War until World War Two, the southern economy lagged somewhat behind the rest of the nation, but the South still experienced modern economic development, as labor shifted out of agriculture. Yet employment in the South was more segregated in 1950 than in 1900. Segregationist ideology, like slavery, was not incompatible with economic growth or structural change. Both took a concerted political effort to fight, and in the end neither was overcome without bloodshed

During the 1980s the American economy has become increasingly integrated into world markets. The forces of international competition have led to a marked shift in employment towards the service sector. One consequence of this shift has been a sharp rise in the earnings of college graduates relative to the earnings of high school graduates. Black college enrollment rates still lag behind white college enrollment rates; demographic trends, however, will create a relatively abundant supply of minority labor in the 1990s. Assuming that aggregate demand conditions are favorable and that the racial gap in college attendance can be narrowed, the 1990s may be a decade of improvement in relative black status. History provides examples of similar opportunities; time will tell if the 1990s will be added to the list.

Notes

Chapter 1

1. A skeptic might blame the Great Depression for the stability in the earnings ratio; as is evident in Figure 1.1, the ratio declined slightly in the 1930s. However, no such explanation can account for the failure of the earnings ratio to rise in the 1920s.

2. My focus throughout is on men because comparable figures for women have not been calculated; based on an analysis of occupation statistics, however, Goldin (1990) suggests that the relative economic status of black women may have deteriorated before World War Two.

3. There is considerable debate over the proper interpretation of the increase in the earnings ratio from 1940 to 1980; a useful introduction to the issues are various chapters in Shulman and Darity (1989). There is little debate, however, that the "new" black middle class is much larger in size that the "old" black middle class of forty years ago, and that middle class blacks today are employed in a broader array of jobs than in the past. Relative improvements in black status slowed after 1975; see Heckman (1990, 243).

4. By contrast, the Great Depression was a negative shock, slowing the absorption of black labor into the nonfarm economy.

5. Here "educational attainment" means highest grade of school completed, or what is commonly meant by the phrase "years of schooling." The racial difference is defined to be the white mean minus the black mean. This difference is always positive for the cohorts analyzed by Smith (1984).

6. The coefficient of the schooling gap is -0.031 with a t-statistic of -6.51. The dependent variable is the cohort-specific black-white earnings ratio (Smith 1984, 695); the independent variables are the schooling gap, white minus black (687), plus dummy variables for census years (1900, 1920–1980; data for 1910 are not available, see Smith 1984, 693).

7. In Chapter 4, however, I analyze racial differences in wages paid to teachers, and in chapters 6 and 7 present some evidence on racial differences in earnings from the 1940 and 1950 public use samples.

8. Smith's (1984) earnings ratios, shown in Figure 1.1, were derived from employment categories. Smith assigned fixed weights (using 1970 census data on earnings) to the proportions of individuals in particular occupations. The sum of the weighted pro-

portions yields an index of "occupational status," and the black-to-white ratio of occupational status is Smith's estimate of the earnings ratio. Thus changes in Smith's proxy reflect shifts in the occupations held by black men relative to white men; shifts in the structure of wages are ignored.

9. A good example involves the analysis of region of employment in Chapter 7. In an earnings function analysis of racial differences, region would be an independent variable: other things held constant (e.g., age, educational attainment), blacks living in the South had lower wages. The earnings function approach fails to address an underlying question: if living in the South was so costly to blacks in terms of earnings, why didn't more blacks move to the North? Posing the question in this manner, as I do in Chapter 7, goes to the heart of the debate between the institutionalist and human capital models.

A limitation of analyses of employment rather than earnings is that effects of schooling on earnings within occupations are ignored. This is an important criticism, but until more earnings data are found for the early twentieth century, the criticism cannot be addressed.

10. See Heckman and Payner (1989) and Butler, Heckman, and Payner (1989).

Chapter 2

1. Slave artisans residing in southern cities and towns may be an exception to the general rule. According to the 1870 census manuscripts, fully 22 percent of urban black artisans were literate, compared with only 5.7 percent of rural southern blacks (Ransom and Sutch 1977). Slave artisans made many economic decisions on their own, frequently hiring themselves out.

2. Strictly speaking, cohort here refers to blacks born in the South in a certain time period *and* remaining in the South, not to all southern blacks born in the time period.

3. In 1910 and after, a person was counted as "in school" if he attended school for at least one day during the census year. A number of adjustments, however, had to be made to the census data for 1880–1900. A question comparable to the one in 1910 was included in the 1880 census form, but the results were not compiled. Instead, the published volumes include figures derived from reports of school superintendents. Attendance rates derived from school reports generally exceed those compiled by the census, because the school reports include a substantial amount of double-counting of enrollments. I devised a procedure to estimate black school attendance in 1880 from child literacy rates (see the notes to Table 2.2). Although I believe the estimates to be plausible, they should be interpreted with care. It is important to note that the census data refer to attendance at a school of any type—public or private, vocational, and so on. For the younger age groups, however, the vast amount of attendance took place in public schools, because private school enrollments were a small fraction of total enrollments.

4. In 1940 and 1950 the specific period was shorter in length than before 1940. Had the 1940 or 1950 census question been used consistently throughout the period, the increase over time in black school attendance rates would have been larger than as measured in Table 2.2; some black children who attended school in 1910 would not have been so counted had the 1940 (or 1950) question been asked.

5. The distinction between "years of schooling" in the literal sense of time spent in school, and "years of schooling" as a measure of grades completed (i.e., a certain level of knowledge) is discussed later in the chapter.

6. Using the procedure to estimate literacy rates in 1940 and 1950, had every black male attended 4.5 years of school ca. 1890, virtually all would have been classified as literate.

7. This explanation is similar to Goldin's (1990) analysis of female labor force participation and labor market experience. After World War Two the labor force participation rate of married women increased sharply, but average years of labor market experience among women in the labor force remained low. Average experience remained low by the addition to the labor force of women with little or no work experience since marriage.

8. White years-per-grade is biased upwards because grade includes foreign whites who were less educated than native whites. Thus census data also overstate schooling for whites.

9. Calculated from figures in Jones (1917, 7).

10. There were sixty-seven high schools, if Missouri and Kansas are included; see Jones (1917, 34).

11. Computed from U.S. Bureau of Education (1893).

12. "Plantation" agriculture was a term used by the U.S. Bureau of the Census (1916) to describe the situation in which a large number of farmers operated separate units under the direction of a single landlord. Plantation counties produced staple crops (such as cotton), had high labor-to-land ratios and little mechanization, high rates of tenancy, and were predominantly black.

13. One should not conclude, however, that the equal part of separate-but-equal was a real possibility in 1954. There were still large differences in expenditures on ancillary services, such as transportation, and the value of school capital per black child was far below that per white child.

14. I have focussed my attention on public elementary and secondary schools because that is where the majority of southerners, black or white, were educated during the first half of the twentieth century, and because comprehensive data on private schools are unavailable. For further discussion of the relative quality of black schools in the South during the segregation era, see Bond (1934, 1939), Harlan (1958), and especially Anderson (1987).

15. Racial differences in class sizes would be considerably larger if expressed on the basis of enrollment rather than average daily attendance.

16. See Center for Studies in Demography and Ecology (1980, 35). Fractional months were not retained in the public use sample; it appears that the answers were rounded up. Thus the estimated average months of school attendance are biased upward, but the degree of upward bias cannot be determined from the sample.

17. This was the procedure used in the 1940 census. Census clerks in Washington were instructed that, if the school attendance question was left blank, column 25 of the census form was to be checked. Then, if an "S" (for student) appeared in column 25, a "Yes" was to be entered in the school attendance column as well.

18. The census reached a similar conclusion; see U.S. Bureau of the Census (1918, 378).

Chapter 3

1. See Jones (1917), Bond (1934, 1939), Harlan (1958), Kousser (1974, 1980a), Pritchett (1985, 1986), and Anderson (1987).

2. The discussion in this section is woven together from a number of sources. The best historical account of disenfranchisement is Kousser (1974); see also Bloom (1987). Foner (1988) is a recent synthesis of scholarship on Reconstruction.

3. Other disenfranchisement methods included the "whites-only" primary and the "Australian" or secret ballot. The introduction of the secret ballot in Arkansas, which was especially effective in eliminating illiterates, prompted the following ditty (quoted in Kousser 1974, 54):

The Australian Ballot works like a charm
It makes them think and scratch,
and when a Negro gets a ballot
He certainly has his match.

4. "Decimate" here does not mean completely eliminate. There were areas in the ex-Confederate South in which blacks voted after disenfranchisement, such as Atlanta; see Dittmer (1977). Blacks were freer to vote in border states like Kentucky, and racial differences in per pupil expenditures were smaller in the border states than elsewhere in the South (Jones 1917).

5. Black turnout was declining before suffrage restrictions were enacted; see Kousser (1974, 242–43).

6. Another way around the obstacle was private support for white public schools. It was common in the late nineteenth century South for "patrons" (parents and other interested parties) to provide supplemental funds when public funds ran out. In this manner white parents could be sure that their "tax dollars" (donations) went to support schools for white children.

7. There is considerable debate over the racial incidence of school taxes in the South ca. 1910 (Smith 1973; Pritchett 1986). However, there is little question that, even if the black schools were still being subsidized by whites in 1910, the amount of the subsidy was less *after* disenfranchisement; see Kousser (1980a).

8. The effects of disenfranchisement on school spending in North Carolina have also been investigated; see the valuable studies by Kousser (1980a) and Pritchett (1985).

9. Calculated from figures in States of Louisiana (1879, 12–15).

10. A Louisiana "parish" is the same as a county in other states.

11. A regression was also estimated in which the interaction term was allowed to have a nonzero coefficient only in the sugar parishes in which Hair (1969) claimed blacks voted freely. Consistent with Hair's argument, the coefficient of this interaction term was positive. The level of statistical significance was somewhat lower, however, than in the equation in the text, suggesting that, in the cotton parishes, the black voter was a real threat at the height of the Populist challenge.

12. Indeed, in light of scholarly discussion of the extent of the fraud (Hair 1969; Kousser 1974), the fact that the coefficient has the "correct sign," let alone approaches conventional levels of statistical significance, is strong evidence of a disenfranchisement effect.

13. Chapter 5 shows that the reasoning was self-serving, insofar as better black schools would have led to higher black attendance rates.

14. Quoted in U.S. Bureau of Education (1893, 1079). The superintendent got his wish. Except for Atlanta, blacks were fully disenfranchised in Georgia by 1908; see Kousser (1974).

15. A subsidy from whites to blacks would have been required because per capita black demand for education was lower than per capita white demand. Consider a school district that opted to open a white high school. According to a strict interpretation of separate-but-equal, the district would have been required to open a black high school, regardless of the level of per capita black demand (the results of Chapter 5 suggest, though, that the level of black demand would not be independent of the existence of the black school). As I discuss in Chapter 5, various legal loopholes emerged to get around the strict interpretation. The required subsidy would have been even larger if compensatory doctrine (unequal schools in favor of blacks) had been put into place to offset the effects of family background on black school attendance.

16. Part of the strategy of the National Association for the Advancement of Colored

People (NAACP) initially was to force an abandonment of separate-but-equal by convincing the South that it was too expensive to maintain, if strictly construed; see Chapter 5.

17. The source of this belief, aside from Myrdal's creed may have been a social norm that blacks were entitled to public school funds equal to what they paid in school taxes; see Kousser (1980a).

18. Of course, any given school district might decide to flout the law by not opening a black school but, as I discuss below, the community then risked losing its black residents, which had economic costs.

19. For example, state courts in the South consistently ruled against statutes requiring that school taxes be segregated, that is, taxes paid by blacks would go to black schools, taxes paid by whites to white schools; see Risen (1935). By gerrymandering school districts, however, it was frequently possible to get around the restriction, as happened in North Carolina; see Pritchett (1985).

20. Following the logic to its conclusion, however, foundation contributions would have stimulated more spending on the white schools as well; some of the contributions may have substituted for public funds that would have been spent on blacks anyway. Moreover, it would make no sense at all for school officials to accept matching grants unless they already were committed to supporting the black public schools. Thus, the existence of philanthropic contributions cannot answer Myrdal's paradox in its most basic form, although it can explain why improvements in the black schools took place.

21. Anderson (1987) demonstrates that many of the philanthropic officials were racist and their motives far from pure. But there is no doubt that philanthropic contributions expanded educational opportunities for southern black children.

23. To attract aid from the Rosenwald Foundation, for example, local matching funds would have to be raised. State agents mustered such support from local school officials.

Chapter 4

1. Because the length of the black school year declined relative to the white school year between 1890 and 1910 (Chapter 2), the decline in the black-to-white ratio of *monthly* teacher salaries was somewhat smaller (see Margo 1985).

2. A variation on this argument emphasizes racial differences in grades taught. Black teachers were disproportionately employed in the elementary grades, where salaries were lower than in high schools, even after accounting for education and experience.

3. Monthly salaries are used rather than annual salaries in order to control for variation across counties in the length of the school year. The purpose of pooling by sex is to increase the sample size, because the number of counties in both states are small. The number of observations in every state is less than the number of counties (or twice the number, in the Florida and Louisiana regressions), because of missing data or because a few counties hired only female teachers.

4. The additional regressions are reported in Margo (1984b, 314–15).

5. Variations in population density across counties may also capture variations in the cost of living, which could not be included in the regressions due to data limitations.

6. To correct for heteroscedasticity, each observation was weighted by the square root of the number of teachers to which the average salary refers.

7. This conclusion is sensitive to how qualifications are measured. White teachers

appear to have received higher returns to education and experience; see Margo (1984b, 315).

8. This data base is part of a larger one constructed for a project on the social and economic history of American teachers; see Perlmann and Margo (1989).

9. The racial difference in the age-salary profile is smaller for weekly earnings. Evidently, older black teachers worked significantly more weeks (were employed in school districts with longer than average school years) than younger black teachers.

10. The South Atlantic region consists of Delaware, Maryland, the District of Columbia, Virginia, West Virginia, North and South Carolina, Georgia, and Florida. States in the East South Central region are Alabama, Mississippi, Kentucky, and Tennessee. States in the West South Central region are Arkansas, Oklahoma, Louisiana, and Texas. The greater locational disparity in black salaries suggests that the market for black teachers may have been less efficient spatially than the market for white teachers. Additional support for this conclusion is obtained if dummy variables for states are substituted for the regional dummies in the regressions; the coefficient of variation of the black state dummies exceeded the coefficient of variation of the white state dummies.

11. I will return to this point in Chapter 5, when I examine the impact of separate-but-equal.

12. See Murray (1949, 63) for a list of cases through early 1948 and their outcomes.

13. This avenue was closed off, however, with the successful resolution of *Morris v. Little Rock* in 1945, which outlawed "rating systems" as a method of discriminating against black teachers; see Marshall (1947, 47).

14. The number of males employed in high schools also fell proportionately to the number of females; see Federal Security Agency, U.S. Office of Education (1951, 83).

15. Class sizes were computed from U.S. Department of Health, Education and Welfare (1954, 98). In the elementary grades the average class size (enrollment per member of the instructional staff) was 38 in 1942 and 37.3 in 1950. In the high schools the average class size was 25.7 in 1942 and 17.4 in 1950.

16. Total black enrollment in the elementary grades fell by 3 percent between 1942 and 1950, while total enrollment in high schools rose by 28 percent; see Federal Security Agency, U.S. Office of Education (1947, 113) and U.S. Department of Health, Education, and Welfare (1954, 98). An improvement in the educational qualifications of black teachers vis-à-vis white teachers, which was associated with the increase in black high school attendance, is also part of the demand story, and helps explain the rise in the black-white salary ratio. Between 1940 and 1950 the proportion of black teachers with 2 years or less of post–high school training fell by 14 percentage points, while the proportion who were college graduates or better increased by 30 percentage points; the corresponding figures for white teachers were 1 percentage point and 12 percentage points (Welch 1973, 43). The black regression coefficients in Table 6.3 imply that the premium (in logs) for up to 2 years of college was 0.171 and for 4 or more years was 0.566 (this lumps persons with 3 years into the "2 year or less category," which will bias upward the total importance of the changes in educational background). The corresponding figures for whites are 0.136 (2 years or less) and 0.40 (4 years or more). If these figures are used to weight the changes in educational background, the implied increase in the black-white salary ratio is 0.096 = (0.133 [blacks] − 0.034 [whites]), or 27 percent of the actual change from 1940 to 1950 (0.096/0.352).

17. In log terms, the increase in black salaries (in 1950 dollars) between 1942 and 1950 was 0.59. If $e = -1$, the log of the number of black teachers employed would have declined by 0.59 which, in 1950, would have corresponded to a reduction of 33,000 in instructional staff. If black enrollment had stayed constant (which, I admit,

is doubtful, because overcrowding would have been horrendous), the pupil-staff ratio would have been 58 (compared with an actual value of 32.1).

Chapter 5

1. My discussion of *Plessy v. Ferguson* draws heavily on Lofgren's (1987) monograph; see also Woodward (1955).

2. Notwithstanding its modern notoriety, there is debate whether *Plessy* was an unexceptional ruling for its time. The conventional wisdom is that there was little in Brown's opinion to excite contemporaries and the decision could have been foreseen by the participants (Lofgren 1987). Recent work by Morgan Kousser (1986, 1988a, 1988b), however, casts doubt on this view. The opinion was a product of its era: popular support for civil rights was at a low ebb in the late nineteenth century, and there was little pressure on the justices to vote in favor of *Plessy* although, in Kousser's view, there was legal precedent to do so.

3. Mangum (1940, 79–83) discusses the various state laws regarding racial segregation in public schools.

4. See Kousser (1980b) for an excellent discussion of *Cummins*.

5. At the time there was a private black high school operating in Augusta; see Kousser (1980b).

6. The import was less extreme because it is unclear whether knowledge of the decision was widespread among school boards. Further, as pointed out earlier, the number of black public high schools in the South increased anyway after World War One.

7. See also Schmidt (1982).

8. Lloyd Gaines, who had sought to enroll in law school, could not be located after the Supreme Court reached its decision, and never directly benefited; see Tushnet (1987, 70–77).

9. Not quite the right statistics, however. The very county and state data that permitted me to write this monograph would not have been sufficient; the right detail was at the school district level, which typically would have to have been collected on site, at great expense.

10. It was legally sound because of the Supreme Court's 1886 decision *Yick Wo v. Hopkins* which, in theory, linked unconstitutionality to the administration of racially based statutes; see Tushnet (1987, 25). It was cheaper because the equalization suits would have been brought in numerous localities, most very distant from NAACP headquarters in New York.

11. That is, as long as the Court was receptive to the argument that *de jure* segregation was morally wrong, there could be no defense of compensating inequalities.

12. I do not wish to imply that no further moral indictment is possible. A case could be made, for example, that separate-but-equal, strictly enforced, would have wasted resources (unnecessary duplication of school facilities); or, alternatively, would have required so large a redistribution of income from whites to blacks that it would not have been too costly to achieve (that is, there would have been strong incentives for whites to prevent the redistribution from taking place).

13. For a good discussion of the difficulties involved, see Hanushek (1986).

14. Orazem (1987, 714) makes a similar point.

15. For a contrary view, see Kiefer and Phillips (1988) and Donohue and Heckman (1989).

16. A recent paper by Card and Krueger (1990) persuasively demonstrates that long-term improvements in the quality of schooling (which they measure by class size,

the length of the school year, and similar variables) did appreciably raise the rate of return to schooling.

17. The major exception is Bond (1934). who conducted a number of pioneering studies of racial differences in educational achievement, but who did not provide a quantitative estimate of the impact of separate-but-equal.

18. As the state-level regressions in Chapter 2 showed, compulsory schooling laws had only a minor effect on black attendance rates; see also Landes and Solmon (1972). Orazem (1987) uses a household model in his study of separate-but-equal and Maryland test scores.

19. The variable refers to attendance in any type of school, not just public schools. But for the age group in question (5–16), the majority must have been enrolled in public elementary schools, because private school enrollments were a tiny fraction of total enrollments in the South in 1900, concentrated at the high school level (that is, older children).

20. Occupational status (available from the 1900 census tape) is constructed by attaching to each occupation a weight derived from 1950 income data (the higher the average income in the occupation, the higher the weight). Thus occupational status is a proxy for income.

21. The school variables were drawn from the published reports of state superintendents of four states in 1900: North and South Carolina, Alabama, and Florida (data for a fifth state, Texas, could not be successfully matched to the 1900 census sample). Observations for the four states from the 1900 census tape make up the sample analyzed.

22. Strictly speaking, positive coefficients could be expected only for children who were at the margin between attending and not attending school. For children already in school, it is possible that an improvement in average school characteristics could lower school attendance. This is not just a theoretical quibble. Black children in northern cities could complete more grades in less time than southern children, because the schools were better. Consequently attendance rates of older urban children were sometimes lower in the North (and in some southern cities). On black education in the North at the turn of the century, see the important recent book by Perlmann (1988).

23. Because most children attended one-teacher schools, variations in class size may capture variations in the availability of schooling, thus accounting for the insignificant coefficients of the school density variable.

24. Because the regression does not control for within-county differences in school characteristics, it is also likely that the urban dummy is partially capturing the positive effect of better urban schools on school attendance.

25. In performing the calculation using the black coefficients, I ignore the negative coefficient of school density (see Table 5.2). If the true impact of school density on black attendance were negative, the calculated impact would be biased upward, but this would simply reinforce the conclusion that racial differences in school characteristics do not explain all of the attendance gap.

26. The calculation is a "partial equilibrium" one. If the equal part of separate-but-equal had been enforced, someone would have had to pay for it. Because strict enforcement would have probably increased the white share of the school tax burden (see Chapter 3), white after-tax incomes would have fallen relative to black after-tax incomes, further lowering the racial attendance gap.

27. Racial differences in child characteristics and geographic location explain only a small amount of the racial attendance gap; see Margo (1987).

28. To estimate per capita incomes at the county level, I devised a procedure that applied fixed income weights from the 1950 census to urban, rural farm, and rural nonfarm population shares; see Margo (1986a, 795). Because of the errors inherent in this

procedure, I tested the sensitivity of the results by estimating regressions including urban and rural nonfarm population shares instead of the income variable. Urban incomes were higher on average than rural nonfarm incomes, so an increase in the urban share should have a larger positive effect on the literacy rate than an increase in the proportion urban. This turned out to be the case. The additional regressions can be found in Margo (1986a, 796).

29. The fixed effects estimator corresponds to a regression with dummy variables for counties and years. On the random effects estimator, see Maddala (1977).

30. School capital was typically valued at its historical production cost; privately owned buildings used as schools (e.g., churches) were frequently not included in the valuation. Consequently the insignificant coefficients may reflect measurement error.

31. Due to the difficulties of interpreting the coefficients of the school capital and percentage one-teacher schools variables (the coefficients are either the "wrong" sign or are statistically insignificant), the calculations do not equalize the value of school capital and the percentage one-teacher schools.

32. Margo (1986a, 799) reports a regression of state-level data in 1930 showing that, holding constant school characteristics and school attendance, child literacy was positively related to adult literacy.

33. Orazem (1987) also estimated regressions combining the black and white schools together (including a race dummy), with no substantive effect on the results.

34. Orazem (1987, 720) also estimated race-specific attendance equations, concluding that equalization of school inputs completely explained the racial attendance gap. It is likely that his omission of family background variables accounts for the larger impact of separate-but-equal than in my analysis of school attendance in Section 5.2 (which did control for family background).

35. The inclusion of dummy variables for counties corresponds to the fixed effects estimator of Section 5.3.

36. If the fixed effects coefficients are used, the average reduction is 27 percent.

Chapter 6

1. Figures for adult males can be constructed for the entire country from published census volumes (as in Smith 1984), but not for regions.

2. Over two-thirds of the black professionals were schoolteachers or clergymen in the 1940 sample. In 1930 there was one black teacher for every 194 southern blacks and one black clergyman for every 495 blacks; the corresponding ratio for lawyers was one for every 21,472 blacks (U.S. Bureau of the Census 1935, 292).

3. In the sample drawn from the 1940 census tape, 87 percent of the fifty-eight black managers labored in trade, financial and business services, or personal services. Only two were employed in manufacturing, compared with 12 percent of southern white managers. Eighty-one percent of the black managers were self-employed, and 79 percent of these worked in wholesale and retail trade. None of the non-self-employed black managers worked in southern manufacturing; 15 percent of non-self-employed white managers did.

4. See Goldin (1990) for an application of this index to measure employment segregation between men and women.

5. The indices would be invariant to the number of categories (below the one-digit level) if and only if the *signs* of the racial differences within categories were the same as the sign at the one-digit level. For example, if the white proportion with skilled blue-collar jobs exceeded the black proportion, the same would have to be true for every skilled trade. Since this is unlikely, the values of the indices are lower bounds.

6. Compared with Smith's (1984) indices, Becker's are based on fewer occupational categories, a broader age grouping, and are *not* cohort specific. However, Becker's index of relative black status in the North shows an *increase* before 1950, which suggests that regional differences were fundamental to the behavior of the aggregate black-white earnings ratio prior to World War Two.

7. Goldin (1990) shows that, prior to World War Two, many large firms had "color bars" prohibiting the employment of blacks in office work and other white-collar jobs.

8. Models of "statistical" discrimination help explain the persistence of social norms involving employment; see Starrett (1976), Lundberg and Startz (1983) and Akerlof (1985). In Lundberg and Startz's model, for example, there are two population groups, W and B; firms base hiring decisions on the expected productivities of workers which, in turn, are assumed to be a weighted average of individual characteristics (e.g., human capital) and the average characteristics of the worker's racial group. It is assumed that the weight attached by firms to group characteristics is greater for the B group than for the W group. Given this assumption, individual members of the B group have less incentive to invest in human capital than do members of W; and over time, the average level of human capital in the B group will be less than the average level in the W group (which, in turn, reinforces the initial beliefs of employers about the relative productivities of the two groups).

9. Roosevelt's order was in response to a threatened march on Washington to be led by A. Philip Randolph, president of the Brotherhood of Sleeping Car Porters, the purpose of which was to demand an end to hiring discrimination in defense plants; see Vatter (1985, 132).

10. Given the categorical nature of the dependent variable, a multinomial logit or probit model might be preferred to the linear probability model. The multinomial logit and probit models, however, are impractical because of the large sample sizes and number of estimations to be performed. I did, however, estimate certain regressions (the agricultural participation regressions) using binomial logit analysis, and all of the regressions were estimated using discriminant analysis (Amemiya 1981). Discriminant function estimates of multinomial logit parameters are biased, but the biases are typically small, and discriminant analysis is much cheaper than maximum likelihood. None of the substantive findings were affected. See also Heckman and Payner (1989), who use the linear probability model in their very similar analysis of racial differences in employment in South Carolina during the twentieth century.

11. Census region and urbanization are included because, as discussed in the text, the extent of the nonfarm economy in the South varied geographically. Marital status is included to control for the possibility (suggested by Wright 1986) that certain occupations (e.g., unskilled nonfarm labor) were avoided by married men because wages in the occupation were too low to support a family. Years of schooling (1940 and 1950) is highest grade completed. Because the census did not ask a separate question about highest grade *attended* in 1940 (the 1950 census did), it is possible that some persons in 1940 reported their highest grade attended instead of highest grade completed, thus overstating their completed schooling level. Experiments with the 1950 census sample indicate that the mean racial difference in years of schooling (for adult males) was only slightly larger if measured by highest grade completed than by highest grade attended. Thus the substantive conclusions of the chapter regarding the effects of schooling on labor market outcomes are unaffected by the use of highest grade completed (as measured by the census) in the 1940 and 1950 regressions.

12. In light of the cohort differences found in the previous section, it would be better to estimate age-specific regressions, rather than include age as an independent variable. Unfortunately, once the dependent variable is disaggregated into one-digit industry and occupation groups, the sample sizes are too small to disaggregate by age.

13. Let α_i be the coefficient of the race variable in, say, the ith occupation. The segregation index is $\Sigma|\alpha_i|$ (since $\alpha_i = b_i - w_i$, controlling for other factors).

14. The regression coefficients were used to predict race-specific values of the industry or occupational probabilities, the p_i's, given the particular values assumed for the independent variables (e.g., that the mean value of years of schooling was the same for whites and blacks).

15. In the 1940 and 1950 census samples, "teachers" were classified in the "professional services" industry, which accounts for black overrepresentation in both years. Because most of the teachers were employees of local governments, had they been correctly classified, blacks would have been more underrepresented in government employment than as measured by census data.

16. Because the 1940 and 1950 regressions use a more accurate measure of educational attainment, it is likely that the estimated increase in employment segregation is biased downward. The industry and occupation regressions for 1940 and 1950 were reestimated with a proxy for literacy instead of years of schooling. A person was deemed literate if his educational attainment was greater than two years, and illiterate otherwise. The values of the segregation indices computed from the race coefficients of these regressions were 36.4 in 1940 and 35.9 in 1950, both exceeding the values in Table 6.5.

17. Bond (1939, 339–44) reported the results of standardized tests conducted in the 1920s showing that black third and sixth graders in Alabama and Louisiana scored a full grade below national norms, controlling for the age of the pupil; not controlling for age, the gap was three years, which is the basis for the adjustment in the text. A similar adjustment for school quality was made by Heckman and Payner (1989). A three-year adjustment is not restrictive; a larger adjustment, say five years, would not alter the conclusions.

18. Calculations equating white and black urbanization and regional population shares reached a similar conclusion.

19. "Earnings" here refer to wage and salary earnings; self-employment income is excluded. Consequently the regression sample excludes a fairly large portion of agricultural employment in both 1940 and 1950. Because the decline in agricultural wage labor among blacks during the 1940s was greater than the overall decline in agricultural employment (compare the means in Table 6.6 with Table 6.1), the earnings data overstate the improvement in relative black *incomes* (including self-employment income) in the South between 1940 and 1950.

20. The sectoral differences in earnings are not adjusted for nonwage benefits. Farm laborers, however, received more nonwage benefits (e.g., food, housing) than nonfarm workers. Adjusting for such benefits would reduce the size of the sectoral gap and therefore the importance of the sectoral shift. On sectoral wage gaps before 1950, see Alston and Hatton (1989) and Williamson and Lindert (1980).

21. The age range 25 to 64 was chosen because, for these cohorts, no adjustment for relative school quality is warranted; see note 22 in this chapter.

22. No adjustment for relative (black-to-white) school quality is appropriate because, for the birth cohorts included in the regressions (1876–80 to 1921–25), no improvement in quality took place for the average black member of the 1940 and 1950 samples; the average birth year of blacks in the 1940 sample was 1900 and in the 1950 sample it was 1909. However, the impact of changing racial differences in schooling is biased downward, because no adjustment is made for "ungraded school bias" (Chapter 2). The 1940 census understated the educational attainments of blacks born in the late nineteenth century; the bias is less in 1950 because these cohorts are a smaller share of the 1950 sample. If all blacks born before 1900 were educated in ungraded schools and the adjustment for ungraded school bias reduces mean educational attainment by two

years, then the reduction in racial differences in years of schooling between 1940 and 1950 would be -0.51 years (instead of -0.26 years; see Table 6.6). Thus adjusting for ungraded school bias among blacks would approximately double the explanatory power of changing racial differences in schooling (Panel C, Table 6.6). I regard this as an upper bound to the true adjustment for ungraded school bias because many southern whites, too, attended ungraded schools.

23. Freeman (1973) argued that educational discrimination slowed the narrowing of racial income differences by reducing the supply of black employers in the South, who would have hired black workers. The results of the chapter support Freeman's hypothesis.

24. Without the public use samples, it would have been impossible to calculate segregation indices controlling for racial differences in schooling.

25. The importance I attach to social norms may be overstated. It is possible that census samples for 1920 and 1930, were they available, would show that the increase in employment segregation was primarily a consequence of setbacks during the Great Depression. On the other hand, the data in Table 6.1 show that the lag in the black shift out of agriculture predated the 1930s (see Table 6.1).

Chapter 7

1. See Epstein (1918), U.S. Department of Labor (1919), Kennedy (1930), Kiser (1932), Vickery (1969), Henri (1975), Gill (1979), Johnson and Campbell (1981), Fligstein (1981), Gottlieb (1987), and Grossman (1989).

2. A major exception is the important study by Leiberson (1978), who applied forward survival techniques to aggregate census data from 1890 to 1950 to show that net migration of southern blacks was higher among literates than illiterates. My analysis differs from Leiberson's in two ways: the measure of migration I use is gross and the data refer to individuals. Gross measures of migration are preferable to net measures because migration theory, economic or otherwise, refers to gross flows, not net. Because the data I use refer to individuals, it is possible to control simultaneously for characteristics other than schooling, which cannot be done with aggregate data.

3. Another possibility is that there may have been a greater census undercount of less-educated blacks in northern cities than in the rural South, but the differential would have to have been very large to account for the migration-schooling relationship.

4. Some persons migrated to attend high school or college in the North and ended up staying. Middle-class black parents in the upper South, for example, sent their teenage offspring to Chicago to attend high school; see Grossman (1989).

5. The variables for 1900 and 1910 are age, age squared, gender, literacy, family size, relationship to head of household, marital status, region of birth within the South, and whether the person's parents were interstate migrants. The last variable was included to test for migration of young children with families or for an intergenerational effect, but none was found. The variables for 1940 and 1950 are the same, except for the following differences. In 1940 and 1950 the schooling variables are years of schooling and years of schooling squared, and parents' interstate migration is excluded. In 1950, veteran status was added. The substantive results are not affected if family size, relationship to head of household, and marital status (which, for migrants, are observed after the move) are excluded.

6. Schooling could be a proxy for ability or some other unobserved characteristic ("motivation"), but the census samples, because they are cross sectional, cannot address this issue (but see Sec. 7.3).

7. For a contrary view, see Fligstein (1981).

8. Consider the calculation for 1940. Suppose that, for black schooling to equal white schooling (including the quality of schooling), the black schooling distribution (as in Table 7.2) would have had to be: 0–1 years of schooling, 3.4%; 2–4, 0%; 5–8, 20%; 9–12, 60%; ≥13, 16.6%. This corresponds to an increase in the mean years of schooling for blacks so that it equalled the mean for whites plus two additional years. Under this assumption, the predicted black migration rate in 1940 would be 28.1% (instead of 23.9; see Table 7.5).

9. The state dummies control for geographic factors that influenced the extent of the migration (e.g., distance to the North, literacy rates, percentage nonfarm employment, wage differentials, and so forth).

10. The regression specification can be criticized because it excludes schooling (although variations in black literacy rates would be captured in the state dummies). To address the criticism, I estimated a logit regression using a sample of southern-born adult blacks from the 1910 census tape, in which the lagged outmigration from the state of birth was included as an independent variable, as well as literacy. The logit coefficient of lagged migration implied a partial probability change of 0.88 (the dp/dx, analogous to the autoregressive coefficient of the state-level regression).

11. The coefficients of the year dummies are also of interest; in particular, the value of the 1930 dummy (0.043) indicates that slightly more than half of the migration between 1910 and 1930 was due to "trend" factors (e.g., schooling, falling costs of migration, etc.).

12. In fact, the coefficient of the lagged migration rate is insignificantly different from one. This implies that the long-run effect of a shock would be to raise permanently the proportion of black migrants (if the coefficient were less than one, the black migration rate would eventually return back to its original level).

13. On the other hand, if black schooling levels had been higher earlier in the century, the autoregression implies that more blacks would have left subsequently. The autoregressive coefficient can be used to calculate how big this "feedback" effect would have been. Suppose, for example, the literacy rate of adult black males in 1910 had equalled its 1940 value. According to Table 7.5, the 1910 migration rate would have then been 1.86 percentage points higher than its actual value. This increase, in turn, would have caused an increase in the migration rate in 1920, 1930, and 1940 (through the feedback effect). The total increase in the migration rate (between 1910 and 1940) can be shown to be 2.93 percentage points, or 34.1 percent (= 2.93/8.5) of the actual increase in the migration rate of adult males between 1910 and 1940 (see Table 7.2).

14. It is also consistent with "learning" by firms; after experimenting with black workers (because of a shock like a war) and finding the experiment to be successful, the firm permanently raises its demand for black labor in the future; see Whatley (1990).

15. The cost-of-living adjustments are described in the notes to Table 7.6. No adjustment is made for nonwage payments, which were quite common among farm laborers (Alston and Hatton 1989). Including these payments, however, would narrow further the regional difference in wages at the lowest schooling levels (because farm laborers were the least schooled occupation), and, hence, would have no effect on the substantive conclusions.

16. If data for all northern blacks were used (instead of data for migrants), the substantive contrasts in Table 7.6 would be unchanged. The North-South wage gap is usually calculated in this manner; see, for example, U.S. Commission on Civil Rights (1986).

17. In Margo (1988b), I specify and estimate an econometric model of the Great Migration, using individual-level data from the 1940 census tape. The model consists of three equations:

$$(1) \qquad\qquad \ln w_m = X\beta_m + \varepsilon_m$$

$$(2) \qquad\qquad \ln w_n = X\beta_n + \varepsilon_n$$

$$(3) \qquad\qquad I^* = \mu(\ln w_m - \ln w_n) + Z\alpha + \delta$$

Equations (1) and (2) are earnings functions for migrants and nonmigrants. Equation (3) is an index function: if $I^* > 0$, the person migrates; if $I^* < 0$, the person stays. The X's are variables that influence earnings, and the Z's are variables that influence the costs of migration. Schooling is included in both X and Z; that is, it has an impact on migration indirectly through its effects on earnings, and it has a direct impact by affecting the costs of migration (or the nonpecuniary benefits). The model is completed by assuming that the error terms (the ε's and δ) are joint normally distributed.

Equations (1)–(3) are estimated in a three-step procedure (see Maddala 1983). First, (1) and (2) are substituted into (3) and a reduced-form probit is estimated. The probit coefficients are used to calculate selectivity-bias correction terms, which are then added to (1) and (2) in a least squares regression (selectivity bias is present unless ε_m and ε_n are uncorrelated, which is highly unlikely). The regression coefficients are used to calculate the expected earnings gains of migration ($\ln w_m - \ln w_n$). Finally, the structural probit (e.q. [3]) is estimated, included the expected earnings gain.

The model was estimated using a sample of 1,147 southern-born black males (ages 14 and over), 284 of whom were migrants. The dependent variable of the earnings functions was the person's weekly wage. In principle, the model's parameters are identified as long as one variable in X is excluded from Z, but in practice, it proved necessary to include occupational and broad sectoral (manufacturing, agriculture) dummies in the earnings functions. In effect, the specification implies that black migrants would have worked in the same occupation and economic sector in both regions, a factually incorrect assumption for many migrants. However, the estimate of μ was insignificantly different from one, and the coefficient of schooling in the structural probit was positive and statistically significant. The higher were the expected earnings gains, the more likely a black would migrate; but, holding constant the expected earnings gains, schooling had a positive effect on the propensity to leave the South. These econometric results, then, are consistent with the conclusions reached in the text.

18. The decline in the earnings gap at the high school level is larger than that reported in U.S. Commission on Civil Rights (1986, 81), but the commission's study did not adjust for regional cost-of-living differences. Another interpretation of the decline is that skill differentials were higher in the South, and, indeed, had been since the antebellum period; see Margo and Villaflor (1987).

19. It is also possible that economic opportunities for better-educated blacks were greater in the North, in ways not fully reflected in earnings; for example, the chances of finding a blue- or white-collar job.

20. A large collection of responses appear in Foner and Lewis (1980, 259–81), from which the examples in the chapter are selected.

21. For example, in the 1940 sample used in Panel C of Table 7.7 below, the average educational attainment of non-southern-born blacks was 8.4 years, compared with 7 years among southern-born black migrants.

22. It is noteworthy that the proportion of black migrants in white-collar jobs exceeded the proportion of blacks in white-collar jobs in the South (see Chapter 6), which is consistent with the schooling-migration relationship.

23. In order to ensure a large enough sample of Recent migrants, the sample definition was extended to include all black males in the labor force (ages 14 and over); see Margo (1989). The percentage differentials were calculated from the logs of the variables, so the sample definition excludes persons who reported no wage and salary earnings in 1939, and who worked zero weeks.

24. Because there were over ten times as many Lifetime migrants as there were Recent migrants, the average earnings of black migrants (Lifetime and Recent) exceeded the average earnings of non-southern blacks. A similar overall difference (not shown) was found using the 1950 census sample.

25. Poorly educated non-southern blacks, too, were atypical of the population from which they were drawn. Their earnings may have been unusually low, biasing the comparison in favor of southern black migrants.

26. The black-white earnings and wage ratios are biased upwards because no adjustment has been made for the 1939 earnings limit (which was $5,000). Proportionately more whites earned above the limit than did blacks. For such adjustments, see U.S. Commission on Civil Rights (1986, 128).

27. The result is consistent with Becker (1957, 113), who found an increase in black-to-white occupational status in the North from 1910 to 1950.

28. According to the 1910 census sample (see Chapter 2), 60 percent of southern black males (ages 20–64) were literate. According to Higgs (1971, 424), every male immigrant group except for two, Portuguese and Turkish, had a higher literacy rate. Higgs's figures pertain to 1909, but the contrast would be larger if late nineteenth century data (e.g., 1880) were used.

29. They also had lower unemployment. A regression analysis of the 1910 census sample shows that, among foreign-born adult men, literacy in any language reduced the annual frequency of unemployment (the probability of experiencing unemployment in a year's time) by 5.6 percentage points (t-statistic = 5.6). The ability to speak English also reduced the unemployment frequency, but by a smaller amount, 2.3 percentage points (t-statistic = 2.6). The regression included age, city size, region of residence, years in the United States, marital status, and a nonwhite (i.e., Asian) dummy. If one-digit industry and occupation dummies are added, the literacy coefficient remains significantly negative, but the English-speaking coefficient no longer is so.

References

Akerlof, George. 1985. Discriminatory, Status-Based Wages Among Tradition-oriented, Stochastically Trading Coconut Producers. *Journal of Political Economy* 93 (April): 265–76.

Alston, Lee J., and Timothy Hatton. 1989. The Wage Gap Between Farm and Factory: Labor Market Integration in the Interwar Years. Typescript. Department of Economics, University of Illinois.

Amemiya, Takeshi. 1981. Qualitative Response Models: A Survey. *Journal of Economic Literature* 19 (December): 1483–1536.

Anderson, James. 1987. *The Education of Blacks in the South, 1860–1935.* Chapel Hill: University of North Carolina Press.

Banfield, Edward. 1968. *The Unheavenly City: The Nature and Future of our Urban Crisis.* Boston: Little, Brown.

Becker, Gary. 1957. *The Economics of Discrimination.* Chicago: University of Chicago Press.

Black, Earl, and Merle Black. 1987. *Politics and Society in the South.* Cambridge, MA: Harvard University Press.

Blalock, Hubert. 1967. *Toward a Theory of Minority Group Relations.* New York: Wiley.

Blinder, Alan. 1973. Wage Discrimination: Reduced Form and Structural Estimates. *Journal of Human Resources* 8 (Fall): 436–55.

Bloom, Jack M. 1987. *Class, Race, and the Civil Rights Movement.* Bloomington: Indiana University Press.

Blose, David, and Ambrose Caliver. 1935. *Statistics of the Education of Negroes, 1929–30 and 1931–32.* U.S. Office of Education, Bulletin No. 13. Washington, D.C.: U.S. Government Printing Office.

———. 1938. *Statistics of the Education of Negroes, 1933–34 and 1935–36.* U.S. Office of Education, Bulletin No. 13. Washington, D.C.: U.S. Government Printing Office.

Bond, Horace Mann. 1934. *The Education of the Negro in the American Social Order.* New York: Prentice-Hall.

———. 1939. *Negro Education in Alabama: A Study in Cotton and Steel.* New York: Associate Publishers.

Bowles, Samuel. 1970. Migration as Investment: Empirical Tests of the Human Capital Approach to Geographic Mobility. *Review of Economics and Statistics* 52 (November): 356–62.

Branch, Taylor. 1988. *Parting the Waters: America in the King Years, 1954–1963.* New York: Simon and Schuster.

Butler, Richard, James J. Heckman, and Brook Payner. 1989. The Impact of the Economy and the State on the Economic Status of Blacks: A Study of South Carolina. In *Markets in History: Economic Studies of the Past,* ed. David W. Galenson, 231–346. New York: Cambridge University Press.

Card, David, and Alan Krueger. 1990. Does School Quality Matter? Returns to Education and the Characteristics of Public Schools in the United States. Typescript. Department of Economics, Princeton University.

Center for Studies in Demography and Ecology, University of Washington. 1980. *United States Census Data, 1900: Public Use Sample.* Ann Arbor, MI: The Inter-University Consortium for Political and Social Research.

Cogan, John. 1982. The Decline in Black Teenage Employment, 1950–1970. *American Economic Review* 72 (September): 621–38.

Coleman, James S. 1966. *Equality of Educational Opportunity.* Washington, D.C.: U.S. Department of Health, Education, and Welfare.

Day, Richard. 1967. The Economics of Technological Change and the Demise of the Sharecropper. *American Economic Review* 57 (June): 427–49.

Dewey, Donald. 1952. Negro Employment in Southern Industry. *Journal of Political Economy* 60 (August): 279–93.

Dittmer, John. 1977. *Black Georgia in the Progressive Era, 1900–1920.* Urbana: University of Illinois Press.

Donohue, John, and James J. Heckman. 1989. Continuous versus Episodic Change: The Impact of Affirmative Action and Civil Rights Policy on the Economic Status of Blacks. Typescript. Department of Economics, Yale University.

Du Bois, W. E. B., and Augustus Dill. 1911. *The Common School and the Negro American.* Atlanta, GA: Atlanta University Press.

Ellwood, David. 1988. *Poor Support: Poverty in the American Family.* New York: Basic Books.

Epstein, Abraham. 1918. *The Negro Migrant in Pittsburgh.* Pittsburgh, PA: School of Economics, University of Pittsburgh.

Federal Security Agency, U.S. Office of Education. 1942. *Biennial Survey of Education in the United States, 1936–38.* Washington, D.C.: U.S. Government Printing Office.

———. 1947. *Biennial Surveys of Education in the United States, 1938–40 and 1940–42.* Washington, D.C.: U.S. Government Printing Office.

———. 1949. *Biennial Survey of Education in the United States, 1942–44.* Washington, D.C.: U.S. Government Printing Office.

———. 1950. *Biennial Survey of Education in the United States, 1944–46.* Washington, D.C.: U.S. Government Printing Office.

———. 1951. *Biennial Survey of Education in the United States, 1946–48.* Washington, D.C.: U.S. Government Printing Office.

Fishback, Price. 1989. Can Competition Among Employers Reduce Governmental Discrimination? Coal Companies and Segregated Schools in West Virginia During the Early 1900s. *Journal of Law and Economics* 32 (October), pt. 1: 311–28.

Fligstein, Neil. 1981. *Going North: Migration of Blacks and Whites from the South, 1900–1950.* New York: Academic Press.

Fogel, Robert W. 1989. *Without Consent or Contract: The Rise and Fall of American Slavery.* New York: W. W. Norton.

Foner, Eric. 1988. *Reconstruction: America's Unfinished Revolution, 1863–1877.* New York: Harper and Row.

Foner, Philip S., and Ronald Lewis. 1980. *The Black Worker: A Documentary History,* vol. 5. Philadelphia: Temple University Press.

Foote, J. M., and M. S. Robertson. 1926. *The Public Schools of East Feliciana Parish.* Baton Rouge, LA: State Department of Education.

Freeman, Richard. 1973. Black-White Income Differences: Why Did They Last So Long? Typescript. Department of Economics, University of Chicago.

———. 1977. Political Power, Desegregation, and Employment of Black Schoolteachers. *Journal of Political Economy* 85 (April): 299–322.

Georgia, State of. 1907. *Annual Report of the State Superintendent of Public Instruction.* Atlanta, GA: State Printer.

Gill, Flora. 1979. *Economics and the Black Exodus: An Analysis of Negro Migration from the Southern United States.* New York: Garland Press.

Goldin, Claudia. 1976. *Urban Slavery in the American South, 1820–1860: A Quantitative History.* Chicago: University of Chicago Press.

———. 1990. *Understanding the Gender Gap: An Economic History of American Women.* New York: Oxford University Press.

Gottlieb, Peter. 1987. *Making Their Own Way: Southern Blacks' Migration to Pittsburgh, 1916–1930.* Urbana: University of Illinois Press.

Greene, Lorenzo J., and Carter G. Woodson. 1930. *The Negro Wage Earner.* Washington, D.C.: The Association for the Study of Negro Life and History.

Grossman, James R. 1989. *Land of Hope: Chicago, Black Southerners, and the Great Migration.* Chicago: University of Chicago Press.

Guzman, Jessie Parkhurst. 1947. *The Negro Yearbook: A Review of Events Affecting Negro Life, 1941–1946.* Tuskegee, Alabama: Department of Records and Research, Tuskegee Institute.

Hair, William Ivy. 1969. *Bourbonism and Agrarian Protest: Louisiana Politics, 1877–1900.* Baton Rouge: Louisiana State University Press.

Hanushek, Eric A. 1986. The Economics of Schooling: Production and Efficiency in the Public Schools. *Journal of Economic Literature* 24 (September): 1141–77.

Harlan, Louis. 1958. *Separate and Unequal: School Campaigns and Racism in the Southern Seaboard States, 1901–1915.* Chapel Hill: University of North Carolina Press.

Harris, Carl V. 1985. Stability and Change in Discrimination Against Black Public Schools: Birmingham, Alabama, 1871–1931. *Journal of Southern History* 51 (August): 375–416.

Harris, Robert J. 1960. *The Quest for Equality: The Constitution, Congress, and the Supreme Court.* Baton Rouge: Louisiana State University Press.

Heckman, James J. 1990. The Central Role of the South in Accounting for the Economic Progress of Black Americans. *American Economic Review* 80 (May): 242–46.

Heckman, James J., and Brooks Payner. 1989. Determining the Impact of Federal Anti-Discrimination Policy on the Economic Status of Blacks: A Study of South Carolina. *American Economic Review* 79 (March): 138–77.

Henri, Florette. 1975. *Black Migration: Movement North, 1900–1920.* Garden City, New York: Anchor Press.

Higgs, Robert. 1971. Race, Skill, and Earnings: American Immigrants in 1909. *Journal of Economic History* 31 (June): 420–28.

———. 1976. The Boll Weevil, the Cotton Economy, and Black Migration. *Agricultural History* 50 (April): 325–50.

———. 1977. *Competition and Coercion: Blacks in the American Economy, 1865–1914.* New York: Cambridge University Press.

———. 1982. Accumulation of Property by Southern Blacks Before World War One. *American Economic Review* 72 (September): 725–37.

———. 1989. Black Progress and the Persistence of Racial Economic Inequalities, 1865–1940. In *The Question of Discrimination: Racial Inequality in the U.S. Labor Market,* eds. W. Darity, Jr., and S. Shulman, 9–49. Middletown, CT: Wesleyan University Press.

Jaynes, Gerald, and Robin Williams. 1989. *A Common Destiny: Blacks and American Society.* Washington, D.C.: National Academy Press.

Johnson, Charles. 1934. *Shadow of the Plantation.* Chicago: University of Chicago Press.

———. 1938. *The Negro College Graduate.* Chapel Hill: University of North Carolina Press.

———. 1941. *Statistical Atlas of Southern Counties.* Chapel Hill: University of North Carolina Press.

Johnson, Daniel, and Rex Campbell. 1981. *Black Migration in America: A Social Demographic History.* Durham, NC: Duke University Press.

Jones, Jacqueline. 1980. *Soldiers of Light and Love: Northern Teachers and Georgia Blacks, 1865–1873.* Chapel Hill: University of North Carolina Press.

Jones, Thomas Jesse. 1917. *Negro Education: A Study of the Private and Higher Schools for Colored People in the United States.* U.S. Office of Education, Bulletin, 1916, vols. 1 (no. 38) and 2 (no. 39). Washington, D.C.: U.S. Government Printing Office.

Joyner, J. W. 1910. *Biennial Report of the State Superintendent of Public Instruction.* Raleigh, NC: State Printer.

Kaestle, Carl. 1983. *Pillars of the Republic: Common Schools and American Society, 1780–1860.* New York: Hill and Wang.

Kennedy, Louise V. 1930. *The Negro Peasant Turns Cityward.* New York: Columbia University Press.

Key, V. O. 1949. *Southern Politics in State and Nation.* New York: Knopf.

Kiefer, David, and Peter Phillips. 1988. Doubts Regarding the Human Capital Theory of Racial Inequality. *Industrial Relations* 27 (Spring): 251–62.

Kirby, Jack T. 1983. The Southern Exodus, 1910–1960: A Primer for Historians. *Journal of Southern History* 49 (November): 585–600.

Kiser, Clyde V. 1932. *Sea Island to City: A Study of St. Helena Islanders in Harlem and Other Urban Centers.* New York: Columbia University Press.

Kluger, Richard. 1977. *Simple Justice: The History of Brown v. Board of Education and Black America's Struggle for Equality.* New York: Vintage Books.

Kousser, J. Morgan. 1974. *The Shaping of Southern Politics: Suffrage Restriction and the Establishment of the One Party South, 1880–1910.* New Haven, CT: Yale University Press.

———. 1980a. Progressivism—For Middle-Class Whites Only: North Carolina Education, 1880–1910. *Journal of Southern History* 46 (May): 169–94.

———. 1980b. Separate but *Not* Equal: The Supreme Court's First Decision on Racial Discrimination. *Journal of Southern History* 46 (February): 17–44.

———. 1986. *Dead End: The Development of Nineteenth-Century Litigation on Racial Discrimination in Schools.* New York: Oxford University Press.

———. 1988a. Before *Plessy,* Before *Brown:* The Development of the Law of Racial Integration in Louisiana and Kansas. Typescript. Division of Social Sciences, California Institute of Technology.

———. 1988b. The Supremacy of Equal Rights: The Struggle Against Racial Discrimination in Antebellum Massachusetts and the Foundations of the Fourteenth Amendment. *Northwestern University Law Review* 82 (Summer): 941–1010.

Landes, William, and Lewis Solmon. 1972. Compulsory Schooling Legislation: An Economic Analysis of Law and Social Change in the Nineteenth Century. *Journal of Economic History* 32 (March): 54–91.

Landry, Bart. 1987. *The New Black Middle Class*. Berkeley: University of California Press.

Leiberson, Stanley. 1978. Selective Black Migration from the South: A Historical View. In *The Demography of Racial and Ethnic Groups*, eds. Frank D. Bean and W. Parker Fresbie, 119–41. New York: Academic Press.

Lofgren, Charles. 1987. *The Plessy Case: A Legal-Historical Interpretation*. New York: Oxford University Press.

Louisiana, State of. 1879, 1887–1912a, 1926, 1946. *Biennial Report of the State Superintendent of Public Education*. Baton Rouge, LA: State Printer.

———. 1892b. *Biennial Report of the Auditor of Public Accounts for the Years 1890 and 1891*. Baton Rouge, LA: State Printer.

———. 1912b. *Biennial Report of the Auditor of Public Accounts for the Years 1910 and 1911*. Baton Rouge, LA: State Printer.

Lundberg, Shelly, and Richard Startz. 1983. Private Discrimination and Social Intervention in Competitive Labor Markets. *American Economic Review* 73 (June): 340–47.

Maddala, G. S. 1977. *Econometrics*. New York: McGraw Hill.

———. 1983. *Limited-Dependent and Qualitative Variables in Econometrics*. New York: Cambridge University Press.

Mangum, Charles. 1940. *The Legal Status of the Negro*. Chapel Hill: University of North Carolina Press.

Mandle, Jay. 1978. *The Roots of Black Poverty: The Southern Plantation Economy After the Civil War*. Durham, NC: Duke University Press.

Margo, Robert A. 1982. Race Differences in Public School Expenditures: Disfranchisement and School Finance in Louisiana, 1890–1910. *Social Science History* 6 (Winter): 9–33.

———. 1984a. Accumulation of Property by Southern Blacks Before World War One: Comment and Further Evidence. *American Economic Review* 74 (September): 768–76.

———. 1984b. "Teacher Salaries in Black and White": The South in 1910. *Explorations in Economic History* 21 (July): 306–26.

———. 1985. *Disfranchisement, School Finance, and the Economics of Segregated Schools in the United States South, 1890–1910*. New York: Garland Press.

———. 1986a. Educational Achievement in Segregated School Systems: The Effects of "Separate-But-Equal". *American Economic Review* 76 (September): 794–801.

———. 1986b. Race and Human Capital: Comment. *American Economic Review* 76 (December): 1221–24.

———. 1986c. Race, Educational Attainment, and the 1940 Census. *Journal of Economic History* 46 (March): 189–98.

———. 1987. Accounting for Racial Differences in School Attendance in the American South, 1900: The Role of Separate-But-Equal. *Review of Economics and Statistics* 69 (November): 661–66.

———. 1988a. Interwar Unemployment in the United States: Evidence from the 1940 Census Sample. In *Interwar Unemployment in International Perspective*, eds. Barry Eichengreen and Timothy Hatton, 325–52. Dordrecht, The Netherlands: Kluwer Academic Publishers.

———. 1988b. Schooling and the Great Migration. National Bureau of Economic Research Working Paper no. 2697. Cambridge, MA: National Bureau of Economic Research.

———. 1989. The Effect of Migration on Black Incomes: Evidence from the 1940 Census. *Economics Letters* 31 (December): 403–6.

———. 1990. Segregated Schools and the Mobility Hypothesis: A Model of Local

Government Discrimination. Typescript. Department of Economics, Vanderbilt University.

Margo, Robert A., and Elyce Rotella. 1981. Sex Differences in Labor Market Outcomes: Houston School Teachers, 1891–1922. Typescript. Department of Economics, Indiana University.

Margo, Robert A., and Georgia Villaflor. 1987. The Growth of Wages in Antebellum America: New Evidence. *Journal of Economic History* 47 (December): 873–95.

Marshall, Thurgood. 1947. Teacher Salary Cases. In *The Negro Handbook, 1946–1947*, ed. Florence Murray, 40–50. New York: A. A. Wynn.

Masters, Stanley. 1975. *Black-White Income Differentials: Empirical Studies and Policy Implications.* New York: Academic Press.

Morris, Aldon D. 1984. *The Origins of the Civil Rights Movement: Black Communities Organizing for Change.* New York: The Free Press.

Morris, Robert C. 1981. *Reading, 'Riting, and Reconstruction: The Education of Freedmen in the South, 1861–1870.* Chicago: University of Chicago Press.

Murray, Charles. 1984. *Losing Ground: American Social Policy, 1950–1980.* New York: Basic Books.

Murray, Florence. 1949. *The Negro Handbook.* New York: Macmillan.

Myrdal, Gunnar. 1944. *An American Dilemma: The Negro Problem and Modern Democracy.* New York: Harper and Row.

Orazem, Peter. 1987. Black-White Differences in Schooling Investment and Human Capital Production in Segregated Schools. *American Economic Review* 77 (September): 714–23.

Perlmann, Joel. 1988. *Ethnic Differences: Schooling and Social Structure Among the Irish, Italians, Jews, and Blacks in an American City, 1880–1935.* New York: Cambridge University Press.

Perlmann, Joel, and Robert A. Margo. 1989. Who Were America's Teachers? Towards a Social History and a Data Archive. *Historical Methods* 22 (Spring): 68–73.

Population Studies Center, University of Pennsylvania. 1989. *Public Use Sample: 1910 Census of Population.* Ann Arbor, MI: The Inter-University Consortium for Political and Social Research.

Pritchett, Jonathan. 1985. North Carolina's Public Schools: Growth and Local Taxation. *Social Science History* 9 (Summer): 277–91.

———. 1986. The Racial Division of Education Expenditures in the South, 1910. Ph.D. diss., Department of Economics, University of Chicago.

———. 1989. The Burden of Negro Schooling: Tax Incidence and Racial Redistribution in Postbellum North Carolina. *Journal of Economic History* 49 (December): 966–73.

Rabinowitz, Howard N. 1974. Half-a-Loaf: The Shift from White to Black Teachers in the Negro Schools of the Urban South, 1865–1890. *Journal of Southern History* 40 (November): 565–94.

Ransom, Roger, and Richard Sutch. 1977. *One Kind of Freedom: The Economic Consequences of Emancipation.* New York: Cambridge University Press.

Risen, Maurice L. 1935. *Legal Aspects of Separation of Races in the Public Schools.* Philadelphia: Temple University Press.

Rosen, Sherwin. 1974. Hedonic Prices and Implicit Markets. *Journal of Political Economy* 82 (January/February): 34–55.

Schmidt, Benno C., Jr. 1982. Principle and Prejudice: The Supreme Court and Race in the Progressive Era. Part 1: The Heyday of Jim Crow. *Columbia Law Review* 82 (April): 444–524.

Shulman, Steven, and William Darity, Jr. 1989. *The Question of Discrimination: Racial Inequality in the U.S. Labor Market.* Middletown, CT: Wesleyan University Press.

Sjaastad, Larry. 1962. The Cost and Returns of Human Migration. *Journal of Political Economy* 52 (October), supp.: 80–93.

Smith, James. 1984. Race and Human Capital. *American Economic Review* 74 (September): 685–98.

———. 1986. Race and Human Capital: Reply. *American Economic Review* 76 (December): 1225–29.

Smith, James, and Finis Welch. 1979. Race Differences in Earnings: A Survey and New Evidence. In *Current Issues in Urban Economics,* eds. P. Mieskowski and M. Straszheim, 40–73. Baltimore, MD: Johns Hopkins University Press.

———. 1989. Black Economic Progress After Myrdal. *Journal of Economic Literature* 27 (June): 519–64.

Smith, Richard K. 1973. The Economics of Education and Discrimination in the U.S. South: 1870–1910. Ph.D. diss., Department of Economics, University of Wisconsin.

Spivey, Donald. 1978. *Schooling for the New Slavery: Black Industrial Education, 1868–1915.* Westport, CT: Greenwood Press.

Starrett, David. 1976. Social Institutions, Imperfect Information, and the Distribution of Income. *Quarterly Journal of Economics* 90 (May): 261–84.

State of Georgia. *See* Georgia, State of

State of Louisiana. *See* Louisiana, State of

Strober, Myra, and Laura Best. 1979. The Female/Male Salary Differential in Public Schools: Some Lessons from San Francisco, 1879. *Economic Inquiry* 17 (April): 218–36.

Summers, Anita, and Barbara Wolfe. 1977. Do Schools Make a Difference? *American Economic Review* 67 (May): 639–52.

Tushnet, Mark V. 1987. *The NAACP's Legal Strategy Against Segregated Education, 1925–1950.* Chapel Hill: University of North Carolina Press.

Tyack, David, Robert Lowe, and Elisabeth Hansot. 1984. *Public Schools in Hard Times: The Great Depression and Recent Years.* Cambridge, MA: Harvard University Press.

U.S. Bureau of the Census. 1913. *Thirteenth Census of the United States, 1910.* Vol. 2: *Population: Reports by States.* Washington, D.C.: U.S. Government Printing Office.

———. 1914. *Thirteenth Census of the United States, 1910.* Vol. 4: *Population: Occupation Statistics.* Washington, D.C.: U.S. Government Printing Office.

———. 1916. *Plantation Farming in the United States.* Washington, D.C.: U.S. Government Printing Office.

———. 1918. *Negro Population, 1890–1915.* Washington, D.C.: U.S. Government Printing Office.

———. 1922. *Fourteenth Census of the United States, 1920.* Vol. 2: *Population: General Report and Analytical Tables.* Washington, D.C.: U.S. Government Printing Office.

———. 1923. *Fourteenth Census of the United States, 1920.* Vol. 4: *Population: Occupations.* Washington, D.C.: U.S. Government Printing Office.

———. 1933. *Fifteenth Census of the United States, 1930.* Vol. 4: *Population: Occupations, by States.* Washington, D.C.: U.S. Government Printing Office.

———. 1935. *Negroes in the United States, 1920–32.* Washington, D.C.: U.S. Government Printing Office.

———. 1943. *Sixteenth Census of the United States, 1940.* Vol. 2: *Population: Characteristics of the Population, Reports by States.* Washington, D.C.: U.S. Government Printing Office.

———. 1944. *United States Census of Population, Special Reports: State of Birth of the Native Population.* Washington, D.C.: U.S. Government Printing Office.

———. 1948. *Special Reports of the United States Census, Current Population Reports,* ser. P-20, no. 20. Washington, D.C.: U.S. Government Printing Office.

———. 1952. *Census of Population 1950.* Vol. 2: *Characteristics of the Population, Reports by States.* Washington, D.C.: U.S. Government Printing Office.

———. 1953. *Census of Population 1950.* Vol. 4: *Special Reports, Part 4, Chapter A, State of Birth.* Washington, D.C.: U.S. Government Printing Office.

———. 1975. *Historical Statistics of the United States.* Washington, D.C.: U.S. Government Printing Office.

———. 1983a. *Census of Population, 1940: Public Use Microdata Sample.* Washington, D.C.: U.S. Bureau of the Census.

———. 1983b. *Census of Population, 1950: Public Use Microdata Sample.* Washington, D.C.: U.S. Bureau of the Census.

U.S. Bureau of Education. 1893. *Report of the Commissioner of Education for the Year 1889–90,* vol. 2. Washington, D.C.: U.S. Government Printing Office.

U.S. Census Office. 1883. *Statistics of the Population of the United States at the Tenth Census.* Washington, D.C.: U.S. Government Printing Office.

———. 1895. *Report on the Population of the United States at the Eleventh Census: 1890,* pt. 1. Washington, D.C.: U.S. Government Printing Office.

———. 1897. *Report on the Population of the United States at the Eleventh Census: 1890,* pt. 2. Washington, D.C.: U.S. Government Printing Office.

———. 1902. *Twelfth Census of the United States, 1900, Population,* pt. 2. Washington, D.C.: U.S. Government Printing Office.

———. 1904. *Occupations at the Twelfth Census.* Washington, D.C.: U.S. Government Printing Office.

U.S. Commission on Civil Rights. 1986. *The Economic Progress of Black Men in America.* Washington, D.C.: U.S. Commission on Civil Rights.

U.S. Department of Health, Education, and Welfare. 1954. *Biennial Survey of Education in the United States, 1948–50.* Washington, D.C.: U.S. Government Printing Office.

———. 1957. *Biennial Survey of Education in the United States, 1950–52.* Washington, D.C.: U.S. Government Printing Office.

———. 1959. *Biennial Survey of Education in the United States, 1952–54.* Washington, D.C.: U.S. Government Printing Office.

U.S. Department of Labor. 1919. *Negro Migration in 1916–1917.* Washington, D.C.: U.S. Government Printing Office.

Vatter, Harold G. 1985. *The U.S. Economy in World War II.* New York: Columbia University Press.

Vickery, William. 1969. The Economics of the Negro Migration. Ph.D. diss., Department of Economics, University of Chicago.

Washburne, Carleton. 1942. *Louisiana Looks at Its Schools.* Baton Rouge: Louisiana Educational Survey Commission.

Welch, Finis. 1973. Education and Racial Discrimination. In *Discrimination in Labor Markets,* eds. O. Ashenfelter and A. Rees, 43–81. Princeton, NJ: Princeton University Press.

Westin, Richard B. 1966. The State and Segregated Schools: Negro Public Education in North Carolina, 1863–1923. Ph.D. diss., Department of History, Duke University.

Whatley, Warren. 1990. Getting a Foot in the Door: "Learning," State Dependence, and the Racial Integration of Firms. *Journal of Economic History* 50 (March): 43–66.

Williamson, Jeffrey G., and Peter Lindert. 1980. *American Inequality: A Macroeconomic History.* New York: Academic Press.

Woodward, C. Vann. 1955. *The Strange Career of Jim Crow.* New York: Oxford University Press.

Wright, Gavin. 1986. *Old South, New South: Revolutions in the Southern Economy Since the Civil War.* New York: Basic Books.

Index